Gender in Medieval Culture

Gender in Medieval Culture

MICHELLE M. SAUER

Bloomsbury Academic
An imprint of Bloomsbury Publishing Plc

B L O O M S B U R Y
LONDON • NEW DELHI • NEW YORK • SYDNEY

Bloomsbury Academic
An imprint of Bloomsbury Publishing Plc

50 Bedford Square
London
WC1B 3DP
UK

1385 Broadway
New York
NY 10018
USA

www.bloomsbury.com

BLOOMSBURY and the Diana logo are trademarks of Bloomsbury Publishing Plc

First published 2015

© Michelle M. Sauer, 2015

Michelle M. Sauer has asserted her right under the Copyright, Designs and Patents Act, 1988, to be identified as Author of this work.

All rights reserved. No part of this publication may be reproduced or transmitted in any form or by any means, electronic or mechanical, including photocopying, recording, or any information storage or retrieval system, without prior permission in writing from the publishers.

No responsibility for loss caused to any individual or organization acting on or refraining from action as a result of the material in this publication can be accepted by Bloomsbury or the author.

British Library Cataloguing-in-Publication Data
A catalogue record for this book is available from the British Library.

ISBN: HB: 978-1-4411-7956-2
PB: 978-1-4411-4262-7
ePDF: 978-1-4411-2160-8
ePub: 978-1-4411-8694-2

Library of Congress Cataloging-in-Publication Data
Sauer, Michelle M., 1972-
Gender in medieval culture / Michelle M. Sauer.
pages cm
Includes bibliographical references and index.
ISBN 978-1-4411-7956-2 (hbk) – ISBN 97814411 42627 (pbk) 1. Women–England–History–To 1500. 2. Women–Europe–History–Middle Ages, 500-1500. 3. Sex role–England–History–To 1500. 4. Sex role–Europe–History–To 1500. I. Title.
HQ1147.E6S28 2015
305.40942'01–dc23
2014047083

Typeset by Newgen Knowledge Works (P) Ltd., Chennai, India

To Annette for her love and support throughout my life

CONTENTS

Acknowledgments viii
A note on texts ix

Introduction: Gender in medieval culture 1
1 The social world: Law, medicine, and science 15
2 The expected ideal: Marriage and virginity 47
3 The unexpected actuality: "Deviance" and transgression 67
4 The gendered Christ: Sexuality and religion 101
5 The political sphere: Power, labor, and economics 125

Notes 149
Further reading 189
Glossary 193
Index 197

ACKNOWLEDGMENTS

As always with a project of this magnitude, I have a number of people to thank for the various ways they have assisted me during the process.

First, I must acknowledge the support of the University of North Dakota's Graduate School, through which I earned a summer professorship, which in turn enabled me to complete a great deal of research. Through their auspices, I was also able to secure the assistance of Michele Eifert, a graduate student in English, for research and organization assistance.

Second, the McNair Program at the University of North Dakota has allowed me the opportunity to mentor two undergraduate English majors, Rachel Piwarski and Kelly Kennedy, both of whom, as part of their program commitments also provided me with research and materials-gathering assistance.

Third, I have a number of friends and colleagues who have helped me in various ways, providing advice, suggestions, corrections, and distraction. Among these, I include Susannah Chewning, Diane Watt, Natalie Grinnell, Madisson Whitman, Amy Stroh, Jason Miller, Heike Bauer, and Audrey Johnson. Thank you one and all for your help—even if you didn't actually realize you were helping! I also want to express gratitude to, collectively, the members of the class I taught on Medieval Sex during the spring semester of 2013 at UND. Their reactions and insights provided me with a number of ideas. Here, also, is where I should mention that this book was written with the aid of three cats: my late feline friend Grendel, my new companion, Gawain, and my latest addition, Hadwisa, all of whom warmed my lap and my heart throughout the days of writing.

Finally, I want to thank the various members of the Continuum/Bloomsbury family, including Michael Greenwood, Emily Drewe, Emma Goode, and Rhodri Mogford. Each has had a hand in developing this volume, and has been both professional and human in every way.

A NOTE ON TEXTS

All Biblical quotations are taken from the Latin Vulgate. The version found at http://www.latinvulgate.com conveniently displays the Vulgate Latin and English versions side-by-side, and is accessible to all.

The Vulgate, a Latin translation of the Hebrew and Greek texts, is primarily the work of St Jerome (ca. 347–420 CE), commissioned in 382 CE by Pope Damasus I (ca. 305–84 CE; r. 366–84). It was the most influential text of Western Christendom, and the official Bible of the Church.

The majority of the quotations from the works of Church Doctors will be taken from the full text archives available from Christian Classics Ethereal Archives (http://www.ccel.org). Again, ease of accessibility is assured.

INTRODUCTION

Gender in medieval culture

Undertaking a project such as this one is both daunting and rewarding. "Gender" is an extensive topic, and one that carries with it a great many political and social ramifications. This volume is not meant to provide definitive answers to many of the questions that can and should be raised, but rather to provide some tools for those who want to pursue inquiry in this area. As such, the ground covered will not necessarily be "new," but rather complementary to study. To begin, I hope to outline some basic concepts and ideas, as well as explain the reasons why I have made some of the choices that I have made. Toward that end, let us begin by looking at the title of this volume in reverse.

First, despite the seemingly wide scope of the title, *Gender in Medieval Culture*, I will, for the most part, be focusing on medieval England. "Culture" is, of course, a broad term, and pairing it with an equally large descriptor, "medieval," makes the subject somewhat untenable in a compact volume meant for initial study. Roughly speaking, culture encompasses the beliefs, customs, arts, and other social institutions of a particular society, group, place, or time. To address the entirety of medieval culture is nigh impossible. The differences in sociopolitical structures, religious beliefs, and cultural practices between Western Europe and the rest of the world simply comprise too much material. Even a discussion limited solely to Western society is complicated. For better or for worse, British literature and culture has become a staple of our educational systems, and so this will be my primary focus. However, there are some parts of medieval culture that transcend national borders, especially in terms of religion, sex, and sexuality. In the portions of this volume that address religious standards, such as sexuality in hagiographies, for example, I draw from all of Western Christianity, not simply England. However, in segments that address such things as female participation in the guild system, I will mostly confine my discussions to English laws and standards. In terms of religion and medicine, much of Western Christendom was interconnected in beliefs, whereas the economy and legislation saw sharp divisions, ones that cover too much to adequately address here. For instance, while female medical professionals trained through an apprenticeship system in England and France, in Italy, where a number of city-states strictly regulated female participation in Craft Guilds, they could attend university after a fashion, as part of a learned group in Salerno. Outlining each country's approach would ultimately prove more confusing in a study such as this where the focus is on highlighting gender relations, rather than examining the historical perspective of the individual profession or country.

Next, despite recent trends against periodization, this book specifies "medieval" as its point of inquiry. Here, I am taking medieval to mean, in England anyway, post-Conquest through the beginnings of the Tudor Dynasty, or, in traditional dates, 1066–1485 CE.[1] Of course such boundaries are fluid, and these dates correspond only to British history. In recent years, the study of English literary and cultural texts has embraced the impulse to examine the borders between medieval and early modern ("Renaissance") in particular, although the idea can be applied backward, too, encompassing the Classical and Patristic eras (sometimes called the "Dark Ages"). Scholars have scrutinized the terms as designating both historical periods and conceptual categories; they have examined the assumptions and analytical frameworks that these terms have invoked and sustained. Their work results in new accounts of relationships between literary texts and cultural practices that move beyond notions of difference and dependence, rupture and continuity, to underscore a more complex historiography, one that pursues diachronic notions of repetition, reinvention, appropriation, renewal, revival, and reciprocity. Assuming neither the foundational status of the medieval nor the cultural superiority of the early modern, this approach to historiography investigates how the various "periods" of the premodern world mutually inform each other. Similarly, Jeffrey Jerome Cohen has asked the question, "What if the medieval were not middle to anything? Instead of a historical lacuna sandwiched between the fall of Rome and the rise of the early modern, what if the medial adjective in the Middle Ages does necessarily signify as intended?"[2] These are indeed important questions to those of us who study the medieval era. One of the most troubling things about strict periodization is the tendency for the familiar "phases of history" to disguise a claim to power as a historical fact. Subjugation in various forms is more easily justified when projected onto the Middle Ages. Periodization thus furnishes one of the most enduring conceptual foundations for the usurpation of equality and the abuse of power, as well as for the continued machinations of patriarchal oppression.

Fredric Jameson brought this "crisis" in periodization to wider attention, stating: "the larger issue is that of the representation History itself. There is in other words a synchronic version of the problem: that of the status of an individual 'period' in which everything becomes so seamlessly interrelated that we confront either a total system or an idealistic 'concept' of a period: and a diachronic one, in which history is seen in some 'linear' way as the succession of such periods, stages, or moments,"[3] However, even Jameson finds periodization pedagogically necessary. Despite our good intentions, periodization is almost inevitable when discussing the process of humanity, which is a development of culture that is tied to temporal unfolding, even if not to temporal "progression." We think in sections of time, perhaps because we have been culturally conditioned that way, but these segments provide for us a useful way to think about the past. David Perkins argues, "[a]t present, we tend to regard periods as necessary because . . . one cannot write history or literary history without periodizing it. Moreover, we require the concept of a unified period in order to deny it."[4] We need to think in terms of confined moments in order to gain understanding of what we are attempting to recover and what we are attempting to live.

In light of this perception of understanding history—not as a progressive narrative, but rather as a section of time—this volume will make use of early sources and references whenever the medieval depends on the Classical, or note when trends continue into the beginnings of modernity, but still depend upon periodization for its boundaries. One has to set boundaries somewhere, and the traditional lines at least provide a starting point. Furthermore, studying gender in the Middle Ages provides an opportunity not only to examine the entrenchment of certain ideas that continue today, but also to explore the ways those concepts were decidedly different in the past than they are now. If gender itself is fluid and unstable, surely the study thereof cannot be confined so simply merely by the act of periodization.

As modern academics, we often speak of gender as "constructed" or "performed" as a standard assumption. While I assume this modern understanding throughout the work, nevertheless, sex and gender ideology in the Middle Ages was basically essentialist, albeit a slightly different essentialist position than the current one and with frequent exceptions. Toward that end, I intend in this introduction not only to provide a general overview of the modern academic concepts of sex and gender, but also to provide a rationale for studying the Middle Ages in this manner. It is important, I believe, that the basic vocabulary and ideas behind the concepts to be discussed are addressed here. With that in mind, I want to begin by looking at gender, sex, and sexuality as we by and large approach them in modern scholarship.

Sexuality has always mattered to Western society. Since Western society is dominated by Judeo-Christian doctrine and patriarchal rhetoric, sexuality is also subjected to those principles, and is generally tied directly to identity and subject to regulation. Jeffrey Weeks calls this the "will-not-to-know," and about it says:

> This is backed up by an assumption which is deeply embedded in perhaps all our cultures, but strongly in the West: that our sexuality is the most spontaneously natural things about us . . . through it we experience ourselves as real people; it gives us our identities, our sense of self . . .[5]

Sexuality defined by faith and biological gender roles views sex and gender as inherent components of human identity. They are an essential part of what makes us who we are. Historically, this has led to sexuality going relatively unchallenged in regards to many components of human life, including family life, reproductive choices, and the division of labor. Sexuality, invisible yet dominant, is functional to the order of society.

Historically and currently, sexuality has been discussed and understood in relation to gender and sex. All three categories—sexuality, gender, and sex—are contentious, particularly in connection to many social, political, cultural, moral, and religious debates. For many years, a concept we now call essentialism prevailed. Essentialism holds that the characteristics of people are generally similar across human history and culture since they are primarily a product of biology. The qualities of being "male" or "female" are inherent in each individual since birth; each individual has an essential "maleness" or "femaleness" that has been determined by chromosomes and chemistry. Essentialists believe that sex and gender are the same thing (or are at least inseparable). Both arise from "nature" or are "God-given." Chromosomal characteristics, visible sex markers (penis, vagina), and gender cannot be separated. Essentialists usually believe that there are only two genders—male and female—and that these are present at birth, remain unchanged for life, and are the only choices. Behaviors or appearances that do not fit these assumptions are viewed as "perversions," and biological "deviations" are often deemed "monstrous."

Essentialism forms the basis of most of Western premodern gender politics. Men and women were viewed as inherently male or female. Yet, premodern essentialism was distinct from post-Enlightenment essentialism in one crucial manner. Premodern societies preserved patriarchal power by focusing on the similarities between men and women, choosing to claim male superiority through the "better use" of human qualities. A different sort of essentialism grew rapidly in the eighteenth century, to some extent as a reaction against lingering traces of the premodern world. As will be discussed in more depth later, while there was not exactly a consensus of opinion, many medieval theorists, although certainly not all, embraced a one-sex model of sex differentiation. The Classical, medieval, and early modern worlds did not always conceptualize male and female bodies in terms of difference; rather, many medical texts focused on the similarities between bodies. This so-called one-sex model, where women were believed to be "inside out" men, was an extension of patriarchal ontology—man was the measuring stick by which all humans were judged. However, the potential for slippage was too much for eighteenth-century Enlightenment scientists to bear. It became crucial for men and women to have multiple physical differences in order to preserve patriarchal power. In the mid-eighteenth century, anatomists increasingly focused on bodily differences between the sexes, and argued that sex was not restricted solely to the reproductive organs, or as one physician put it: "the essence of sex is not confined to a single organ but extends, through more or less perceptible nuances, into every part."[6] In this way, male and female bodies become conceptualized in terms of opposition and difference, structured within a system of dominance and submission. Physiological "facts" (instead of religious beliefs) were used to explain the natural passivity of women, becoming the benchmark for all sociocultural–political debates.

Within an essentialist framework, physical rhetoric is privileged and disguised as normal, such as socially prescribed sexuality, gender, and sex. Therefore, sexuality, gender, and sex ideologies are perceived as natural, even masked as biological, preventing many from questioning everyday arrangements and practices. Sexuality's major role in everyday interactions is thus understood as vital and necessary to the function of society, but often goes unnoticed unless presented as outside social scripts and norms. Further, sexuality is connected to various cultural practices, boundaries, and rewards, making it difficult to notice and question such ideologies. Hence, it is assumed that all individuals are born with a sexuality, sex, and gender, and that these three categories are aligned and function harmoniously in unison. For example, the social construct "sex" exists as its own act and category, but in conjunction with sexuality is used to define normal and abnormal activities. Sex—defined in this understanding as intercourse between a man and woman—is described as natural and functional to gender. Sex between males and females, heterosexuality, is highly valued and valorized, but also used to demoralize all "unnatural" or "other" sexual acts. Therefore, any individual that deviates from "natural" sexuality, sex, or gender is assumed to be transcending all three categories and does not receive protection or benefits from heterosexuality.

While more traditional perspectives have seen all of these categories as being stable, natural, and tied directly to the human body, feminist, poststructuralist, social constructionist, and queer frameworks challenge assumption of sexuality as inherent and natural. Scholars in these areas argue that sexuality is a social product, a social fiction, as well as a hegemonic construction created out of cultural meanings, social relationships, and power politics.[7] Thus, sexuality is influenced by cultural and political power structures, creating social norms and scripts.

In *Paradoxes of Gender*, Judith Lorber argues, "for humans the social is the natural."[8] The social constructivist view of gender builds upon this notion, explaining multiple experiences and positions in society by challenging all that is assumed to be natural. By challenging natural assumptions of identity, social constructionism recognizes that identity is a social process that continually evolves on both structural and individual levels. Social constructionism questions social institutions that have been associated with natural frameworks, promoting identity and presentation—specifically sexuality, gender, and sex—as finite and static. Conversely, social constructionism argues that identity is malleable and flexible, shifting and transforming with cultural, social, and political events. Often social constructionists speak of "doing gender" as a given.[9] The language of "accomplishment of gender," the "doing of gender," and "gender as an emergent feature" all make gender an action of individuals in contact with one another and an ongoing and never-ending process. The social category of gender (and also gender inequality) for social constructionists arises from interaction.

For the poststructuralists, gender, gender inequality, and sexuality arise from discourse instead of solely from interactions. Discourse is the site in which language is used and where meaning and subjectivity are constructed and contested; thus, accordingly, it "offer[s] the individual a range of modes of subjectivity."[10] Judith Butler's poststructuralist theorizing on gender and sexuality is, in many ways, a version of social constructionism, although it has been given its own designation of gender performance theory. Butler agrees with social constructionists that there is no biological or essential basis for gender and that gender does not correspond to biological sex. She also views gender, and subsequently sexuality, as performative in acts, gestures, and enactments, meaning that "the gendered body is performative suggests that it has no ontological status apart from the various acts which constitute its reality."[11] There is no category of gender outside of enacting gender. Differing from constructivism, however, is the idea that gender is not found, or at least not exclusively found, in interaction; rather, it is predominately found in discourse. Thus, gender and sexuality are constituted effects of performance or of discourse. This eliminates the potentially dangerous situation that social constructionism can fall into: "doing gender" can make gender seem as if it is an expression of an underlying masculine or feminine nature, whereas the performance of gender naturalizes the categories of gender. Instead, gender becomes an effected illusion as essential representation of a real, natural, and underlying core in individuals.

Performance theory dictates that all meaning is constructed through the use of signifiers and the signified. This creates a system that obscures the social relationships making aspects such as power, privilege, and social agency hard to see. Performance theory looks at the different "stages" that gender is performed on and the relationship between those performances. Butler concludes that it is not only sexualized gender that is produced in discourse (as a coherent, stable, essential, underlying core), but also the self (the "I") is fashioned. Therefore, subjectivity is disunified, incomplete, and incoherent; gender is performative, but not "done by" a performer. There is no prior subject who freely and willingly performs gender. The appearance of such a prior, volitional subject is also an effect of the performance.

The notion that sexuality is socially constructed or performative is not limited to formations of nonheteronormative sexualities. Heterosexuality, the identity and practice assigned to male–female sexual relations, is just as much of a construct as its so-called deviant counterparts. Like its counterparts, it is a practice consistently performed and used in social interactions.[12] Prior to the late nineteenth century, heterosexuality as a category of identity did not technically exist. Men and women were expected to marry and to procreate as a functional, productive unit of society. Marriage was a duty and an expectation unless another specified life was chosen. In the Middle Ages, monasteries and convents supplied an alternative to marriage. However, the social expectations of heterosexual functionality followed the individual into such a life. For instance, men and women lived in separate housing since, having given up sex, proximity to the opposite sex would have been the source of too much temptation. The societal assumption underlying this division is that every man and every woman would automatically seek sexual release from the opposite sex. Neither same-sex sexual activity nor noninterest in sexual activity was considered by the dominant discourse. In other words, both the social and the ecclesiastical worlds assumed that human beings would be interested in having sex with the opposite biological sex if they were not constrained by the laws of Church and state, and even if they indulged in other sexual practices as well.

The Reformation brought with it an emphasis on marriage and reproduction rather than virginity and abstinence. Still, the expectation remained that everyone would ultimately end up in a heterosexual partnership, even if an individual participated in homosexual acts. The heterosexual family remained the basis of the economy and the functionality of the state. This perception of heterosexuality cannot be separated from the social institutions of marriage and family. Men and women were not "heterosexual" per se as such an identity did not exist—and because sexuality and marriage did not occupy disparate spheres. Sex was a function of marriage, family, religion, and cultural expectations. This expectation continued until post-industrialization. By the close of the nineteenth century and the start of the twentieth, people began understanding sex as an activity not necessarily connected with reproduction and economy.

As well, the early twentieth century saw a more visible organization of a sexual minority, the "homosexual," which, in turn, contributed to the formation of a heterosexual identity. Heterosexuality became Western society's common, default, and reference sexuality—the "true" sexuality at the top of the hierarchy; thus, the invention of heterosexuality was absolutely vital for the sexual majority to maintain social and legal control over a society. Thus, doing and being a part of heterosexuality allows for the regulation of all sexual and social interactions. As an institution and a practice, heterosexuality maintains its dominance through its relationship with gender and the assignment of genders. For the most part, children are labeled "male" or "female" at birth, and society attaches meaning systems to those (hetero)genders that correspond with an assumed heterosexual sexual identity. In turn, these (hetero)genders instruct everyone how to act according to gendered scripts, and are supported by many social institutions—making heterosexuality intrinsic to all human existence. This is called heteronormativity.[13] Before the term heteronormativity was created, the concept existed; male–female intercourse was the only acknowledgeable sexual relationship in premodern Western society, and according to the pre-Reformation Church, this was only made acceptable through the bonds of matrimony. Men and women who engaged in same-sex relations were thought of in the same light as adulterers—sodomites, fornicators, and deviants. Thus we face an interesting conundrum with using modern terminology to discuss past behavior—heterosexual adulterous relations were aligned with the same unnaturalness as same-sex relations. It's not so much heterosexuality in general that is privileged in this case, but rather sanctioned heterosexuality. This is why, in part, I have chosen to open the book with a chapter on the expected ideal. While the expected ideal in the Middle Ages may have been based in "presumed heterosexuality," it also held virginity in the highest regard. In the sexual hierarchy of the medieval era, active heterosexual relations fell further down the list than both active virginity and chaste widowhood.

Our discussion of the so-called invention of heterosexuality also leads into a conversation about the relevance and privileging of such. Karma Lochrie, in her recent work *Heterosyncrasies: Female Sexuality when Normal Wasn't*, laments the "hardwired" association between heterosexuality and heteronormativity that even the majority of queer theorists rely upon. She fears the "terrible presumption of transhistorical heteronormativity."[14] Lochrie believes that it is possible to construct premodern sexualities as existing outside the common structure of opposition and normativity. This is certainly not the common approach. By the late 1980s, many feminist theorists came to agree that in society heterosexuality is deemed normative, and deviant or subordinated sexualities are ridiculed, policed, and repressed, and most theorists at least acknowledged heterosexuality's role in reaffirming patriarchal oppression. With heterosexuality assumed as society's standard lifestyle, men remained in control of the economic, religious, political, educational, and other institutions of authority.[15] In fact, under this rubric, men use both heterosexual and homosocial situations to remain in control.[16]

Furthermore, as Michel Foucault's *History of Sexuality* (1976–84) demonstrated, the definition and regulation of sexuality were the primary means by which power has been organized in Western society. In societies regulated by a monolithic state institution, power is polymorphous, polyvalent, and omnipresent. Foucault also traced the advent of increasingly structured discourses about sex and sexuality that regulated, classified, and analyzed it. The culmination of this trend was the advent of sexology in the late nineteenth century, which scientifically participated in the debate to maintain the female body as saturated with sexuality and to sustain heterosexual monogamy as the norm. It was during this time (the late nineteenth century) that many of the terms used in today's discourse originated. Sexology developed alongside the other emerging social sciences, such as anthropology, sociology, and psychology, at a time when understanding humanity via classification systems was the standard. Three men, Havelock Ellis, Richard von Krafft-Ebing, and Magnus Hirschfeld, are considered the founders of modern sexology. They sought to produce an exhaustive classification of the multiple aspects of sexuality by tracing its etiology, scrutinizing its fantasies, fetishes, and pleasures, and constructing new pathologized individual identities. Although useful in certain ways, overall the early discipline of sexology has left a legacy of terminology that we are still struggling to escape.

One of the most complicated aspects of discussing gender in the premodern world is the modern association of gender, sex, and sexuality with identity. This identification, in turn, creates a dependence upon a certain type of discourse about sexuality that permeates the scholarship of social history. As Richard Godbeer notes:

> The meanings ascribed to sex vary from one culture to another, from one place to another, and from one time to another. Although members of different societies may experience similar physical impulses and engage in similar acts, they understand them differently. Sexual categories have no universal signification; they are cultural products . . . Thus, if we are to understand past people's experience of sex, we need to jettison our own notions of sexuality in favor of the categories that they used . . . Sex acquires meaning in many cultures only as a function of political, economic, social, and religious ideologies.[17]

Humans never just have sex, "do" gender, or perform roles. Such activities are always scripted by the culture involved, and our interpretations of such are, in turn, scripted by our own expectations. Sexuality is not a thing, but rather is a process. It is dynamic and complex, shifting over time, behaviors, and cultures. It connects to and collides with social identities as they change. Bruce R. Smith addressed the problem within the context of the early modern era, noting that for the sixteenth and seventeenth centuries, "sexuality was not, as it is for us, the starting place for anyone's self-definition."[18] The same is also true for medieval society. No medieval person thought of him or herself as "heterosexual" any more than he or she thought of him or herself as "homosexual."

Returning to the idea of gender construction, a number of years ago, Karma Lochrie, Peggy McCracken, and James A. Schultz wrote, "looking carefully at medieval texts and images, one discovers that gender is constructed according to a number of paradigms, that these entail different sorts of sexuality, and that neither the categories of gender nor the sexualities they entail are as stable as one might have expected."[19] This statement encapsulates the travails faced by scholars seeking to unravel the complexities of premodern "gender," whatever that concept may mean. Further, applying sexual categories such as "homosexual" to earlier periods is problematic both because of cultural complications, and because of the vexed periodization of history. Unfortunately, we have very little other vocabulary by which to discuss such issues than our modern one. Smith carefully delineates the distinction between "homosexuality" and "homosexual behavior," for instance, since the action can be trans-historical and trans-temporal, while the categorization cannot be. Valerie Traub suggests referring to the early modern era as one of "domestic heterosexuality," referring to the new Protestant rhetoric of marriage based on friendship with an expectation of sex for companionship's sake as well as procreation.[20] Both these ideas, as well as a number of others stemming from early modern studies, are on the right path, and it is time for medieval studies to follow in their wake. Several years ago, I noted a trend: medieval scholars often rely upon nonmedieval sources in order to inform their discussions of sexuality, from providing theoretical framework to creating vocabulary, because they are not only forced to do so because of a lack of texts, but also expected to do so because of the constraints of periodization.[21] I hope to rectify this situation at least somewhat here by relying upon nuanced readings of polyvalent situations, rather than upon indeterminate terms such as "homosexual." This is not to say that one cannot speak of a "medieval lesbian experience," just that one must understand that the experience may be lesbian in nature, but the persons involved did not consider themselves to *be* lesbians.

The concept of "norms" did not actually exist as a social phenomenon until the nineteenth century. This does not mean, of course, that all behaviors were acceptable or accepted. Rather, this means that the notion of "normal" and "norming" is a function of the development of the social sciences. Lochrie maintains, "before the advent of the normal, no sexuality or any other cultural ideal was normative."[22] Although generically normative means relating to an ideal standard, more specifically normative has come to mean habitual, average, and natural. All these descriptors are dangerously exclusionary, especially when applied to sexuality, and they lend themselves to the further prescriptive enhancement of "correct."

Knowing that norms are a product of the nineteenth century, and that neither heterosexuality nor homosexuality as they exist today were the same in the Middle Ages, is it fair to divide a book into chapters that address topics such as "The Expected Ideal: Marriage and Virginity" and "The Unexpected Actuality: 'Deviance' and Transgression"? Do the chapter titles and subtitles serve to reinforce a hetero/homo binary? I do not believe so for a very simple reason: the ideal of the Middle Ages is *not* a typical, (re)productive heterosexual marriage, even if it involved heterosexual behaviors. As well, deviance from that ideal involves numerous practices, at least some of which are heterosexual in action. Similarly, the two most significant portions of medieval life were church and state—or, religion and the social world. In essence, then, I have attempted to make the sections of our discussion mirror actual medieval life. In written life, as in active life, however, there is a great deal of overlap, messy boundaries, and unclear limitations. Each section builds within itself as well as upon the others.

In fact, I chose the chapter titles deliberately, at least in part because of the fraught definition of normative and what it means to medieval scholarship today. The study of gender in medieval culture necessitates, for the most part, a discussion of male and female roles in society. How were people expected to live? If we are to understand gender as a construct of society, then the society's expectations are crucial to that understanding. By collapsing heterosexual activity, virginity, and chastity into a discussion also populated by masculinity and femininity, normative and natural become changed from the twenty-first-century understanding of those concepts into the medieval ones. Once the expectations are established, then looking at how those presumptions are flouted, who transgresses when and how, becomes a necessary addition to the discussion. To denote deviance only to align it with heterosexual practices is to undermine the potentially norming value of the term. The social and religious worlds provide the additional cultural context for creating the concepts of masculinity, femininity, and whatever exists outside the binary. While religious discourse permeates the Middle Ages, there is a distinction between speaking about chaste marriages and discussing the gendered body of Christ, and the social world of law, economics, and medicine presents a complementary view of gender politics.

Aside from theoretical discussions about gender and sexuality, a good portion of this volume focuses on what men and women actually did or did not do. Like Butler's performance theory approach, looking at repetitive actions may point us in the direction of gender concerns, as much as they cannot provide a stable identity. As Natalie Zemon Davis reminds us, "gender conventions are used and manipulated so that women and men can manage their lives, make do as best they can, or advance," especially during an era when such conventions were "often accepted ... [but] also on occasion defied, challenged, or simply ignored."[23] By offering aspects of men's and women's lives in the Middle Ages, I hope to reveal their acceptance, negotiation, or dismissal of the gender conventions as these manifested and changed in this time and culture. Accordingly, the issues discussed should illustrate responses to gender conventions, and gender deviations, during the medieval era.

We are at a moment of transition in the historiography of sexuality as scholars move beyond the Foucauldian dichotomy of sexual acts versus sexual identity. The latter, Foucault contends, is an entirely modern construct; as a result, it would be anachronistic to speak of premodern people as having sexual identities. More recent notions of identity as performance have helped break down that dichotomy. Still, the tendency in contemporary Western culture to imagine gender identity as generally "fixed" by biology, a side effect of the sex/gender schema, permeates investigations. According to Diana Fuss, the sex/gender schema encourages us to think of sexual characteristics as things that are natural, "hardwired," and therefore largely immutable: as she puts it, we tend to assume that "nature and fixity . . . go together."[24] As we have discussed, to some extent the Middle Ages shared that view, yet there were many exceptions to the rule. Many functions of gender in medieval culture were ultimately determined by actions, rather than biology, although the relationship between the two was by and large interdependent.

Therefore, I propose thinking about the gender continuum that is observable in the Middle Ages as a function of "performative essentialism"—biology, social roles, and personal actions not only can determine gender, but also can change it. In the medieval era, many ideas about gender and sexuality were based on biology and the "natural" distinctions between men and women; however, that medieval people recognized the role of "nature v nurture" is evident in a great many texts, including philosophical treatises, theological expositions, and popular fiction. Moreover, according to Laqueur, the notion that "sex" was (at least potentially) malleable went hand-in-hand with the notion that male and female bodies were structurally homologous, with women merely having "inside out," and therefore inferior, penises; thus, changes in humoral makeup or corporeal structure could move an individual along the gendered continuum. As well, performing the social functions of the opposite sex could cause gender change, either physically or perceptively. For instance, the hero/ine of the tale *Yde et Olive*, an early medieval *chanson de geste*, dresses and acts like a knight, performing great feats of chivalry, and is "rewarded" in the end by being transformed into a physical male, capable of fathering offspring. Numerous female saints "became male" by ignoring their female instincts, remaining chaste, and living an ascetic life. Still other women assumed male rights through guild memberships or *feme sole* (single woman) status, even if only temporarily. Instances of men sliding toward feminine are less common, but still exist. Physically, castrated men entered a "not-man" status with the removal of their male parts. Spiritually, priests were feminized through their dress, their chastity, and even their passivity. "Real" men fought and labored; clerics often did neither. Thus, literature and history offer a full range of gender potential, suggesting that the gendered body is permeable and variable, imprecise in its categories. Biology is not necessarily destiny, and gender participates in a series of taxonomies that structure the social order, such as religion, the law, and chivalry, and it therefore participates in processes beyond itself. With that notion in mind, then, let us look at the main aspects of medieval life—marriage, sex, religion, and society—as places where nature and nurture interact.

CHAPTER ONE

The social world: Law, medicine, and science

Although the Church had a significant impact on the development of gender roles and sexual ideals, the social world also influenced sexual codification and reflected the systematic patriarchal society of medieval Europe. Understanding how women were treated under the law and how medicine viewed them reveals the great discrepancies in medieval society—ones that still underpin many attitudes in today's society. Medieval women were subjugated to men legally in practically every way, thus making them almost wholly dependent upon men economically. While religion provided the basis for many of the attitudes toward women, medicine and law also provided the basis for discrimination; in fact, these disciplines worked in tandem to create a pervasive view of woman as naturally subordinate to man, and nonhuman as subordinate to human.

Sex discrimination regarding wealth and property was built into the legal system under English common law. Coverture was the legal doctrine whereby, upon marriage, a husband subsumed a wife's legal rights.[1] One of the earliest and clearest writers on this practice was English jurist Henry of Bracton (ca. 1210–68 CE). Around 1235 CE, he wrote a treatise called *De legibus et consuetudinibus Angliae* (*On the Laws and Customs of England*). In it, he identified the legal rights of individuals, placing women in an inferior position to men by defining women's legal standing by categorizing women as living under the legal guardianship of their husbands. Upon marriage, a man and woman became "one flesh, one blood," so the woman gained access to a male body with all its rights and privileges. Therefore, a woman could only be defined as a person under the law if she was married—an unmarried woman could not be a person since she had no male body to become part of—although she was only a person as far as being an extension of her husband.[2] Although in theory this was meant to strengthen the marital relationship, as it would remove discord from the union, as Sara M. Butler notes, "the implication in reality, however, was total erasure of a woman's legal personality."[3] An examination of English Year Books (condensed reports of legal cases that went before the common law courts) reveals that coverture grew increasingly restrictive as the Middle Ages drew to a close. Early Year Books indicate ways around the restrictions of coverture, especially where necessities or maintenance were concerned. For instance, a wife could clothe herself without her husband's express permission as long as she remained within the bounds of her social status. Similarly, she could purchase items in the marketplace as long as they were for the good of the household. However, by the fifteenth century, these so-called laws of necessities greater restrictions came into play, as even for basic goods, "the husband's consent, implicit or explicit, before or after the purchase, was needed."[4] Presumably this practice served to decrease debt, as a husband was liable for his wife's debts, even if she acted without his knowledge. In practice, however, it decreased women's agency, increased their dependency, and reduced their adult status. Butler further asserts that "coverture reared its ugly head primarily in times of crisis," but there is a little more to it than that.[5] Certainly, the rights of coverture were invoked more assiduously when men were faced with a potentially lowering situation, such as divorce or property challenges. Since a woman had no legal rights apart from her husband, he was almost assured a victory in such cases. In turn, women who may have otherwise sought to escape untenable situations likely chose to remain simply because they had no other recourse.

Furthermore, while the legal impact on women's everyday lives might have been slight, culturally, coverture, coupled with religion, gave husbands the right to govern wives. Governance with a firm hand was expected: "late medieval English people perceived violence as an instrument and a sign of good social order . . . violence was normatively thought to be rightly exercised in the maintenance of divinely instituted order."[6] Both canon law and secular law acknowledge the rights, and the duty, of husbands to control their wives, and the complete subordination of women. Restraint and confinement were expected methods of control, as was physical punishment.[7] The law addressed this topic only vaguely, admonishing husbands to, "treat and govern her [your wife] well and honestly, and to do no injury to her body other than that permitted lawfully and reasonably to a husband for the purpose of control and punishment of his wife."[8] The boundaries of spousal control are difficult to discern, and this writ merely implies limits, it does not actually set them. Thus, marital violence was inscribed within the culture both through religion and through the law, both of which placed women completely in the power of their spouse.[9] Women were not "people" with full rights and privileges; instead, they were objects to be used as necessary for pleasure and profit.[10]

One part of medieval law codes that typify both the reduction of women to chattel and the use of women for male pleasure are laws that address rape and ravishment. Such laws demonstrate the gender imbalance within the culture. Women were, for the most part, legal property, so laws reflected damage and compensated the "rightful owners," not the actual victims.[11] These laws illustrate the extreme commodification of women, and even when prosecution became technically more possible, the success rate dropped dramatically, indicating that as women grew more visible and gained small victories, in general, society feared female empowerment, and sought to control women's bodies even more vigorously. When women did attempt to exercise their rights by appealing or pursuing prosecution, they were subjected to an exacting pretrial process that was physically and emotionally draining and damaging to their reputation, only for the majority of the cases to be dismissed. In some cases, the victim was then prosecuted herself for a "false appeal." These private problems were thus publicly made into a spectacle, and like all spectacles, these trials carried a message of social control, here more specifically connecting to the subjugation of women.

Medieval medical perspectives of gender and sexuality are reflected in rape laws. Corrine J. Saunders asserts, "rape became a kind of touchstone for medical thinkers, an instance of female weakness as well as an example of the way that the reproductive processes worked."[12] For one thing, the pervasive guilt of the female body is present in medieval law—derived from the Galenic physiological model—that a woman could not conceive a child unless she consented to intercourse because she could conceive only by the releasing of female sperm through orgasm; therefore, she had to take at least a modicum of pleasure in the act. If a woman would then subsequently conceive, her right to appeal was lost.[13] This exception was generally held true throughout English rape law history, perhaps most notably in Bracton's treatise and *Fleta*, another late-thirteenth-century legal commentary.[14] This dual notion of female weakness and susceptibility to pleasure becomes intertwined in rape legislation. Saunders notes, for instance, that William of Conches writes, "and if the start of the act of rape is displeasing, in the end as a result of the weakness of the flesh, it becomes pleasing," which corresponds to the English medical text *The Prose Salernitan Questions* (ca. 1200 CE), which asserts that women were particularly disposed to pleasure.[15] Here, woman's tendency toward temptation is integrated with the legal discourse in order to reduce the potentially criminal actions of men. While no English rape laws went so far as to say that rape was always inherently pleasurable, the lack of prosecution and punishment speaks to the prevailing view on the subject—women somehow "asked for it," at least in many cases.[16] Coupled with legal exposition, "medical theory and natural philosophy intersected with ideas of theologians regarding gender, sexuality, and the frailty and bodiliness of women to form a powerful and insidious set of cultural assumptions."[17] The female body was firmly inscribed as being the source of human frailty, sinfulness, and at least to some extent, criminal behavior. In turn, one of the most problematic constructions of the female body created through the conflation of all these discourses is their combined insistence that women desired to be ravished and dominated.[18]

Although medical texts support the theories about female weakness in the face of temptation, an even more significant aspect of medieval medicine as far as gender studies is concerned is the idea of the "one-sex" model. This idea originated during the Classical era and held sway through the eighteenth century. Under this concept, women and men as essentially the same beings, only women's bodies are "inside out" men. However, as a response to cultural demands, post-Enlightenment science developed the "two-sex model" out of fear of women possessing power. To further differentiate the power held by men and women, two models were formed so that a woman would not simply be seen as an unfinished man, but rather as a different and inferior being. The two-sex model was an attempt to take power from women, making them the "other" sex. As with the "one-sex" model, the male body serves as the paradigm.[19] While the "one-sex" model is just as inherently patriarchal as the "two-sex" model, it opens up different possibilities for gender fluidity and even transformation, such as hermaphrodism.

Alongside the one-sex model, the "two-seed" theory of conception, wherein both male and female sperm were required for an embryo, seemingly provides for a measure of biological equality. On the contrary, however, the two-seed model works in tandem with the rest of Galenic and Hippocratic theories to reinscribe biological inferiority through the establishment of women as cold, wet, and composed of inferior biological matter. Moreover, just as the two-seed model made women responsible for rape and conception, it similarly made them responsible for infertility, since they were clearly incapable of producing enough passion (heat) to properly release their seed. Similarly, the desire to release their semen could account for vulnerability to lust or for falsely inducing passion in an unsuspecting man. The inherent inferiority and vulnerability to temptation made women susceptible to disease and disorder. Finally, the attempts by women to control their own bodies and their own fertility were first construed as medically and socially dangerous, and eventually interpreted as interference with God and nature, both hallmarks of witchcraft, the ultimate defiance of male authority.

Rape and *raptus*

Scholars have long lamented the lack of cohesive studies regarding rape in the Middle Ages, and while some of that dearth has been rectified, there is still more work to be done. In particular, the voice of rape victims is rarely heard in these studies. Rape was a vexed crime in the Middle Ages, problematized by the conflicts between secular and canon law as well as by varying medical and social perceptions. Unlike modern definitions of the term, which rely primarily on constructions of power, medieval "rape," at least early on, carried the explicit sense of sexual violation. Although this perception gradually shifted toward one of power—expressed in medieval terms as "ravishment"—the sense of sexuality was only lessened, and not erased. Further, issues of consent, sin, and consequences swirled almost impenetrably around the topic.

Medieval rape laws descended from the Roman legacy surrounding *raptus*, literally "carrying off by force," which in its original conception did not even require sexual intercourse, and could be used to describe property theft.[20] *Raptus* did not become a public crime until after Constantine (ca. 272–337 CE). Constantine was also the first to address women who conspired to stage their own abduction—they, as well as their abductor, would be subject to the death penalty.[21] Here the problem is not so much the removal of the daughter from the family home, but rather the damage done to parental property through marriage without approval. In the sixth century, Justinian added a new penalty, the confiscation of property, and further more narrowly defined *raptus* as being applicable only to unmarried women, widows, or nuns. Married women—women who regularly engaged in sexual activity—could not be raped. The theft of innocence was a requirement for rape, and married women could never be fully innocent since they owed their husbands the marriage debt.

English laws regarding rape have their basis in Roman law codes as well as the elaborate Anglo-Saxon justice system. Problematically, these two systems are directly oppositional in their approach. Roman law basically treated rape as "a blemish on the woman rather than as an offence committed against her," whereas Anglo-Saxon laws "recognized rape as a serious crime of devaluation."[22] In both systems, the woman herself is less important than the subsequent consequences; however, the Anglo-Saxon approach insisted on some form of restitution, whereas the Roman tradition resulted in the permanent disgrace, if not death, of the victim. The earliest English laws insisted on monetary payment, if not marriage, as restitution, and the early penitentials follow this lead. For instance:

> If anyone carry off a maiden by force, [he is to pay] to the owner 50 shillings, and afterwards buy from the owner his consent [to the marriage].[23]
>
> If it be rape of a maiden, seven half-*cumals* (is the fine) for it.[24]

The injured party is not the one to receive recompense, and while the gravity of the crime is at least acknowledged, the severity of the crime is more dependent upon collateral damage to property than to personal violation.

Both secular and canon law addressed rape, and both definitions and prosecution became intertwined. In the early twelfth century, Johannes Gratian (d. ca. 1155 CE), defined rape as a "sexual corruption" that included both abduction and unwanted sexual intercourse.[25] Thomas Aquinas (1225–74 CE) further specified that rape meant the use of force to violate a virgin, but that force could be directed at fathers whose daughters conspired with abductors as well as at the victim herself. Aquinas also allowed for "rape without seduction if a man abduct[s] a widow or one who is not a virgin."[26] In other words, although rape is more detrimental if the violated woman is a virgin, rape without force is impossible. It was up to the victim, however, to prove that force was involved.

Rape prosecution continued to be the burden of the victim. A treatise of unknown authorship, written shortly after the Norman Conquest (ca. 1188 CE) states that the courts required both the presentation of the bloody and/or torn clothing worn during the attack as proof of force, and a detailed report made directly to trustworthy men prior to any attempt at prosecution.[27] Similarly, around 1235 CE, English jurist Henry of Bracton wrote *De legibus et consuetudinibus Angliae* (*On the Laws and Customs of England*), in which he placed a heavy burden of proof and a multitude of requirements upon the rape victim. First, in order to be classified as rape, the woman's virginity or sworn chastity must have been lost during a forced sexual encounter.[28] Then an elaborate process had to be followed, including raising the hue and cry, relating details of the encounter to men of good repute in a neighboring township, explaining the circumstances to the reeve, detailing the experience to other officials such as the king's sergeant and the sheriff, making an appeal at the county court, and having their appeals copied verbatim into court rolls.[29] If the victim managed to accomplish all of this, and the court actually convicted the antagonist, then Bracton determined that the punishment should be blinding and castration—unless the victim agreed to marriage. In this early period, there was also a distinction made between *raptus* (abduction) and *violentus concubitus* (violent sexual intercourse). However, as Saunders notes, the Norman patriarchal system combined with the Church's singular focus on the violation of virgins (and by extension, nuns), and the two aspects of rape became elided into one, with abduction taking precedence over violation.[30] This is a troubled tableau of medieval sexuality—who controls it, who urges it, who desires it, who prevents it. There is also here an interesting conflation of virginity and sworn chastity, both of which enhance a woman's value, either for her family or for God.

The later Middle Ages witnessed changes in rape laws. Before the late thirteenth century, with a few exceptions, rapes could be prosecuted only by appeal, which in medieval England simply means "private prosecution," as opposed to public prosecution, which is called "presentment." In 1285, the Parliament under Edward I (1239–1307 CE) altered the definition and legality of rape in chapter 34 of the Statute of Westminster II:

1. It is provided, that if a man from henceforth do ravish a married woman, maid, or other, where she did not consent, neither before nor after, he shall have judgment of life and member.
2. And likewise where a man ravisheth a woman, married lady, maid, or other, with force, although she consent after, he shall have judgment as before is said, if he be convicted at the king's suit, and there the king shall have the suit.[31]

On the surface, this seems to be a step forward in rape prosecution. Under this law, women could independently prosecute men for rape without waiting for a male relative to make the case for them. By increasing the penalty involved, from imprisonment to execution, a woman's right not to engage in unwanted sexual activity was seemingly upheld. Furthermore, it also appears that this Parliament considered rape a serious and prosecutable offense. In reality, however, the provision provided neither deterrent nor successful prosecution. Court records show that the royal and local courts never sentenced convicted rapists to the penalties prescribed by Westminster II, and the majority of rape cases that were even heard resulted in acquittals.[32]

Since women knew that in practice, jurors and judges would not actually apply the new rape laws, many rape victims were apparently reluctant or unwilling to appeal the men who raped them.[33] Possibly, the women involved found it unlikely that the courts would not recognize the extent of their trauma. Or, perhaps they believed that the courts would also be reluctant to impose the new severe punishment of death. A number of scholars have suggested that the rape laws included in Westminster II were unable to ensure that rape victims could convict their rapists because local court jurors did not agree with the idea of women's right to self-representation, and therefore refused to implement the new rape laws. Others suggest that the new rape laws were never designed to prevent rape or protect women's right to prosecute rapists; instead, they were designed to defend the interests of male heads of families. In particular, the secular courts now joined with the ecclesiastical courts to pressure rape victims to marry their rapists. By transforming the law of rape into one of abduction and elopement, by incorporating cases of elopement into rape law, Edward diminished the legal severity of rape, transforming it into a less serious act of unacceptable marriage. The "afterwards clause" in Section 34 allowed the courts to prosecute cases in which the defendant consented afterward, in turn protecting male heads of families from the dangers associated with elopement.

On a more practical level, bribery, kidnapping, or coercion may have reduced the number of complaints.[34] Certainly, a large number of women chose private settlement of their cases over the much more public and riskier court appeal. Women who settled privately gained material rewards, such as money or property, or, perhaps more often, marriage. Despite the offense to modern sensibilities, this was often the most practical and desirable outcome in the Middle Ages, and English laws encouraged this solution. However, a number of other European countries, including France, discouraged this practice.[35] This has led some scholars to postulate that jilted women brought false accusations of rape against men in order to secure their desired or expected spouse. While this certainly may have been the case in some instances, acceptance of this as a "commonality" is more likely the result of modern rape culture rather than actual medieval fact.[36] Marriage was a desirable outcome not necessarily because of personal feelings, but rather because the raped woman was considered "damaged goods." If the victim could not secure a spouse, then monetary compensation could at least augment her dowry, providing a financial security that had been significantly diminished upon her loss of virginity. Finally, as Daniel Klerman notes, "Monetary settlements reflect some continuity with the early medieval criminal law, in which monetary payments were the most common official penalty for crime."[37] The difference between early medieval and late medieval settlements was the possibility that a woman could receive some sort of compensation personally.

Furthermore, while the new rape statutes should have increased the likelihood of conviction, instead they did nothing of the sort. Analysis of local court records from varying towns and cities between 1218 and 1276 indicates that the local courts acquitted 76 percent of accused rapists, and after the enactment of Westminster II in 1285, records reveal that the local courts acquitted an even higher percentage of accused rapists.[38] And, in cases resulting in conviction, juries almost never assigned any punishment harsher than imprisonment, and in those cases, for less than two years.[39] By disregarding the proscribed punishments, the courts demonstrated that they considered rape to be a minor offense, and by failing to convict in most cases, they demonstrated that they would not harshly punish men for committing rape. Popular literature of the day reflects this struggle. In Geoffrey Chaucer's "Wife of Bath's Tale," a knight comes across a maiden while he is out hunting and proceeds to take her maidenhead by force. Although Chaucer readily admits in the course of the Tale that the knight should have "lost his head" because of his crime, instead, Queen Guinevere charges him with a quest. He completes the quest with the assistance of a loathly lady whom he subsequently marries, and she becomes a beautiful and faithful wife. Thus, the rapist knight is richly rewarded, while the rape victim is not heard from again. Far from being an atypical depiction of society created for the benefit of literature, this scenario is instead the commonplace of medieval Britain.[40]

Rape laws, especially in later medieval England, demonstrate an interesting dichotomy, whereby women are given the unusual legal privilege of being able to wage a suit on their own reckoning, but then generally are unable to see those suits come to fruition. Women who did attempt to appeal without settlement were put through a grueling process that rarely resulted in satisfaction, and likely suffered from secondary victimization. Secondary victimization is the re-traumatization of a sexual assault victim that occurs indirectly through the responses of individuals and institutions.[41] Families may have encouraged women to prosecute not only for potential gain, but also to publicly proclaim that she was a victim, an unwilling participant, so as to lessen the consequences of loss of virginity. Then, as now, women were conditioned to be victimized and to be at fault for the actions of men, in particular for the sexual reactions of men. Several early penitentials reflect this idea, by stating that a man who had sex with, by force or otherwise, an ugly woman was more guilty of lust than a man who had sex with a beautiful woman, since she was too tempting and in essence compelled him to act.[42] Similarly, the literature of the era reflects the male viewpoint that women either desire to be ravished, or that at the very least, sexual violence did not harm the woman involved. Rape scenes often take place in almost a *locus amoenus*, where "the springtime landscape, dainty gestures, controlled emotional expression, and elegant costumes all serve to prettify the rape."[43] Indeed, places that should provide safety and comfort instead become locations of terror, just as the courts, which seemingly promised justice, also become spaces of fear. Overall, in the Middle Ages, rape and rape legislation was another way to restrain female sexuality and to control female bodies, to commodify women, and to silence them.

The majority of scholarship has focused on medieval English rape laws; however, this is not a deterrent to understanding the medieval mindset: "secular law on rape was fairly consistent throughout medieval Europe, although each country maintained its own procedures."[44] For instance, in medieval France, the punishment for rape reflected the Roman practice and paralleled the English one by imposing a formal sentence of death. Most cases were, however, handled through levied fines, and extant cases indicate that the female victims were often assessed steeper fines for "allowing carnal knowledge" than the perpetrators were for "forcing sexual congress."[45] Medieval German law also officially called for the death penalty, with the particularly gruesome practices of being buried alive or decapitated as the suggested methods. In practice, the punishment was usually mitigated to blinding or imprisonment—or exoneration through marriage. Italian law was, perhaps, the most casual. Only cases involving incest, the elderly, or very young girls were taken seriously at all. Rape of any other woman was treated as a matter of course, typical of action against women.[46] Of course, the ecclesiastical courts embraced the same perspective no matter the country, and the Church's attitude toward sex was based, at least in part, on medical views of the female body.

Medicine, science, gender, and sexuality[47]

Although it would be impossible to cover all of medieval medicine here, it is valuable to situate some of the ideas about gender and sexuality within the context of medieval medicine and science. For instance, it is important to the construction of both gender and sexuality to look at what makes a male body male and a female body female, as well as how conception occurs. The mystery of embryology carries with it the seeds of misogyny. Fertility control, still a controversial topic in modern society, divided religion and science as well as men and women, and the result strengthened patriarchal and ecclesiastical dominance. Similarly, a number of diseases, such as syphilis, leprosy, greensickness, and hysteria are all closely connected with intimate relations, and with maintaining the sexual status quo, with men in power and women in a subordinate position.

Overall, all medical writing is fundamentally gendered because it deals with human biology and the human body, which is to some extent a cultural artifact fixed in a particular historical moment. If bodies are culturally specific, produced by the society in which they exist, then medicine is one of the many discourses that (re)inscribe meaning (back) on to the body. The medieval medical tradition is deeply indebted to—in fact is inseparable from—its Classical roots, particularly to Aristotle (384–322 BCE) and Galen (129–ca. 200/ca. 216 CE). Galen combined two medical philosophies—the Empiricists and the Dogmatists—into one approach, and this became the foundation of the majority of medieval medicine.[48] Galenic principles dominated early medieval medicine; however, in the twelfth century, new Latin translations of Aristotle, as well as the arrival of Arabic works by Rhazes (854–925 CE), Avicenna (ca. 980–1037 CE), and Averroes (1126–98 CE), brought a shift toward combining the two approaches.[49]

One of the main bases of premodern medicine is the basic philosophy of the four bodily humors, or the four liquids of which each human body is composed: blood, phlegm, black bile, and yellow bile. A healthy individual has all of these in balance, and humoral disposition can determine, among other things, which diseases will pose the largest threat to an individual. These fluids also determine a person's personality traits, depending on which is predominant. These humoral interactions could be interconnected to make more complex personality assessments. As well, in this system, humans are inherently connected to the natural elements. The complete

Table 1 The four humors and corresponding attributes

Humor	Temperament	Character	Temperature	Season	Element
Blood	Sanguine	Optimistic, cheerful, fun-loving	Hot and moist	Spring	Air
Phlegm	Phlegmatic	Calm, unemotional, shy	Cold and moist	Winter	Water
Black bile	Melancholic	Considerate, creative, perfectionist	Cold and dry	Autumn	Earth
Yellow bile	Choleric	Ambitious, dominant	Hot and dry	Summer	Fire

schema of these was set out in Galen's *On the Temperaments*.[50] Finally, the humoral system also connected to gender. In short, men were hot and dry, while women were cold and moist (see Table 1).

Biology and reproduction

One of the primary functions of medical texts is to define the human body by means of an idealized, centralized figure that stands as the model for all other bodies. By default in patriarchal societies, this body is male. When the female body is discussed, it is revealed through its difference from (and inferiority to) the male body; "man occupies the absolute position from which, at times, woman diverges, and on which she is completely dependent, for the female sex is not explicable in its own right, but only in relation to the male."[51] This difference is generally constructed on Aristotelian principles: the male is active, and associated with form; the female is passive, and associated with matter. This solidifies the male body as perfect, and the female body as flawed. Medieval philosophy embraced this belief completely:

> The male passiþ þe femel in parfite complexion and wirkyng, in wiþ and discrecioun, in miȝt and in lordschippe: in parfit complexioun for in comparisoun to þe femel þe male is hoot and drie, and þe femel aȝenward. In the male beþ vertues formal and of schapinge and werchinge, and in þe femel material, suffringe, and passiue.[52]

The social is natural, here, because it is believed that women are specifically designed to live sedentary lives at home, while men are made to deal with the things outside. These Aristotelian gender categories have a direct influence on medieval notions of physiology since activity links to heat, and passivity to coolness. Similarly, Galen's understanding of the differences between men and women was dependent upon his theory of "vital heat."[53] The amount of vital heat produced by an individual directly reflected that person's hierarchical order of rank in relation to degrees of perfection. Men, who produced the highest levels of vital heat, were more perfect than women; thus, the male body, being superior, is hot, while the female body is cold. The male body is dry and stable, with strictly defined boundaries. The female body is cold and wet, with porous and leaky boundaries. Moistness is an unavoidable characteristic of being female: "the main collection of gynecological writings—*Diseases of Women* . . . argues that women's flesh is softer, wetter, and more spongy than male flesh; it therefore absorbs more fluid from the diet than does that of men's flesh; *Glands* explains that women's bodies retain moisture because they are loose textured (*araios*), spongy (*chaunos*), and like wool (*eirion*)."[54] Women's bodies are characterized by a superfluity of fluids that cannot be fully contained within the body.

Given these differences, then, male and female bodies should be impossible to confuse. In fact, as Thomas Laqueur has elaborated, in premodern medicine, male and female bodies exist as different points on a continuum, with the disturbing possibility of slippage between the two. Instead of the maleness or femaleness of the physical body depending on its different genitalia, and thus on its reproductive capacity, Laqueur argues that the dominant model from antiquity into the early modern period stressed not the difference between male and female bodies, but rather the similarity between them. He contends that male and female bodies, in premodern thought, differ mainly in the positioning of the genitals. According to Galenic biology, male and female reproductive parts were identical, with the difference being that women were merely inversions of men. Basically, in female bodies, the penis and testicles failed to descend before birth, and instead remained inside to form the vagina and ovaries:

> All the parts, then, that men have, women have, too, the difference between them lying in only one thing . . . namely that in women the parts are within [the body], whereas in men they are outside . . . Consider first whichever ones you please, turn outward the woman's, turn inward, so to speak, and fold double the man's, and you will find them the same in both in every respect . . . for the parts that are inside in woman are outside in man.[55]

Female genitals were an inverse of male genitals, basically a "negative" version of the male "positive," with the ovaries and uterus being, essentially, an "inside-out" penis and testicles. This inversion happened because the female body was too cold to produce perfect, external genitals. In this one-sex model, there was no such thing as a specifically female body; instead, there was just one body, which if it was cold, weak, and passive was female, and if it was hot, strong, and active was male.[56]

Laqueur's argument is sound, if a bit reductive. Ruth Mazo Karras reminds us that "the binary opposition between men and women was extraordinarily strong in medieval society. Although theorists might write that females were defective males, their defects were significant enough that no one seriously considered them the same as males."[57] In other words, regardless of the beliefs in the Middle Ages regarding the physical body and reproductive organs, and despite the view that women were viewed, to some extent, anyway, as "defective" men because of their incomplete sexual development, women were also clearly seen as something different from, albeit still inferior to, men. Thus, the one-sex body is never an egalitarian one; instead, it is slanted in favor of the idea that the male is the primary form, and that women are in some way inadequate. Women are passive, colder, wetter, and more prone to instability. This inferiority makes them more prone to irrationality; they cannot control themselves in the way that men can. Such theories subsequently justify a hierarchy in which the male is innately superior to the female.

Theories of conception and reproduction reflect these gendered differences as well, primarily in regards to the contributions of the sexes. The most distinct contrast was found between Aristotle's "one-seed" theory and Hippocratic and Galenic "two-seed" theories.[58] Under Aristotelian principles, the male is active, and associated with form, while the female is passive, and associated with matter. These polarities are especially evident in the Aristotelian theory of conception, in which the sperm, the "formal cause" of conception, shapes the passive matter (the "material cause") provided by the female, which, in turn, had a direct impact on the theology of ensoulment put forth by Thomas Aquinas. In this model, the woman serves merely as an incubator full of disorganized matter (menstrual blood), waiting to be formed through fertilization by the male sperm, which carries with it "life force." By contrast, in the Hippocratic text *On the Nature of the Child*, the process was said to begin when the male and female seeds mixed. The ensuing seed inflated and formed a membrane through which it received breath (*pneuma*), and then menstrual blood is drawn into the membrane where it coagulates. Eventually flesh formed, and by the thirtieth day for boys and the forty-second day for girls, the fetus was formed and continued to develop thereafter.[59] Galen's work was built on this concept. For Galen, sexual pleasure and orgasm for both female and male were necessary to generate enough heat to release and combine the two seeds into matter, thereby creating a fetus. The male heats up to a point at which blood is transformed into semen (seed), and is transmitted through ejaculation (orgasm). Galen believed that the female requires similar stimulation in order to produce semen (seed). Although both contradictory theories coexisted, Galen's "two-seed" model held sway throughout most of the Middle Ages, even after Aquinas incorporated Aristotle's ideas into his own Natural Law. Hildegard of Bingen's (1098–1179 CE) twelfth-century description of the female orgasm illuminates this idea:

> When a woman is making love with a man, a sense of heat in her brain, which brings with is sensual delight, communicates the taste of that delight during the act and summons forth the emission of the man's seed. And when the seed has fallen into its place, that vehement heat descending from her brain draws the seed to itself and holds it, and soon the woman's sexual organs contract, and all the parts that are ready to open up during the time of menstruation now close, in the same way as a strong man can hold something enclosed in his fist.[60]

Hildegard here depends on the mechanics of conception to create her depiction of the orgasm, as is evident from the woman's release waiting for the man's—otherwise it would be useless, and potentially even damaging. Although women supposedly were more lustful than men by nature, once impregnated, a woman's duty was to temper her ardor so she could nourish the fetus. Nevertheless, the woman's orgasm was essential to generation, at least in this system.

Unfortunately, however, the existence of an alternate theory of conception neither seriously challenged the association of women with matter, nor produced an egalitarian view of conception and humanity.[61] For instance, despite believing that both parents contributed to the formation of a fetus, Galen also speculated that male fetuses were conceived on the right side of the uterus and female fetuses on the left side. The inferiority of women can be attributed to their association with the left side. In his classic article "On the Pre-eminence of the Right Hand," Robert Hertz elucidates how dualism was essential to premodern societies: "so on one side, there is the pole of strength, good, and life; while on the other there is the pole of weakness, evil, and death . . . All oppositions presented by nature [e.g. light/dark, north/south, male/female, and so forth] exhibit this fundamental dualism."[62] A dichotomy between the right and left sides of the body was a natural outgrowth of this viewpoint, with the right representing everything sacred, strong, and male, and the left standing for secularity, weakness, and female. This assumption was implicit in Greek culture and became the basis of medical conceptions of sexual differentiation. While Hippocratic texts set out the women/left and men/right conception placement, Galen refined this further. He believed that the uterus had two distinct chambers, mirroring women's two (milk-producing) breasts. The left side of the uterus in the female and the left testis in the male received impure blood, full of residue, which had passed through the kidneys, while the right side of the uterus, and the right testis, received cleansed blood directly from the great artery. Thus, the seed from the right testis is purer and warmer, and the environment of the right side of the uterus is more nourishing, so the embryo becomes a warm, dry male. Qualitative differences between the sexes begin in utero. Men are engendered from quality material and grow in warm and dry conditions, resulting in a superior specimen. Women, on the other hand, are created from impure residue and struggle under cold and wet uterine conditions, making them a substandard product. Social and political inferiority is thus very simply biologically justified.

Medicine + philosophy + theology

Alongside actual medical texts are the philosophically oriented theological works of Thomas Aquinas (1225–74 CE), arguably the most influential medieval philosopher and theologian. He, in turn, while inspired to some degree by the Patristic Fathers, was most heavily influenced by Aristotle, particularly his arguments on biology, philosophy, and their intersection. Some have termed this approach Christian Aristotelianism, and indeed, it is a complex synthesis of the two traditions, although ultimately still misogynist. In his *Commentary on Aristotle's Metaphysics*, Aquinas addresses the questions of biological sex as well as gender relations, and combined with his *Commentary on St. Paul's First Epistle to the Corinthians*, in which he addresses questions about equality within the species, Aquinas effectively establishes the foundations of Western thought for the centuries to come, and in doing so, also assures male superiority.

Aquinas did not consider woman to be a separate species from man; rather, both belong to the same species (humanity), have the same nature, and possess a rational soul. They are essentially equal in these regards, and this is the substantial form of all humans. For Aquinas, then, sexual difference is something that pertains not to the form, or the soul, but to the matter, that is the body. Humanity is a singular composition of soul and body, but form and matter affect each other. The form of a thing determines its nature or essence, gives the thing its definition, and makes it part of a species.

However, to Aquinas, the "image of God" was presented more perfectly by men than by women. This is an "accidental" difference between men and women, not an essential one, yet it is a significant one. Man is the principle of his species as God is the principle of all being, like man reflects the glory of God and woman reflects the glory of man. Aquinas most assuredly does not say that woman is a mistake of nature. She is wholly necessary to the human species not only for generative purposes, but also as a way to complete and perfect human nature. In other words, women are saved through childbearing only if they are also faithful and holy. Temporal salvation occurs because of their necessity in reproduction; eternal salvation is achieved only through faith, holiness, and temperance.

As has been indicated, the difference between men and women for Aquinas arises not from their souls or substantial form, but from their bodies or matter—the difference is a physical one, accidental and not specific. Thomas considered women to be less strong physically than men, and he refers to them as the "weaker sex" on numerous occasions. However, women's frailty can be attributed to their sexual (biological) difference from men. Because the only physical purpose for two sexes is reproduction, it is to reproduction that Aquinas turns in order to situate feminine inferiority as determined by sexual differentiation. Like Aristotle, Thomas identifies the male as the active principle in generation and the female as the passive principle, given the necessity of both an active and a passive principle in every act of generation. As passive principle of the generated being, the female supplies the matter or passive element, thought to be menstrual blood; the male seed as active principle supplies the form, actualizes the matter, and in fact does the generating with the matter supplied by the female.

On one hand, this attributes the passing along of Original Sin to the male generative principle. If Eve alone had sinned, her passive nature would have been unable to transmit it to future generations. On the other hand, Aquinas is constrained to see masculinity as the superior perfection to femininity, since activity is superior to passivity. Men provide the seed; women provide the blood that is transformed by it. Men provide generative force, ensoulment, and life; women provide a space for development. Because women are the passive principle in generation, the production of female offspring must arise because of something going wrong; hence women are defective, misbegotten men. In fact, Aquinas further suggests that a defect or weakness in the matter, or even the direction of the wind might interfere with the natural course of generating a male child and result in an imperfectly generated female one. Of course this assumes that the intention in any generative act is to produce male offspring, especially since the active principle tends to a perfect likeness of itself. This does not mean that the female is holistically a mistake; rather, that each individual woman is a mistake, although women in general needed to exist in order to propagate the species. Overall, then, Aquinas agrees with Aristotle that women are accidental insofar as they are generated against the tendency of nature; he disagrees, however, with the conclusion that they are for this reason not intended to exist.

In terms of gender, then, we have the following: men and women are only equal as part of the human species; as individual entities, men are superior to women because the active masculine sex is superior to the feminine passive sex; masculinity in form and function is superior to femininity and its entailments because it is the more active construction. Thus, women who performed masculinity—or at least avoided performing femininity—could gain some measure of superiority.

In general, though, women are inferior in bodily strength and in temperament and constitution. They are inferior because femininity is an inferior quality and they were passively and accidentally generated. Even the souls of men are more perfect than women's. The soul and body are related according to form and matter; therefore, inferior matter results in inferior form, which in turn leads to inferior moral turpitude. Just as male bodies are stronger than female ones, male souls withstand. Men and women differ in rational abilities, and in such virtues as courage, continence, and fortitude. In particular, women are incontinent because of their instability of reason, which in turn comes from having a weak temperament—women cannot resist passion.[63] Weak temperament and lack of reason also make women fickle and easily mislead. Unlike Jerome, who suggested that women could "become men" in essence by suppressing femininity (rather than by performing masculinity), Aquinas does not suggest that women have a reliable way of doing that. Instead, he concentrates on men who can be classified as effeminate. He names vacillation, the vice that opposes constancy, "effeminacy." He further says that men who are soft and womanish, those who yield readily, are effeminate.[64] Thus, gendered performances are flexible for Aquinas even if the gendered body is not.

This is, I suggest, a clear demonstration of the concept of "performative essentialism." For Aquinas, biology determines gender and its accompanying characteristics. Women are inconstant precisely because they were born women. However, biology can also change gender performances, even in Aquinas's system. Men who yield act like women and become effeminate. He also clearly allows for exceptional women. Aside from Mary, who embodied perfection in every way, including correctness of reason, he points to other exceptional women. He suggests that moral virtues are habits and can be cultivated with a resulting increase in virtue, as long as they are accompanied by grace. Women can overcome inferior reasoning through practice and education, and they can overcome temptation by training in moral fortitude. Of course women can never be as perfect as men, but they change act outside their biologically inscribed gender norms if they apply virtue, grace, prayer, and practice to the sole purpose of overcoming them.[65]

Fertility control

In the Classical world, both contraception and abortion were acceptable, if not necessarily encouraged. Hippocrates offered pessaries to his patients, describing their ingredients as conducive to inciting menses. A particularly efficacious plant called silphion was (sadly) harvested to extinction in Cyrene, the only location in which it was known to grow.[66] Although the Bible does not specifically mention birth control, it may be implied in at least one place.[67] Furthermore, abortion is mentioned in the Bible on at least one direct occasion as a chastity test.[68] As in today's world, the ability to control fertility is directly tied to gender relations. Freedom from constant pregnancy allows women the ability to have control over their own bodies. Margaret Sanger, the American birth control pioneer, saw family planning as a means for women to escape poverty and as step toward full gender equality.[69] While women in the premodern world would not have seen fertility control in these same political terms, they would have understood it as both lifesaving, due to high childbirth mortality rates, and economically sound. Moreover, in some cases, such as a single woman or an adulterous wife getting pregnant, it was simply a wise decision to either prevent conception or childbirth from happening.

Christianity, for the most part, did not alter this perspective initially. Certainly some theologians spoke out against fertility control of all sorts. Jerome, for instance, complained about women who drank concoctions to prevent conception or to terminate birth.[70] John Chrysostom (ca. 349–407 CE) also roundly condemned such practices with vivid imagery, such as referring to the womb as a "chamber for murder."[71] However, the most widely accepted Church view stemmed from Augustine of Hippo (354–430 CE) and Gregory of Nyssa (ca. 335–95 CE), and was based on Aristotle's "proposition that *psyche* [animation] did not enter the embryo until the fetus had 'formed,'" culminating in the position that "the unformed embryo could not be considered a human being."[72] This becomes an issue of ensoulment for the Church—just when did a human become "fully human?" In this mixture of ecclesiastical and Classical philosophy, the answer became this: humanity came with "quickening," which occurred roughly around the fourth month.[73] Medieval people did not believe that the soul existed at conception; therefore, purging of a womb before ensoulment was not abortion, although it was birth control. Birth control was tolerated, if not especially approved, as, indeed, abortion even was to some degree. Penitentials commonly assign a penance of "forty days" to women who admit ingesting herbs that prevent conception. The 40-day penance signifies that it is a minor sin, not a major one. At the same time, however, Augustinian doctrine equated sexual pleasure with sin, and held that couples should engage in sex for procreation only. This then negates the need for contraception since it negates the reason for sexual relations. Still, the vast amount of penitential literature that discusses various sexual infractions indicates that sex-for-pleasure was a thriving pastime, and therefore people still wanted to use contraceptives.

Sanctions against birth control grew stronger among theologians from the thirteenth century onward, especially after the Black Death ravaged the population. The changing outlook really began with Aquinas, who voiced the Church's changing stance on fertility control as being universally unacceptable, as opposed to acceptable up to a certain time as Augustine allowed. As noted earlier, Aquinas incorporates Aristotelian views into his Natural Law, insisting that the efficient cause of human generation is the male, while the female is only the material cause[74]: "In perfect animals, generated by coitus, the active power [*virtus*] is in the semen of the male, according to the Philosopher in *De Generatione Animalium*, but the matter of the fetus is what is provided by the female," with menstrual blood being the matter contributed by the incubating female.⁷⁵ The problem becomes how to explain the generative process of the male occurring in the body of the female. The solution, for both Aquinas and Aristotle is to place the *"virtus formativa,"* the formative power that organizes the matter provided by the female in the menstrual blood, within the male's semen. Unlike his predecessors, however, for Aquinas, God immediately creates the human soul and infuses it into the body when the human parents have, by their generative act, produced a material substance that is disposed to receive and to be informed by a rational human soul, with the length of time being determined by the biological sex of the child—40 days for males; 90 days for females.⁷⁶ The actual soul existed prior to its installment, however, and was already part of God's design. Thus, to interfere with conception in any way was to be unnatural by going against God; only He could decide who was going to be born when. As a result, the Church formally condemned "human interference" of all sorts, and medieval contraceptive practices grew more furtive. Fourteenth century popular literature reflects this trend, with comments about birth control potions buried in veiled references.⁷⁷ Certainly, however, women must have continued to brew their own concoctions, and clearly other methods were still employed.

Herbal potions, teas, and pessaries comprised the major forms of medieval contraceptive attempts. Many of the herbal draughts contained the same ingredients as "abortion potions," since the purpose of such things was to stimulate menstrual flow. Commonly used herbs included rue, sage, and cabbage blossoms. Teas and tisanes made from tansy and pennyroyal were common. Pessaries, or vaginal suppositories, were also covered in Classical texts and passed down to the Middle Ages. These are a little more frightening to a modern reader than even some of the more noxious draughts, as many include ingredients such as lead, resin, animal dung, and wool. Aside from medicinal remedies, there were a number of physical methods of contraception that were also in use in the premodern world. The most common was *coitus interruptus*, the "withdrawal method," although the efficacy rate was certainly lowered by the lack of true understanding of how conception takes place. It is not mentioned with much frequency in Classical texts, but becomes a growing concern of the later medieval Church. As Roberta Gilchrist observes, "in the early 14th century the authors of English pastoral manuals were concerned that illicit birth control was being practiced through *coitus interruptus* and extended breastfeeding."⁷⁸ In this case, the Church is censuring not only the birth control attempt, but also the "sin of Onan," or the essentially masturbatory effect that withdrawing had. Other physical remedies likely included "unnatural" sexual activities, such as oral or anal sex. Some medical treatises recommended sneezing, squatting, holding one's breath, and twisting around during sex.⁷⁹ Of these various methods, only one received universal acclaim from the Church—abstinence. Caesarius of Arles (ca. 468/470–542 CE) writes, "a woman who does not want to have children should enter into a religious pact with her husband: for, chastity is the only sterility for a Christian woman."[80] This position makes it very clear that sex is exclusively procreative in nature, that women bear the brunt of sexual responsibility, and that reproduction is a woman's duty. Caesarius further denounced abortion, numbering it among the most grievous of sins, and of course lay full accountability for it on the pregnant woman.

Methods of abortion varied, with medicinal potions, such as medicinal contraceptives, being the most common. Most medical manuals as well as informal "receipt books" have suggested herbal concoctions for bringing on menses, curing "sickness in the womb," easing menstrual irregularities, or even expelling a dead fetus. Certainly these tonics may have been intended for those designated purposes; however, they may just as easily have been intended as abortifacients. A number of different remedies include the ingredients rue, sage, and pennyroyal;[81] however, there are numerous other herbs that show up in various combinations: anise, artemisia, calamint, catmint, cumin, fennel, hyssop, parsley, pellitory, rosemary, savory, thyme, and wormwood being the most common. Usually these herbal draughts were prepared with boiled wine and water as a base, which probably augmented the concoction with a sedative effect.[82] The prospect of an abortion was generally a dangerous undertaking as well, since these "concoctions were too revolting to drink in adequate doses," not to mention "fatal" or "useless."[83] Despite these drawbacks, however, these recipes were clearly used.[84]

While herbal potions were common abortion inducers, more physical solutions were also suggested. Avicenna recommended exercise, especially jumping backward, and, along with *Trotula*, also advocated (induced) sneezing.[85] One Hippocratic treatise proposes that the woman should, on the sixth day of her pregnancy, perform a number of mighty leaps, making her heels touch her buttocks, so that on the seventh day the "seed" would fall out of her with a clatter.[86] Still another physician, Soranus of Ephesus (first/second century CE), commented that vigorous shaking could assist with difficult births, which could also have had an abortifacient result if performed too soon.[87] Midwives were known to press strongly on the stomach and womb in order to hasten birth; similarly, women who wanted to cause a miscarriage might sleep exclusively on their stomachs. Related to these practices is a violent method of abortion with far-reaching consequences, the so-called abortion by assault, which was also considered a felony punishable by death, under English law.[88] This could take the form of beating the woman, or pressing on her womb so as to kill the fetus. Hanawalt notes that English writers, specifically Bracton and *Fleta*, were the first to link abortion with manslaughter in this manner, with Bracton linking "poison" drinks and "striking [her]" as equally problematic.[89] Medieval common law endowed fetuses with human rights by equating abortion with homicide; however, the law defined abortion as any interference with a fetus after ensoulment. Before ensoulment, the Church considered any intervention to be contraception instead, thus carrying a lighter penalty.[90] In these cases, however, the woman herself is not guilty of the manslaughter—her assailant is.[91]

Abortion was a complicated issue in the late Middle Ages, made more convoluted when social class and sexual desire were introduced into the mix. In the third century, for instance, Hippolytus (170–235 CE) denounced Pope Callixtus (r. ca. 218–23 CE) for his lax policies concerning forgiveness of sexual transgressions, among these validating marriages between noblewomen who partnered with lower class spouses or their own slaves because of their own overwhelming desire. Supposedly, his primary concern was the "criminal means" by which these women would prevent the birth of offspring of such unions, fearing for their elevated lineage and great wealth. Hippolytus specifically suggests that the women bound themselves tightly with bandages as well as taking herbal potions. Although he crafts his charge to make it look like his concern is for the supposedly rampant "godlessness of unchastity and murder," it is rather apparent that the real issue Hippolytus has is with the mixing of social classes as well as with the sexual agency of the upper class women who would rather marry and be sexually active than to remain chaste.[92] Here, abortion is specifically discouraged as a punitive measure against women who exhibit desire. That is a common theme echoed throughout early Church history: that women use contraception and abortion as licenses for promiscuous behavior without consequence. In early penitentials, a section called "Simulated Virgins and Their Morals" castigates young women for using birth control to conceal their love affairs, assuming both no other motivation for use and the idea of pregnancy as (appropriate) divine punishment of unchaste women.[93] Similarly, as mentioned earlier, Caesarius of Arles railed against abortion practices in a series of sermons (at least five) deemed *admonitiones*, or didactic pieces for lay audiences.[94] He condemned women who practiced abortion as selfish murderers with no regard for God's workings, possibly in league with the devil, and distinctly "unnatural." Abortion existed in direct opposition to the feminine ideal of maternity, harming not only the individual woman's soul, but also the entirety of female nature and Mother Church. To women fell the task of perpetuating the social order and theological order since children would become secular heirs to their earthly fathers, and spiritual heirs of God as new Christians. Thus, women who procured abortions were abominations who cared only for sexual diversion. In only one instance (Sermon 52) does Caesarius note that women might contemplate abortion for economic reasons, which he quickly dismisses in favor of spiritual riches. However, other clerics were not so hasty in this regard, and moderated their views on contraception and abortion when the woman's economic conditions were poor. A number of penitentials advise the cleric to determine whether the woman in question was merely a lustful fornicator trying to cover up her iniquity, was involved with something more sinister such as witchcraft, or was motivated by her impoverished circumstances—in which case the penance was half as much as in the other cases.[95] In so doing, these men tacitly acknowledged (not condoned) the occurrence of illicit sexuality and its consequences within the different social classes. Another canonist, Johannes Andreae (1270– 1348 CE), observed that there might be "many reasons why a woman would want to take a contraceptive: she might not want to bear a child because of her relations with the father; she might not want an heir to his estate; she might not want a child."[96] Andreae's concern over the woman's desire to bear children is extremely unusual in the Middle Ages, an era where reproduction was an expected duty of all married, sexually active women.

The motivation behind seeking an abortion is crucial to the understanding of an unusual link between sanctity and abortion in the so-called abortion miracles found in some early hagiographies, and points toward the complex position fertility control occupied in medieval society and ecclesiastical thought. Intriguingly, the majority of saints involved in these miraculous occurrences are male. One, Germain of Paris (ca. 496–576 CE), was still in the womb when he performed his miracle. Before his birth, Germain's mother, Eusebia, moved by "womanly shame" (*muliebra pudor*) because she had conceived her children so close together, wanted to eliminate the child from her womb. Since a potion did not work, she took to lying on her stomach to suffocate (*praefocaret*) the fetus. Germain fought back and was born, rendering his mother innocent (*et matrem redderet innocentem*).[97] There are a number of interesting things going on here. First of all, Germain's mother is ashamed because of her speedy pregnancy, presumably because it is a sign of her rampant lust. Clearly she could not forbear from having sex with her husband, perhaps even before proper churching had taken place, and as is typical in medieval culture, the burden of sin lay with the woman. John Kitchen suggests that this is a deliberate action by the hagiographer to ameliorate any potential compassion the audience may have felt for Eusebia, because giving "greater prominence to the emotional factor by elaborating on it would risk casting the mother in a sympathetic light."[98] In turn, this also neatly eliminates approval of her original plan to eliminate the fetus. Second, Eusebia, a Christian woman of rank, was plainly familiar with herbal abortifacients, and was willing to employ them to ease her own life. Third, when the herbal remedy failed, she turned to other physical methods to seek her release, as suggested by the medical texts. The Latin term *praefocaret* is the third person singular imperfect active subjunctive conjugation of *praefoco*, which usually means "suffocate," but can also mean "choke" or "obstruct." In terms of female anatomy, each of these meanings carries an interesting connotation. Besides termination, "suffocate" also recalls the womanly condition of "uterine suffocation" or "suffocation of the mother"—hysteria—which will be discussed later in this section. In uterine suffocation, the womb is choked by lack of space in the abdominal cavity among other things. As well, Germain's entrance into the world is obstructed by his mother's attempt at terminating her pregnancy. Finally, Germain's successful fight to live certainly displays his saintly prowess, but more importantly here, also renders his mother "innocent." The word innocent (*innocentem*, accusative feminine singular of *innocens*) is a provocative choice because it carries with it a sense of removing blame and guilt, not just forgiving it. Through Germain's birth, then, his mother is returned to a pure state, and through it, Fortunatus also sends the message that virginity is the preferred lifestyle and carries with it much fewer spiritual risks than even chaste marital relations.

A similar return to purity can be seen in several other recorded "abortion miracles." Maeve B. Callan observes, "Ireland has no less than four abortionist saints—Ciarán of Saigir, Áed mac Brice, Cainnech of Aghaboe, and Brigid of Kildare—all of whom reputedly lived in the central lowlands during the fifth and sixth centuries."[99] In Brigid's *vita*, the abortion is contextualized within a host of other pregnancy-related miracles, and is described in terms of sparing the woman the pangs of childbirth. This concern for the life of the mother, rather than simply for her restored virginity, speaks to a female perspective over a male ecclesiastical one.[100] The male hagiographies, on the other hand, are primarily concerned with reinstatement of the female body. After a local king raped one of Ciarán's disciples, Bruinnech, she became pregnant and applied to Ciarán for a cure. Because he despised the crime, the cure meant that he pressed on her womb, blessed it, and emptied it.[101] Callan suggests that this demonstrates that Bruinnech's body was a battleground for the struggle between secular and ecclesiastical (male) power. I would also point out that the methodology employed by Ciarán, the physical pressing of her womb, follows the medical advice of the day. The blessing implies that she is returned to the state of consecrated virgin. In the hagiographies of Áed mac Brice and Cainnech of Aghaboe, each is faced with a (former) consecrated virgin who is pregnant—in these instances because she had secretly fornicated, not because she was raped—and once the saint has blessed her womb, all traces of pregnancy vanish as if they had never existed.[102] Thus, a woman who had sinned is fully restored—rendered innocent—and the power of the saint is aptly demonstrated.[103] Aelred of Rievaulx (1110–67 CE) records a similar incident in England. He relates the story of the Nun of Watton, a Gilbertine sister who became pregnant and was imprisoned until she gave birth, but then claimed that two saintly women who visited her in a dream removed the infant. Her (not surprisingly) skeptical fellow nuns insisted on making a physical inspection of her body, whereupon they discovered that she now had a "girlish if not virginal look" about her, a flat belly and dry breasts, and they "found no sign of childbirth, no indication even of pregnancy." Like the Irish women, the Nun of Watton had her innocence restored, in this case directly because she "moved the tender heart of Jesus."[104] Again, male supremacy and mercy is demonstrated as soon as the woman admits her failing. These stories all have a similar theme: women are spiritually frail, and particularly susceptible to sins of the flesh, so it is the responsibility of men to guard their chastity.[105] In none of these instances, however, is the saint's reputation for holiness affected by his or her support of abortion.[106] In fact, in each instance, the saint's support of virginity and chastity as proper feminine attributes is the focus of celebration.

Disease and illness

The medieval concept of illness is rooted firmly in the humoral system. When all of them are in balance (*eucrasia*), the individual is healthy; imbalance indicates infirmity. The balance of humors was achieved by diet, medicines, and bloodletting. In the Middle Ages, diet was sometimes difficult to control due to lack of ability to store food properly, or even at all, and to purchase a variety of foods. The majority of the population, whether wealthy or impoverished, would have consumed meats and grains, adding in vegetables, herbs, and fruits that were seasonally available. Nevertheless, if an imbalance was perceived, efforts were usually made to adjust the affected person's diet as possible. Medicines were composed primarily of herbs or other natural substances, some rather noxious by modern standards, others that did no harm, but also produced no results (such as magic stones).

Of all the medical techniques used during the Middle Ages, bloodletting was by far the most preferred. Bloodletting involves the release of small amounts of blood from the body through small, precise incisions. The practice is based on Hippocrates's, and subsequently Galen's, belief that menstruation functioned to purge women of bad humors caught in their wet and spongy flesh. In fact, the Hippocratic opine that if menstruation does not occur, then the surplus blood will come out through another orifice or continue to build up in the body, putting pressure on different organs until disease or even death results. If such a process assisted women, Galen reasoned, then a physician could recreate a similar experience for both men and women to adjust the levels of humors according to the desired effect. There are two main types of bloodletting: derivation and revulsion. Derivation meant letting of blood at a point close to the affected area, and revulsion meant that blood was let at the most remote point to the affected area. Over the centuries, medical practitioners painstakingly drew up extensive manuals detailing every vein and its corresponding response. Bloodletting was used as both a curative and a preventative. For instance, monastic rules usually contained a chapter on bloodletting regulations, as periodic bloodletting was a requirement for most orders: "from at least the ninth through the sixteenth century, healthy men and women were bled for reasons of physical and spiritual prophylaxis at regulated intervals throughout the year."[107] Whatever the reason for its instigation, it was understood that bloodletting would restore balance to an imbalanced body.

As an extension of his humoral theory, Galen believed that immoderation caused illness because it caused an imbalance in the humors. This perspective had a significant impact on medieval Christians, not the least of which is the idea that the plague was a direct result of sinful human behavior. However, the direct correlation between certain diseases and sexual sins was noticeable even to medieval physicians. The Middle Ages did not have a sense of "sexually transmitted diseases" the way we do today, but the connection between disease and sex had been noticed for centuries. Ancient, Classical, and medieval texts all make note of diseases that today we can recognize as gonorrhea and syphilis, or "venereal disease."[108] It is debatable whether or not they were directly associated with sexual activity, and often the two diseases were conflated into one, with the symptoms of gonorrhea being thought of as the early stages of syphilis. While both diseases were present, it wasn't until the large outbreaks in the late fifteenth century that it became evident that "syphilis was at least primarily a venereal disease, and often the consequence of sexual immorality, making it not just a shameful physical condition, but a religious one as well."[109] The buboes and scabs of syphilis are often readily visible on the penis or labia. Religious injunctions against fornication thus became not only soul-saving, but also life-saving, and the infected were deemed sinners. Syphilis spread throughout Europe in the 1490s, and was definitely in England by 1493–4, where it was recorded that in the town of Shrewsbury "about thys tyme began the fowle scabe and horrible sickness called the freanche pocks."[110] The main treatment for syphilis from the Middle Ages until the early years of the twentieth century consisted of the application of a mercury ointment which was then steamed into the body, or occasionally other metals such as gold or silver were powdered, made into a solution, and injected into or under the skin. Soranus of Ephesus, a second-century Greek physician, supposedly named gonorrhea, the oldest and most common of the venereal diseases. He identified the disorder in both men and women as frequent emission of semen without sexual arousal, which he believed occurred because of a weakness of the body as a whole. In this perspective, gonorrhea became a clear example of the ill-effects of insufficient tension in the body, and so he prescribed constrictives (binding weights made of lead) to strengthen the ailing body.[111] Medieval medicine followed suit, at least to some degree, as one treatment included binding an afflicted person with strips of cloth that had been dipped in a lead-based solution. Like its venereal counterpart, syphilis, gonorrhea is clearly the result of excess in sexual indulgences, and in both cases, too many orgasms.

The social effects of the medical discourse surrounding sexually transmitted diseases are also interesting to the study of gender. Although bathing was not usually encouraged in the Middle Ages for a number of reasons, as the link between having sexual intercourse with an infected person and getting a disease became more firmly recognized, so did sexual responsibility—medieval physicians began advising patients to wash their genitals after sex.[112] This led, also, to the belief that some people are "clean" and others "dirty," leading to the stigmatizing of patients and the refusal to seek treatment. Moreover, women came to be seen as particular sources of disease as well, since they were considered the weaker sex, and predisposed to sin and lust, it followed that if women were chaste, the disease would disappear.[113] Eventually, this led to the widespread myth of the "virgin cure," the idea that sexual relations with a virgin would cure an infected man of venereal disease.[114]

Despite the occasional conflation of bodily illness with spiritual illness, even in the case of venereal disease, "individual sin was seldom seen as the cause of sickness, whether mental illness or physical ailments. One notable exception was leprosy, which was associated with a variety of sins, but especially with lust and pride."[115] Leprosy has a complicated medieval history, at various times being considered akin to a venereal disease, and being connected to gender and religious identity as well. Unpacking its position is further complicated by the conflation of leprosy proper with any skin disorder or disfiguring disease. In fact, it seems quite likely that leprosy and syphilis were confused to a great extent, which perhaps explains leprosy's fate as a venereal disease. Leprosy was greatly feared in the Middle Ages. Treatments were few, and the main approach was expulsion from the community. Many communities required citizens to denounce suspected lepers and employed a special jury of doctors or even other lepers to examine the accused.[116] A formal ceremony was conducted, at which a priest read-off a list of prohibited behaviors that included restrictions on washing, eating, speaking, clothing, touching, and, of course, sexual intercourse.[117] Lepers lived communally in leprosaria, which existed in Europe from the eleventh century on.[118] Leprosaria were subject to both ecclesiastical and royal control, with the way of life of the patients being very similar to that of a religious order: praying in peaceful surroundings for the salvation of their benefactors and living and working together. Carole Rawcliffe notes that leper houses were places of security and refuge, offering clothing, warmth, friendship, food, and palliative care; moreover, leprosaria were strategically built so as to acquire the most charitable donations.[119] Such donations assisted both the lepers inside the community and the person tendering the donation, who often received an indulgence or other sort of religious reward. Leper houses reached their zenith in the thirteenth century, but saw steady decline through the fourteenth and fifteenth centuries, with many leprosaria being turned into regular hospitals. Causes for the decline are not entirely clear. Some scholars believe that changing medical practices understood the disease better, while others suggest that a wider immunity level was achieved in the population, or a general improvement in diet and housing. Most recently, however,

Rawcliffe has suggested a combination of social and cultural factors. Lay piety no longer favored the monastic life to which leper houses were tied, but rather the mendicant one, to which general hospitals were connected. Thus a competition for alms and bequests, alongside the devastating effect of the Black Death, led to economic crippling from which many of the communities could not recover.[120]

The leper occupied an unusual place in medieval thought. On one hand, lepers offered good Christians the opportunity to practice charity. To some extent, the "Church sought to establish lepers as God's anointed, singled out by Christ for extreme suffering, destined to live out their purgatory on earth."[121] However, numerous other discourses, including Leviticus, implied that leprosy was a punishment for sin.[122] Many early commentators noted that lepers were prone to quick anger (wrath), while others observed greed or envy as the main faults, all of which tie back to Leviticus, and all of which connect leprosy to a sinful nature.[123] As a result, many of the medical treatments combined a scientific and moral approach. For instance, Susan Zimmerman reports that Guy de Chauliac (ca. 1300–68 CE),[124] a well-known French physician, suggested treating lepers with "gentleness," and also to advise them that "sayde disease is to make them penitent for theyr sinnes," while referring to them as "monsters," and noting the connection between the disease and "*luxuria*" (lust; lechery).[125] Thus, leprosy became, in the Middle Ages anyway, a type of sexually transmitted disease, and "contagion was deemed to be effected by sexual relations, by contact, and by breath."[126] Perhaps the competing discourses about syphilis and leprosy as well as their similar symptoms caused the cross-contamination; nevertheless, it becomes quite clear that leprosy eventually became associated with transgressive sexual behavior as well as other sins of excess.[127] Grigsby argues that according to the medieval mindset, "leprosy is transmitted [in sexual intercourse] because the lecherous desire already exists in an individual's body."[128] It is not sex that causes leprosy; rather, lechery—sex that shouldn't happen—causes it. Gilbert the Englishman (fl. 1250 CE) notes that lepers look for sexual pleasure both more than they used to and more than they should, implying that leprosy is both the cause of their lust and the result.[129] Popular literature upholds this connection between sexual transgression and leprosy. For example, John Gower (1330–1408 CE), in his *Mirour de l'omme* (*The Mirror of Humanity*, ca. 1376–9), writes: "Leprosy is so virulent that it corrupts the air together with all the wind that blows by its side, and in this respect stands for Lechery. Wherever Lechery goes, she perverts the people who hold to her."[130] Leprosy is foul air tainted by sexual immorality. Likewise, in the *Book of Margery Kempe*, she warns her debauched son to "kepe þi bodi klene" and to abstain from "womanys feleschep" lest he be punished—which he is, after he falls "into the synne of letchery," when his face "wex ful of wheyls and bloberys as it had ben a lepyr."[131] Clearly, improper sexual relations lay at the root of his illness. Perhaps the most famous literary example is found in Robert Henryson's (fl.

1460–1500 CE) *The Testament of Cresseid*, a fifteenth-century continuation of Chaucer's *Troilus and Criseyde* (1380s), in which he describes Cresseid as being afflicted with leprosy, presumably as fitting punishment for her sexual betrayal of Troilus with Diomedes, and, perhaps, resorting to prostitution after Diomedes has subsequently cast her aside.[132] However, despite this cause-and-effect relationship between lustful actions and resultant leper sores, a number of the supposed cures, or at least treatments, for the disease also involve sex. Numerous medical texts suggested sexual intercourse as a palliative for leprosy, although just as many suggested abstinence.[133] Still others suggest castration as a remedy.[134] More confusingly, a number of texts suggest both sex and abstinence as cures.[135]

Two further associations with leprosy also have a direct impact on the study of gender: menstrual blood and Jewish identity. Specifically, the *De secretis mulierum* states, "whenever men have sexual intercourse with menstruating women they are made leprous," and also warns, "a man should be especially careful not to have sexual intercourse with women who have their periods, because by doing so he can contract leprosy . . . this stink will corrupt a man's insides."[136] In the Middle Ages, leprosy was, fundamentally, an impurity, of both the body and the soul. Menstrual blood, as a particular pollutant, is directly tied to poisoning the system. Thus, women and their tempting sexuality were causes of leprosy. The alleged immunity of women to leprosy highlights this connection. It was noted by a number of medical practitioners that women who had sex with a leper often did not (or seemingly did not) contract the disease themselves, but instead passed it on to the next man who had sexual relations with her. This supposed immunity fits the cultural myth of the promiscuous woman who brings about men's downfalls while escaping the consequences, coupled with the idea that women somehow desired to bring about male destruction. The link to Jews is dependent upon this suspicion of the female: "a common mode of denigrating the Jew in the Middle Ages was to accuse him of an underlying femaleness," and this association was mostly accomplished through the suggestion that Jewish men "menstruated" like women.[137] Like lepers, Jews and women exuded poison; like lepers, Jews and women were impure; like lepers, Jews and women could have an unbearable stench; like lepers, Jews and women were inherently sinful, especially in regards to sex. There is even a tenuous connection to medieval blood libel beliefs about Jews and supposed cures for leprosy—the blood of Christian infants.[138] Although this cure was seemingly never enacted, it is referenced in several medical texts and popular literature, such as the late thirteenth-century romance, *Amis and Amiloun*. In real life, however, the closest example is the Shepherd's Crusade of 1320 during which over 300 Jews were massacred alongside numerous lepers, ostensibly as an act of purification, although more realistically as a blow to royal power.[139] Additionally, leper property was often confiscated and given to monastic houses just as Jewish property was, and, of course, women's right to own property was shaky at best.[140]

Just as too many orgasms brought on sexually transmitted diseases, too few orgasms caused a different set of problems. Although virginity was prized in the Middle Ages, and was considered the ideal lifestyle, it brought with it medical issues. According to Galenic theory, without regular, or at the very least intermittent, orgasms, women's bodies would retain an excess of menstrual blood. As well, without orgasms, it was thought that women might become overly desirous of sex. The "closed" body of the virgin was therefore vulnerable to ailments such as "greensickness," also occasionally called "heaviness," and the sufferers needed to be treated—not only to alleviate their symptoms, but also to preserve their chastity. The initial cure for this disease was bloodletting, as it would allow for the body to release the built up excess of blood. As noted earlier, monastic regulations called for regular bloodletting, so for nuns, who presumably lived a life without regular sexual release, the practice was essential. However, sometimes bloodletting was not enough. In these instances, medieval medical writers suggested that a responsible and trained midwife apply special unguents and assist them in manual medical masturbation.[141] It is especially interesting to note that medieval medicine acknowledged an inherent need for sexual release as part of human nature. Virginity and chastity were not protections against this absolute physical requirement, even though they were protection against the harm sexual intercourse could do to one's soul. Moreover, the approved treatments involved either a simulated orgasm achieved through bloodletting, or an actual orgasm brought about by same-sex digital manipulation—yet in neither instance was the sufferer accused of impurity. In fact, because the process relieved the restrained fluids, the woman would actually become chaster as a result of the treatment.[142]

The fear of this disease grew disproportionately in the Renaissance, especially after the Protestant Reformation encouraged marriage as the preferred life choice over virginity. Dubbed the "virgin's disease," in sixteenth-century Europe, greensickness was seen as a common disorder affecting young unmarried girls. Its symptoms included weakness, diminished appetite, lack of menstruation, and, most significantly, a change in skin color. Puritan teaching raised the bar even higher, by classing the disease as potentially fatal unless immediately controlled, seeing women's virginity as a sign for an incomplete and unnatural state in which to remain. Puberty and virginity were thus neatly turned into medical problems needing to be cured (by men). Although bloodletting and exercise were still suggested treatments, the only cure, propelled by a fear of female sexuality and a fear of masturbation, became marriage, as quickly as possible, to a man who desired to have sex with the girl.[143] Greensickness, it should be noted, could be cured by anyone of the opposite sex; therefore, "a Renaissance diagnosis of greensickness could compel a woman to take a husband she did not desire . . . or engage in sexual intercourse against her will . . . ostensibly for therapeutic reasons."[144] If only sex, preferably through marriage, could cure this disease, it also became very difficult for women to defend a claim or rape or abduction. Since her body needed and desired sexual intercourse, the case would have been easy for a male defendant to make that she welcomed the encounter rather than resisting it.

Another, similar, concern has received a great deal more attention. Recently, much has been made of the affliction called "hysteria" and its impact on women and the sex toy industry.[145] However, medical descriptions of the "disorder" known as "hysteria" have been around for centuries.[146] Hysteria (from the Greek word for womb, *hystera*) is wandering womb syndrome. Early medical writers theorized that when a woman wasn't pregnant, the uterus could actually detach and move around the body like an erratic animal, roaming throughout the female body "hither and thither."[147] This movement could cause injury to vital organs, causing a number of symptoms, including incoherence, delusions, and numbness. Women suffering from hysteria were seen as imbalanced or disturbed, for example due to extreme emotions such as jealousy or love. In extreme cases, where the uterus was attracted upward by a delightful scent, and remained there for some time, the woman could experience choking, gasping, muteness, and perhaps even convulsions. Such cases were often termed *suffocatio matricis* (uterine suffocation), and were a form of advanced hysteria. Because all women have wombs, and all wombs have the potential to move and cause emotional instability, all women were therefore weak, frail, and volatile. Further, the animalistic nature of the womb added to the discussion surrounding the humanity (or lack thereof) of the female sex. Suggested cures involved applying scented oils to women's sexual organs and using scents to coax the womb back into its accustomed place through genital massage. In other words, physicians used digital manipulation to bring female patients to orgasm to cure hysteria; thus, "though all women were endangered by their unpredictable anatomy, women without the benefit of marriage—virgins, nuns, and widows—were especially prone to hysteria."[148] In this way, hysteria was like greensickness, as was its cure. Overall, sexual intercourse was seen to have healing powers, while pursuing unnatural, "manly" interests exacerbated the trouble. This, in turn, had the effect of pressing women into their social roles as wives and mothers, and keeping them in both sexual and intellectual subservience.

Conclusions

Overall, economic and legal discourses comprise a history of patriarchy. As Judith Bennett notes, "the ways in which the institutions and structures of past times worked to maintain male privilege and female disadvantage."[149] While women were viable members of the economy of medieval towns in the Middle Ages, they were not able to participate in the formal political process of the towns, and men had the exclusive right to be citizens and serve in the governmental structure. Yet, women made their testaments, witnessed charters and deeds to property, could own property within reason, and create wills. Although subordinate, the rights women did exercise introduced a conflicting set of meanings about the position of women in society.

Barbara A. Hanawalt acknowledges that women did have a place within London's economic system, yet their primary economic contribution continued to be through dower portions of land and money—capital—that they could pour into their spouse's endeavors.[150] In looking at women in connection to the real estate markets, she notes that women could inherit property, and that property could be leased, sold, and bequeathed. Their dower properties usually remained untouchable even by a husband in debt, preserved for a woman's children. However, the theory of the law and the practice of the law rarely met. Only rarely did women collect their shares on their own. As well, by the sixteenth century, women's property ownership rights had eroded to the point that the majority of wills left all lands to sons and only "moveable goods" to daughters. Here we see gender oppression in action, and to some degree, a re-gendering of the female body. Women, through marriage, become "one flesh" with their male spouse. Thus in legal practice, they cease to function as a sole entity, and instead exist only as an extension of the male body to which they are grafted. Similarly, in a study of Chancery cases, Anna Dronzek finds that "people in medieval England more readily accepted women's claims to property from marriage than from family inheritance, again demonstrating the strength of women's identities as wives and widows."[151] Women did not have identities—legal or otherwise—beyond their relationships to men.

Even laws that seemingly equalize gender constraints ultimately prove to reinscribe patriarchal oppression. The most significant of these is the peculiar concept of *feme sole*. This is the idea that under the law, a married woman, who was usually referred to as a *feme covert* (being under the coverture of her spouse), could act as a single woman in her own right. Theoretically, then, any profit she made, as well as debts she owed, were her own gains and obligations. The law was seemingly designed, at least on the surface, to "protect" women; however, this status was rarely used, and even when it was called upon, it generally did not benefit the woman in question, but rather her husband. Men, and the women married to them, used this legal standing to manipulate the system in order to avoid repayment of debts and seizure of property. Instead of rendering them equal under the law, or at least allowing the women to temporarily gain a sense of "maleness," the law served male purposes, while keeping women bound just as firmly to their male counterparts as under *feme covert* status. Very little measure of independence was truly achieved. Furthermore, in the few instances where women did gain victories, the favorable judgments were nullified if the victors subsequently fell victim to female failings, such as slander, gossip, and lustful pastimes.[152] The law was never intended to allow women to act as men, even temporarily. Rather, it was meant to give men another tool by which to retain economic power, and the flexibility of medieval coverture is "evident in the fact that when coverture was inconvenient for men, the courts ignored it."[153] Karma Lochrie addresses the idea of coverture as tied to the reinscription of gendered binaries. Under coverture, the association of the female with the domestic and the private is reinforced, since it "established a domain of the secret and the private that women were made to inhabit and that came to be identified with the feminine and domestic spheres of daily life in opposition to the masculine domain of publicity."[154] Men, who were rational and controlled, deservingly inhabited the public spaces of society, whereas women, who were irrational and unruly, were just as deservingly relegated to the private spaces.

All of these economic and legal discourses are supported by the medical science of the day, which saw women as inherently and impossibly different from men in ways that rendered them less capable holistically. Biology supported the social and political position that women were inherently inferior to men, meant to be passive and protected. Their cool and moist bodies, although necessary for human reproduction, were full of secrets and problems and needed to be controlled. Menstruation provided evidence of the lack of control the female body truly had. Galen believes that men, who are warmer than women, are better able to process their bodily fluids and expel any excess through perspiration and excretion. Although he viewed menstruation as a necessary part of staying healthy, he also believed menstrual blood was poisonous and full of noxious fumes, leading to an assortment of problems both for the women who produced it and the men who inadvertently came into contact with it. Aristotle differed in his approach, as he understands blood as nourishment, so excess blood becomes bodily residue. Men, who are hot and dry, are better able to convert this residue into a generative force—semen—whereas women, who are cold and moist, cannot fully or properly process this residue, and must expunge it through menstruation. Menstrual blood thereby becomes a manifestation of female incapacity, and, in Aristotle's words, an outward symbol of her "deformity."[155] Men are warm, perfect, and complete; women are not-men. The biological inferiority of women makes their legal, social, and religious suppression natural, and the gender divide almost insurmountable.

CHAPTER TWO

The expected ideal: Marriage and virginity

Although modern conceptions of sex and sexuality place active heterosexuality, along with its procreative potential, in the "normative" position, that was not precisely the case in Christian premodern Western Europe. Pre-Reformation Christianity rejected the duty to procreate as a fundamental value of personal religious life and cast procreation as a social value. By this I mean that the Church extolled celibacy as a nobler platform for salvation than sexual congress. Accordingly, patristic writers held that virgins received a more significant reward in heaven than wives, chaste or otherwise. This position remained unchanged throughout pre-Reformation society. In the seventh century, Aldhelm (ca. 639–709 CE) wrote: "that virginity is gold, chastity silver, conjugality bronze; that virginity is riches, chastity an average income, conjugality poverty; that virginity is freedom, chastity ransom, conjugality captivity."[1] Several hundred years later, in the twelfth century, the treatise *Holy Maidenhood*, which can be read either as a pro-virginity text or an anti-marriage piece, relates a similar sentiment: "If marriage is the third of these three states, you can understand by the degrees of their happiness which one surpasses the others and by how much. For marriage brings forth her fruit thirtyfold in heaven, widowhood sixtyfold; maidenhood with a hundredfold, outdoes both."[2] Virginity was precious, both literally and figuratively. Virginity added to the value of a bride, since she would produce only legitimate heirs. Beyond that practicality, however, "the virgin's body was described as a jewel, a treasure, a sacred vessel, a temple of God which was to be cherished and honored."[3] Thus, while "norm" was not a medieval concept, there was an expected ideal state of humanity, and that ideal was virginity—and even to some extent, a fundamental lack of sexual awareness. This perspective is tied directly to the development of the concept of Original Sin and the sexuality of Adam and Eve in the Garden.

However, despite the Church's strict insistence on virginity as a preferred state, medieval people regularly chose marriage. In response, several things happened. Chaste marriage, or spiritual marriage, that is an asexual relationship between partners, developed. As well, widowhood was not only praised, but also a state of "vowed widowhood" was created. Of course, secular virginity, or the concerns of medieval men and women in ensuring that women remained virgins until marriage, is connected to each of these vocations as well, not only due to Church doctrine, but also due to the importance of lineage, especially for the nobility and gentry. Chastity is the standard practice expected of all women, and to some extent of men also. Ruth Mazo Karras points out that in the Middle Ages, chastity referred to "absence of sexual activity," and celibacy was indicative of being unmarried, not necessarily of refraining from sexual intercourse as part of a vocation, so one could technically be celibate, but not chaste.[4] Although treatises on virginity were addressed to both women and men, most of them concerned women's virginity, both because of the example of the Virgin Mary and women's questionable capacity for virtue. Jerome remarks, "For this reason virginity is more abundantly poured on women, because it began with a woman."[5] Eve failed; later women had to redeem her failing through steadfastness. Male virginity was important to, but not essential for, salvation, and was more important to religious than secular life. Finally, marriage, once a purely social concept, was incorporated into the Church as a religious ritual and, eventually, as a sacrament (although not until post-Reformation). It was also prioritized for the secular world, and removed, at least officially, from the ecclesiastical sphere. Each development in human relationships was fundamentally tied to sexuality and the control the medieval Church exerted upon it.

Virginity

The ideal state of perfection for human existence was virginity.[6] This began in the Patristic era with the early Church Fathers, and continued throughout the Middle Ages, culminating in a change only after the Reformation, and then only for Protestants. Stoicism, an ancient Greek philosophy that advocated emotional control, and asceticism, a lifestyle, both pagan and Christian, that advocated bodily discipline and renunciation, were the two primary influences on development of this position. Numerous Church fathers wrote about the avoidance of sex, and while they differed on the relative sinfulness of the act, almost everyone agreed that the best choice was no sex.[7] This position is tied most clearly to two underlying concepts—the emulation of Christ and/or the Virgin Mary and the idea of Original Sin. In this chapter, I want to look at the idea of the Fall, Original Sin, and the privileging of virginity for women. Religious implications and male virginity will be addressed more thoroughly in Chapter Three.

Adam and Eve's existence in the Garden of Eden proved to be a challenge to Patristic writers attempting to determine the place of sexuality in religion. Many of the arguments centered on whether or not Adam and Eve had sex in the Garden. Although sex was not the actual Original Sin—that was the disobedience of consuming the fruit from the forbidden Tree of Knowledge—it was inextricably tied to it as the first realization Adam and Eve had upon gaining "knowledge" was of their nakedness. Before their eyes were opened to sin, clothing was not necessary because nakedness meant nothing "impure." These acts were not in dispute; however, the amount, type, and effect of human sexual intercourse in the Garden of Eden were a matter of great concern to early theologians. A number, most prominently Ambrose (337–97 CE) and Jerome (347–420 CE), believed that there would have been no sex in the Garden at all. Marriage, sex, and procreation were all seen as direct consequences of the Fall. Still others believed that the reproduction of humans would have happened, but through divine creation, not sexual union. Just how this would have happened was also debated, with no real resolution reached.

Augustine's (354–430 CE) views were more elaborate. For him earthly sexuality is the result of the sin that brought about Adam and Eve's expulsion from Paradise. Concupiscence, the chaotic consequence of the original sin, shows the great distance between the soul and the body. The human body, obedient and docile in the beginning, became rebellious as a consequence of having disobeyed God; hence, humans have difficulties while attempting to dominate and accommodate our body to the spirit's precepts. The genital organs are the portion of our body that more radically comes to show this insubordination, that is the disjuncture between will and corporeity. After the expulsion from Paradise, "the flesh began to lust against the spirit . . . It is this tyranny of lust that makes men ashamed. They hate to have such uncontrollable movements."[8] In other words, according to Augustine, there was indeed sex in the Garden of Eden, but it was sex without pleasure. Edenic sexual intercourse would have been unemotional and purely for reproductive purposes. It is this view of sexuality that influenced Augustine's, and thus Church doctrine, about marital sex. Similarly, since lust is the direct consequence of the Fall, then avoidance of lust—virginity—becomes the way to reproduce Edenic conditions on earth. Finally, Augustine, and subsequent theologians, such as Alexander of Hales (ca. 1185–1245 CE), held that human reproduction in the Garden would have further preserved perfect "innocence" because there would have been no breakage of the hymen.[9] Once the relationship with God was sundered, the hymen was subsequently rent, making virginity a symbolic reunification through an intact body.

Later theologians struggled with the rejection of sexual pleasure, the necessity of procreation, and the literalness of early definitions of virginity. Bonaventure (1221–74 CE), for example, held that there may have been sexual pleasure in the Garden, but it would have been under control and not "shameful." Excessive sexual pleasure is humanity's punishment for disobedience. Thomas Aquinas (1225–74 CE) reinstated the centrality of procreation in Christian theology (*Summa Theologica* II, 2, Q152, reply to the first objection). He, however, emphasized that the duty to procreate lies on the "multitude of humanity," not on every single individual. In this way, he praised those who chose the nobler path of virginity and chastity, but still supported legitimate sexual congress within marriage. Aquinas supported the idea that sexual congress existed in the Garden of Eden, but became more shameful after the Fall. Similarly, he posited that sexual sins within marriage were more plentiful than outside it, primarily because of misplaced desire.

No matter the position on sexual intercourse occurring within the garden, medieval theologians agreed on two points almost across the board: nudity was free from shame and that childbirth was free from pain. Both shame and pain were direct results of the Fall, were caused by Eve's unwise choice, and were therefore the fault of women. Thus it is only fair that women are lower than men. They caused the expulsion from Paradise. They caused shame and pain to be visited upon humanity. They caused sex to happen—and are therefore creatures of lust. A woman practicing chastity distanced herself from the negative qualities associated with women. Because of Eve's sin, women were thought to be carnal and deceitful, easily susceptible to pride, loquacious, and the source of the world's problems. If a man lusted, it was always the woman's fault. Women were seen as being so tied to their sexual nature that to renounce it was to go completely against that nature; a phenomenal achievement representing a completely altered, as it were sexless, state like that in which the angels were said to live. Choosing celibacy broke the bond of their subjection to original sin; but those not able to encompass this, or those attempting it and failing were represented as an actual danger to the Christian life; therefore any woman was inherently dangerous.[10] The only way to overcome that lustful nature is to embrace purity. Virginity is a way to return to the perfection that was Eden and to degender women, since their gendering means dangerous sexuality. Male virginity simply proved the ultimate rational self-control, also connected to Edenic fantasy, since Adam lacked proper self-control and ate Eve's offering.

The association of lack of sexual desire with the Garden of Eden led to a burgeoning amount of the *hortus conclusus* (enclosed garden) in Marian iconography. Similarly, the tradition of the lover's garden grew stronger, as evidenced famously in *Romance of the Rose* as well as countless poems, romances, and paintings.[11] Set apart from the normal realm of moral judgment, the medieval garden of love is usually seen as a site that embodies the carnal human desires that must be renounced in order to find God, but are lustily embraced in earthly gardens. Women, often associated with the natural world because of their fertility, heavily populated lover's gardens in poems. However, by the end of the fourteenth century, images of the Virgin Mary enclosed in a garden were also common in Western Europe. Verse 4:12 of the *Song of Songs* is generally viewed as the source of inspiration for Marian garden iconography: "Hortus conclusus, soror mea sponsa; hortus conclusus, fons signatus," or "my sister, my spouse, is a garden enclosed, a garden enclosed, a fountain sealed up." This verse was first interpreted as an expression of Mary's perpetual virginity. Eventually the *Song* was written into the Latin liturgy as a way to honor Mary's Assumption (her bodily ascension, after death, into heaven). A shift from the liturgical application to a more devotional form of commentary gathered momentum in the twelfth century when the *Song of Songs* became the most popular Biblical book on which to comment. Interpretation of verse 4:12 was expanded to include Mary as an embodiment of the Church, with Mary representing the new or virginal Church—and as such, a Bride of Christ. Eventually the verse inspired a great many visual symbols of Mary as vehicle of the Incarnation: she is the perpetual virgin, garden of everlasting life, and source of nourishment for that life, and exemplar of the feminine ideal in medieval Christian imaginations. The *hortus conclusus* became a symbolic microcosm of the new Garden of Eden in which the Virgin Mary, antitype of Eve, reigns. Just as Eve symbolized humanity's fall in the original Garden of Eden, Mary symbolized humanity's rebirth through the Incarnation. The Virgin Mary in her enclosed garden offers protection and nourishment yet is perpetually virginal and pure. Moreover, the enclosed garden represents a microcosm of the larger world, "completeness," a "mirror of the soul, of man, the cosmos, paradise ... the whole and its parts are analogous." The symbolic language of medieval *hortus conclusus* images can express the Church's doctrine of the Incarnation. By God becoming human, the human is a reflection of the divine; the orderly world contained in the *hortus conclusus* is a mirror of God's overall divine plan.[12] Virginity and chastity brought stability and purity to a world full of instability, sin, and danger.

By its very nature, the concept of female virginity revolves around socially constructed binaries: pure/spoiled, innocent/experienced, intact/damaged. In the Middle Ages, virginity was a signifier of both spiritual and physical wholeness. However, that did not necessarily mean that virginity was understood only as a physiological state. Religious discourses tended to emphasize "spiritual" virginity, and warn against privileging the integrity of the mortal body over the purity of the immortal soul. In this way, virginity was also defined as a moral or spiritual state worthy of a relationship with God, not simply having an intact hymen or lack of sexual experience. In other words, the potential exists for a medieval woman to no longer physically be a virgin but to have reacquired her "virginity" due to her chastity and spiritual devotion to God. However, just as physical virginity could be lost through physical actions, so, too, could spiritual virginity be easily destroyed or corrupted by failure to perform the acts and identifications that produced it. As such, a stray thought could condemn a virgin. For example, Jerome writes, "Virginity can be lost even by a thought," and Gregory of Nyssa (335–94 CE) observes, "Virginity of the body is devised to further such disposition of the soul."[13] A virgin must have *integritas*, or total virginity, meaning both body and mind were uncorrupted and pure. Additionally, Clarissa Atkinson argues, "By the end of the Middle Ages, although the physical definition survived, the moral definition prevailed—in part . . . because of the experience and the reputations of the late medieval saints."[14] Women such as Angela of Foligno, Birgitta of Sweden, and Dorothy of Montau became holy women after leading a secular life.[15] Such women provided models of chastity to both physical virgins and to widows regaining their "virginity."

Widow(er)hood

A virgin or widow was free from a husband's authority and from the inferior legal and social status a woman suffered as a wife; thus, she had a degree of independence and selfhood not known to a wife. However, since virgins were precious, and women had questionable self-control, they had to be closely guarded, unlike widows. Virginity was considered a grace given by God (thus it was sinful for virgins to take credit for remaining chaste, although it was also sinful to fail in that endeavor); widowhood was an active choice, one that gave community status in their communities. The Church chastised women who chose not to remarry for the wrong reasons, such as to receive independence from men, although they often touted this latter point to entice women to remain chaste. Widowhood places a woman outside the sexual economy of marriage thereby creating a desexualized notion of womanhood that was capable of wielding authority, even in a patriarchal culture. Generally, widows had the most independence of any group of women, although they were not equals with men.

The experience of widowhood was deeply gendered. Although it is a condition shared by men and women, their contrasting experiences reflected the patriarchal society in which they lived. Widowers were more likely to remarry than widows, although the loss of a wife rarely altered a man's social or financial status the way the loss of a husband affected a woman's. Men remarried quickly for a variety of reasons, many of them practical. Wives provided men with heirs, housekeeping, and "comforts," including ready access to sex. In the lower classes, wives also provided economic partnership and/or labor assistance. Widowers also had fewer inheritance concerns—a man who remarried was less likely to endanger his children's legacy for the most part, as firstborn heirs usually took precedence over later ones. Like the widow, the widower could be seen as destabilizing to the marital and reproductive order if he remained alone too long. Widowed men sometimes joined monastic orders. Others relied on family members, especially elder daughters, for assistance. To some extent, then, widowerhood acquired invisibility as remarriage and other support structures relieved the widower from the trappings that accompanied widowhood. Overall, however, examining the social and cultural tensions created by uncontrolled women, underscores the centrality of marriage as an organizing principle of late medieval and early modern society. As such, its significance encompassed both genders.

A common theme in discussions of medieval widowhood is the potential problem posed to family, church, and state by an adult woman neither governed nor maintained by a husband. This problem was both conceptual and practical. Families and social institutions attempted various strategies to cope with the problem of widowed women, sometimes seeking to recontain them within marriage or monasticism, and occasionally cooperating to construct a viable identity and space for the independent widow. As well, both Church and society viewed widows with suspicion since they were both sexually experienced and sexually available. When viewed as a drain of resources, or as a danger to transmission of property, or a religious challenge, male relatives and government officials could be quick to push widows back under available forms of male stewardship. These attempts were often facilitated by the inability of authorities to imagine a natural social role for autonomous adult women. Both secular and ecclesiastical officials believed that the widow had only two possible futures—monastic withdrawal or remarriage. Remarriage was often the quickest solution for widowhood, although it posed a number of problems, both secular and sacred. On one hand, widows were encouraged to remain single because of the rewards they would gain in heaven. They were considered to be in a better spiritual position than wives. In addition, there was concern, based on John 4:18 (the story of Jesus and the Samaritan woman who had married five times), that a second marriage didn't count in the eyes of heaven and would therefore be considered fornication.[16] On the other hand, monetary issues, especially inheritance concerns, also affected remarriage. The laws regarding inheritance varied from place to place, but the most general rule was that a widow was the guardian of her deceased husband's property until her children came of age. In some cases, the portion that was her dowry belonged to her and her daughters, and the rest went to her sons. In other cases, she could keep the entire property but forfeited it if she remarried. As will be discussed in Chapter Four, guilds typically allowed widows to maintain their late spouse's membership and apprentices, providing both a living wage and a family legacy.

Widows could also join a monastic order. No restrictions were placed on them because they had been married, and presumably sexually active, before joining. In these cases, any property involved reverted to the Church's possession unless there were surviving male children. In the early medieval period, monasteries were founded "not as retreats from the world but as a means of spreading the Christian faith to all parts of the various kingdoms, of establishing centres of educational, political, and social significances . . . [as] places of learning and [for providing] essential pastoral care for the rural population in their vicinity."[17] Because of this, it was common for upper class widows to join such establishments. They were often already educated, and also could oversee the interests of their family or other supporters of the institution. In other cases, wealthy widows actually founded the monastic house in which she went to dwell. Sometimes these women even assumed the position of abbess, with her donation securing the position, but her widowhood representing a pivotal position between married life and sexual renunciation, and aptly demonstrating a transition from the concerns of secular society to the institutions of a professed religious. In fact, a number of saints were widows. Their hagiographies were carefully constructed to demonstrate their sanctity, since "she who was 'really a widow' was the wife of just one husband, lived chastely, and carried out numerous good works."[18] In other words, because she was once married, the potential saint had to overcome her initial sexual activity by proving her recommitment to faith and chastity, but also had to demonstrate that the potential for sanctity was always within her. Still, even widows who chose a life of religious devotion could give rise to tension. Although the Church supported enclosure, convents often did not have the facilities to support more members. Sometimes families preferred that a widow remarry so as to forge new alliances or provide dynastic heirs. In these cases, widows often acted as sponsors of ecclesiastical institutions, thus extending the influence of the family as a whole. Sometimes honorific posts in convents and hospitals accompanied this support, and, by taking an active role in these institutions, these widows were able, if not to escape from their families, then at least to distance themselves in all-female households where they retained some power.

Although enclosure or remarriage were the two main options for widows, there were a number of women who remained unmarried and outside the ecclesiastical structure. Such a life involved legal challenges, especially if any negotiations or contracts were needed, but also allowed for a relative level of freedom not experienced by most medieval women. As well, a rather unique religious vocation grew out of the desire for chaste widowhood without the rigors of enclosure—the vowess. A vowess took a public vow of chastity (not poverty or obedience) in front of a bishop, but continued to dwell in her own home. By becoming a vowess, a widow could not be forced to remarry, nor would a new husband gain her money and property. Moreover, it put her under Episcopal protection, which made her less likely to be a victim of rape or ravishment. Mary Erler suggests that these women often did not necessarily choose a life of chastity because of any overwhelming spiritual desire, but rather because they needed to negotiate the legal, political, and social systems of their communities.[19] At the ceremony, two men "gave" the widow to the bishop, who symbolically received her and publicly recorded her vow, mimicking a marriage ceremony. She also received dark clothing, a special ring, and a veil, and took her vows while lying prostrate at the bishop's feet, emulating a nun's profession. It is unclear whether or not vowesses were restricted in their movements or in their dress, since little about them survives. However, the mere fact that such a quasi-professed state exists suggests that medieval society understood that women required a position from which to negotiate boundaries. Consecrated chastity offered widows a safe space in which to remain, although instead of becoming Brides of Christ, they essentially remained "spiritual widows."[20]

Finally, widowhood is generally defined as the phase of marriage following the death of one of the partners. To some extent, medieval widowhood might also be able to encompass the monastic profession of both marriage partners, which effectively ended the marriage through the "spiritual death" of enclosure. Theologians were torn about this undertaking. On one hand, they certainly encouraged Christians to embrace fully the religious life and dedicate themselves to God and prayer. On the other hand, while marriage was neither sacrament nor fully religious ritual, it was a legal and moral binding contract, whereby both parties agreed to mutually support each other financially, physically, spiritually, and sexually. However, in three instances, monastic profession after marriage was possible. In the case of an unconsummated marriage, either (or both) spouse was able to enter a monastic house without consent. In fact, the remaining spouse was free to contract another lawful marriage. If the marriage had been consummated, however, the Church required both spouses to undertake religious profession, or at least a private vow of chastity. This was allowed only if the spouse was so old as to be considered past sexual desire. Finally, in the case of adultery, the innocent spouse was allowed to take monastic vows without consent of the adulterous party, who then relinquished all claims.[21] To some extent, in each of these cases, the remaining spouse (if there was one) was treated in a similar fashion to a widow(er), since they were not barred from remarriage and their former partner was "dead" to the secular world.

Chaste marriage[22]

Because of the inherent sinfulness of human sex, the Church came to recognize chaste marriages as a valid form of relationship. A chaste marriage is one that is like a standard marriage in every way except the partners refrain from sexual activity with each other or anyone else. Some scholars refer to such an institution as a "spiritual marriage" instead of a chaste marriage. However, "spiritual marriage" was a term that was often used in connection to the allegorical marriage between Christ and the Church, or between Christ and nuns/monks, or even the relationship between confessor and holy woman. For this reason, I will here refer to a marriage in which the spouses practice sexual abstinence as a chaste marriage, much as medieval writers generally did. Aside from continent contractual unions, however, the issue of chaste marriage is connected to clerical celibacy and to spiritual widowhood. Occasionally, chaste marriages resulted in one or both spouses leaving the secular world for the monastic life. Finally, the late Middle Ages witnessed a rise in a different type of chaste marriage, one in which the partners originally had sexual intercourse and even children, but later agreed to live chastely together. This signaled a return to marriage as idealized by Augustine of Hippo. He suggested that sexual passion, while acceptable in youth, would fade with age; therefore, married couples could spend their elder years in "ordered love," without the need for sex. Furthermore, he held that the "better the couple are, the earlier they have begun, by mutual consent, to refrain from sexual intercourse." Presumably because they could have sex lawfully and within the passion of youth but chose to refrain makes them holier, since self-control is praiseworthy.[23] Even within the lawful bounds of matrimony, sexual intercourse was viewed with suspicion. However, at the same time, it was an expected part of married life.

There were two schools of general thought in medieval theology as to what made a marriage valid: consent theory and consummation theory. In the former, only consent to the ritual was necessary to make a valid marriage; in the latter, sexual intercourse was required. Problematically, consummation theory invalidated the most holy of marriages, that of Joseph and Mary.[24] As such, consent theory, sometimes referred to as betrothal (*desponsatio*), eventually prevailed. Under this philosophy, the betrothal contract seals the marriage through consent alone. Betrothal theory also served to strengthen Church control over marriage. Ecclesiastical authorities often reserved the right to determine whether or not proper consent had been obtained from both parties, in effect, weakening the power of the head of the family. Whatever the cause, however, the result was the validation of unconsummated marriages—as long as those marriages were sanctioned by the Church. Joseph and Mary, then, had a firm and perfect marriage sealed within their betrothal contract and mutual affirmation of the marriage, rather than through sexual intercourse. The doctrine of the perpetual virginity of Mary was generally accepted as early as the fourth century and almost universally agreed upon by the seventh.[25] This relationship became the model for chaste marriage, a practice that the Church reluctantly supported. Aside from the Biblical model of Christ's parents, a number of hagiographies emphasize the saints' chaste marriages. The most famous of these was St Cecilia, whose life was not only preserved in numerous hagiographies including the *Golden*

Legend, but also in Chaucer's *Canterbury Tales* as the "Second Nun's Tale." According to legend, Cecilia was an upper class Roman woman who on her wedding night convinced her husband, Valerian, that an angel of the Lord was guarding her chastity and would kill him if he attempted to consummate the union. When Valerian asked to see the angel, she directed him to Pope Urban I for baptism. Valerian did so, and then later converted his brother, Tiburtius, and a soldier, Maximus. All were martyred for their faith. Interestingly, Cecilia and Valerian did not share a mutual agreement about having a chaste marriage before their ceremony. Instead, Cecilia had secretly converted to Christianity before her marriage and made a private vow of chastity. Valerian went into the marriage completely unknowingly. Instead of agreeing to live in continence because of his own faith, Cecilia threatened him with death via angelic execution. Fear and curiosity compelled him to baptism, yet Valerian converted two more men through his actions. Nevertheless, aside from Mary and Joseph, Cecilia and Valerian are considered role models for chaste marriages. St Alexis upheld the male version of chaste marriage. Son of a wealthy Roman family, Alexis married his chosen bride, but then left her on their wedding night. He gained her permission to seek a life of chastity and prayer, and although she remained in society, she also, supposedly, remained a pure and faithful wife. Once again, as with Valerian, the saint's spouse is co-opted into a chaste marriage without foreknowledge of the commitment.

Historical records of individual chaste marriages are generally not found among the peasant ranks, not only because of extant records, but also probably because they could not afford to give up the contribution of children to a household, or to risk the loss of family monies. Several of these chaste unions involve royalty. Queen Æthelthryth (ca. 636–79 CE), for instance, remained chaste throughout both of her marriages. In between marriages, she retired to the Isle of Ely, and after being expelled by her second husband, Ecgfrith of Northumbria (ca. 645–85 CE), retired back to the island and founded a double monastery there. Even more famously, King Edward the Confessor of England (1003–66; r. 1042–66 CE) and his queen, Edith (ca. 1025–75 CE), supposedly had a chaste marriage. This case was unusual because there were no formal declarations of chaste intent, nor did either party make a formal or public profession of virginity. Instead, the idea of a chaste marriage was retrofitted onto a royal marriage that produced no heirs and essentially resulted in the Norman Conquest. Edward's marriage to Edith, daughter of Godwin, the Earl of Wessex, early in his reign can be taken as a sign of baronial pressure to enmesh himself within Anglo-Saxon politics after his years in Normandy, as well as pressure to produce an heir.[26] The choice of Godwin's daughter associated him with the most powerful barony in the land, and it seems likely that he hoped for an heir from Edith until a feud broke out between Edward and the Godwins. Nevertheless, the feud was resolved and Harold Godwinson (ca. 1022–66 CE), the new earl, became Edward's successor.

During his life, Edward had a reputation for maintaining connections with the church and promoting a religious life in England, and he founded a number of founding monastic houses, including Westminster Abbey. The process of formal, papal canonization of Edward began when his incorrupt body was found in 1102, with the first petition begun in 1038, and his canonization in 1161. Still, contemporary accounts portray Edward not as a particularly saintly individual and most of his church appointments were politically motivated or expedient. As well, the lack of a direct heir resulted in political chaos and the end of Anglo-Saxon England. In order to correct this political disaster, hagiographers recast Edward and Edith as a type of Mary and Joseph. For instance, the *Vita Aedwardi Regis*, an anonymous history of the reign of King Edward and of the Norman Conquest that followed, written around 1067, suggests that both monarchs enjoyed the privileges of parenthood through the foundation of abbeys and the joys of heaven increased by their stalwart virginity.[27]

A different type of chaste marriage emerged in the later Middle Ages. In this case, the spouses were not virgins, but rather chose to mutually end their sexual interactions. Augustine had suggested, as pointed out earlier, that as spouses aged, sex would stop. Medieval tradition saw Sts Anne and Joachim, the Virgin Mary's parents, as a model for this type of marriage. Anne and Joachim had tried to conceive for many years with no luck, and when Anne passed into menopause, they assumed they would remain childless. However, an angel visited Joachim in a dream, instructing him to meet Anne at the Golden Gate of Jerusalem. When the couple was reunited at the gate, they exchanged a chaste kiss, and the Virgin Mary was instantly conceived without sin. Being an older married couple past childbearing age, Anne and Joachim supposedly no longer shared sexual relations, as both desire and the ability to procreate had passed them by. Moreover, Augustine had implied that couples who chose to end their sexual interactions before age withered them would gain spiritual rewards. A number of women seized upon this stance as a way of aligning themselves with the more traditional aspects of saintliness, in essence "re-virginating" themselves. Among this group of women are the canonized saints Birgitta of Sweden (1303–73 CE), Dorothy of Montau (1347–94 CE), Hedwig of Silesia (1174–1243 CE), and Frances of Rome (1384–1440 CE). Each of these women had physical children, and two of them (Birgitta and Frances) founded religious orders, providing them with spiritual heirs as well.[28] The hagiographies of these women tend to extol the virtues they displayed even before they practiced abstinence. Many performed works of great charity and penance or self-mortification. Virtually all of them were described as not enjoying sex, submitting only to the whims of their husbands or the need for an heir. Many of the women were also mystics and visionaries, and their sexual renunciation assisted them with their divine calling, and added to their overall sense of asceticism. That this lifestyle, a reclaimed chaste marriage, was an available option is confirmed by Margery Kempe

(d. after 1438) in her *Book*.[29] The *Book of Margery Kempe*, dictated to two confessors, is considered the first autobiography in English. In it, Margery discusses her life and her saintly aspirations. Margery and her husband John had 14 children. After receiving a vision from Christ, Margery managed to convince John to agree to a chaste marriage by agreeing to pay off all of his acquired debts. In this way, she combines both chaste marriage traditions—she can be re-virginated, as is symbolized in the *Book* by her donning white garments, and she imposes her saintly choice on her spouse, since John regrets his agreement several times. Margery clearly draws on elements from Birgitta of Sweden and Dorothy of Montau's lives. Like Dorothy, Margery is a member of the artisan class. Like Birgitta, she sees herself as a visionary and leader. Margery was never canonized, yet her *Book* amply demonstrates that the desire for sanctity as acquired through sexual renunciation was a strong undercurrent in late medieval society.

The notion of chaste marriage is tied intimately to the question of clerical celibacy. Early on, clerical celibacy was not an issue. The apostles, their direct followers, and the earliest popes were all married. However, as the pressure grew to define virginity as the ideal state, the concern over potential impurity of the clergy grew, too. Redefining virginity as a sort of spiritual marriage contract between the virgin and God allowed the Church to uphold marriage as an institution while simultaneously supporting virginity as a spiritual state. Debates further arose about the distraction married life causes to spiritual pursuits. On the basis of ideas found in the works of Jerome and Cassian (ca. 360–435 CE) as well as St Paul, there is a disconnection between a married life of lust and earthly pleasure and a spiritual life of denial and spiritual fulfillment. To some extent, this resulted in supposed "chaste marriages." Both the Council of Elvira (ca. 305 CE) and the Council of Carthage (390 CE) forbid clergy to marry after ordination, and suggested that it is the duty of those already married to abstain from sexual contact with their wives. Ambrose (ca. 333–97 CE) took up this question in several of his treatises, opining that married men—even those who had fathered children—could be ordained, but not raised to the bishopric. Moreover, those married men who were ordained were subsequently obliged to live lives of purity and restraint afterward. Finally, a number of theologians cast the priesthood as the representation of Jesus's life on earth, and since Jesus was not married, a priest should not be, either. Despite these theological positions, priests continue to marry and to father children. Even if clerical celibacy was the preferred practice from the time of Pope St Leo the Great (440–61 CE) forward, it did not become an actual Church rule until the eleventh century during the Gregorian Reform. Pope Gregory VII (1073–85 CE) issued a papal encyclical in 1074 absolving people from obedience to bishops who allowed married priests, and the following year, he issued another renouncing clerical marriage entirely. These were accompanied by his aggressive moves against simony (paying to receive sacraments), and as such have been rightfully tied to the preservation of Church lands and goods. If priests marry and have children, their heirs stand to interfere with Church monies and properties, but also they might expect to inherit a Church office. As Helen L. Parish notes, "priestly celibacy was not just a matter of ecclesiastical discipline, but of political import and social function."[30] A clerical wife posed all kinds of threats to the ecclesiastical system. Inheritance was only one of these potential problems. Wives occupied too much space, created the need for social networks, and, perhaps most easily acknowledged, damaged clerical purity. Not only would a wife tempt a priest to sexual intercourse, but also her constant presence in or near the church potentially defiled it with her lust, her menstruating body, and her womanly failure. In order to preserve clerical masculinity, medieval priests have to renounce the very act that made medieval men manly—sex. The marital debt was a complicated concept.

Despite the warnings of Church authorities on the sinfulness of sex, those same authorities also acceded that it was a part of marriage and both parties were responsible for honoring the marital debt. And, as Dyan Elliott discusses, "release from sexual duties, moreover, is often perceived as potentially altering traditional gender-dictated roles and challenging normative concepts like female submission. From the perspective of the hierarchy of sexes, spiritual marriage may then have posed a parallel threat to both husband and society."[31] Certainly perpetual virginity offered women a measure of independence and even regendering, as will be discussed in Chapter Three. Widowhood, and its freedom from sexual congress, was also liberating. Sexual liberation challenged male authority. Married women who refused to pay the marriage debt veered toward independence. Margery Kempe, for instance, was able to go on pilgrimages and to experience more heavenly visions once freed from sexual duties. Thus the concern of the patriarchal state was realized. The best way to contain women was to subsume them under male control, and most often that meant marriage.

Marriage

Marriage was the least spiritual state of earthly existence, but was the most commonly chosen one. Medieval marriage was the adoption of something already in existence, originating in the practice of ancient Rome. Eric Carlson observes, "reliance on Roman law for ideas and language reinforced the view of marriage as a secular matter, and priests were rarely involved even in ceremonial aspects."[32] In fact, before the eleventh century, there were no uniform church regulations for marriage in the Church. For the first few centuries of Christianity, the community simply adopted familial customs of marriage in the home. Church leaders relied primarily on the civil government of Rome to regulate marriage and divorce between Christians and non-Christians alike. With the fall of the Roman Empire, the Church gradually began to take legal control over marriage and make it an official church function. In the Middle Ages, the Church began looking into the sacramentality of marriage, making it something that would be regulated by the Church not the state, although it would not become a formal sacrament until the Council of Trent (1545–63 CE). As mentioned earlier, the Church held the exchange of consent between the spouses to be the indispensable element of a valid marriage, not consummation. However, the lines between consent and consummation were repeatedly blurred. In essence, however, if consent is lacking, there is no marriage, but if consummation is lacking, the marriage may still exist. Mostly, however, marriage was regarded as a business in the matter of society, state, and church rather than a union established solely for the concern of the two individuals who would perform it.

Marriage was first and foremost a social contract. Church involvement primarily changed attitudes toward marital sex, not necessarily toward the contractual nature. Feudalism and its literary offshoots such as courtly love also had effects. For instance, marriage in pre-Conquest England differed significantly from later versions. Men paid a bride price for a woman. She retained rights to his lands and properties after his death, receiving half if she bore a child, less if she did not. She was also given the right to leave the marriage and take the children if she desired, or to leave the children with him. On the morning after the wedding night, a man gave a morning gift to his wife, which remained her property during the marriage and after her husband's death or separation. Inheritance laws also allowed women to buy, sell, inherit, and bequeath land and movable goods. Although some historians may argue that women were not treated as property, others maintain that what looks like purchase and ownership actually is just that, only with different parameters.[33] Legislation reflects an ideal situation that is unlikely to have represented the true state of affairs. Women were still very much under the control of their husbands. For instance, while monogamy was theoretically the accepted practice, men regularly took lovers and concubines, while women were punished for adultery, sometimes with physical mutilation. As well, although married women were allowed to make wills to bequeath their property, they could not do this during their husband's lifetime without his consent. In fact, women had very few legal rights outside of marriage, and upon marrying became the chattel of their husband. There was really no such thing as divorce, even if the remote possibility existed. Marriage was viewed as a means to cement alliances with families or to make peace with an enemy, and daughters were not typically consulted in the matter. The king might also be involved in the marriage negotiations, occasionally using marriage between children of noble families to settle disputes between warring families.

Christianity and feudalism brought changes to marriage practices. One significant difference was the institution of primogeniture, meaning only the eldest (legitimate) male offspring could inherit. In this effort to have legitimate male heirs, it was important to have a wife of good breeding. Since control of land was necessary, the king required all noble marriages to be approved by him in order to prevent his enemies from gaining strength. Widows and heiresses thus became wards of the king, a relationship that in later years became a profitable business—the king could sell wardships and levy fines to remain unmarried. This led to the formation of an aristocratic group that intermarried within itself to maintain family power and to increase wealth and land. Instead of the morning gift, women now received a dower portion, which consisted of one-third of the property of her husband, with the remaining two-thirds inherited by the heir. Most noble marriages set out by contract before the marriage the exact amount of the wife's dower. Although the dower did not belong to the wife alone during the marriage, and she had no power over it until her husband's death, he could not sell it without her consent. As well, although medieval marriage patterns generally involved partners in their early twenties among the lower classes, early marriage was more common among the nobility and the gentry. A higher social status narrowed the pool of potential partners, and also made the necessity of gaining allies more immediate.[34]

The process of selecting a marriage partner was something families took great care with. Generally, the criteria included "the advancement of the individual and the family, [and] the ideal of parity."[35] Certainly, a measure of personal affection between spouses was preferable, but it was not tantamount. The most important purpose of a suitable marriage was to gain new and potentially useful kin, even among the lower classes. Material substance was always taken into consideration very seriously. A marriage contract set up the conditions that made it possible for the couple to live on their own, but it could include a wide range of other matters. Bargaining was a complicated subject. The contributions of one side had to match those of the other side and future incidents which could not have been foreseen were also dealt with. Still, the major focus of negotiations was often the dowry. Commentaries on Gratian's *Decretum*, a twelfth-century collection of canon law, and other papal letters suggested that the dowry be at least four times the income of the bridegroom in order to contribute to the capital of the new household, although certainly that was not always possible.[36] An attractive woman or a woman of higher status might even be excused from part of her dowry. The ideal of parity between marriage partners was also taken into consideration.

Similarity of ages was considered, but was not necessarily essential, especially for older men seeking male heirs. Similarly, age parity assumed, at least to some extent, that the parties involved were old enough to consider their consent. However, many upper class marriages were contracted when either one or both of the parties were children. This could be an advantage, because the children would grow up together and grow to love each other, but the Church frowned on consummation of marriages until the girl was at least 12 years old, although at the time of the marriage the girl might be as young as 6. Occasionally a betrothal occurred, but marriage actually took place when she was older. The Church required consent of both parties to complete the marriage, and there are some instances of marriages that took place when the girl and boy were very young, and by the time they reached the age of consent, they refused the marriage and it was annulled. The lower classes married at later ages, at least until the period after the Black Death (1348–50 CE).

The most important consideration was parity of rank. Women had more flexibility in this regard than men. Widows could choose a partner for remarriage with more freedom, and some nobles married "excess" daughters into the gentry class. Occasionally, a wealthy merchant married a daughter into one of the higher classes for the sake of her dowry, but merchants' sons were rarely allowed to marry into the landed classes. Finally, character of the individuals involved and the potential for affection was sometimes considered, but rarely was the motivation for marriage. Instead, marriage was an economic relationship, or, essentially, a "two-person career."[37] Personal affection was often not considered when contracting a marriage, although the Church did advocate marriage to avoid the occasion of sin (fornication) as well as for procreation. In fact, according to Church teaching, husband and wife owed each other a conjugal debt. This was one of the very few reciprocal aspects of medieval marriage, and on the surface, almost appears to encourage equality, at least in one area. However, the debt really worked to the advantage of male sexuality. Dyan Elliott notes that discussions of the conjugal debt were "padded" in ways that were prejudicial to women. Women were instructed to dress to capture their husbands' attentions. They could not fast without permission because that diminished sexual appeal. They were also encouraged to undergo "churching" (a purifying rite performed after childbirth) as soon as possible so as to be sexually available. These may appear to be small concerns; however, together they demonstrate that the Church was anxious to channel women's sex drive. Clothing, food intake, and vaginal care were all aspects of the female body that should have been under female control. Instead, they were regulated and objectified as spaces for male sexual pleasure.[38] In every other way, the wife owed complete and immediate obedience to her husband. This position was supported by Church and state, as well as by popular culture and tradition. Men were superior to women; husbands ruled wives. In fact, any man who allowed himself to be controlled by his wife was considered to be lacking in masculinity. "Real men" controlled women properly. The law, the ultimate masculine presence, controlled women completely.

Marriage was seen as a matter of concern not only to those joined together in it, but also to their parents in the eyes of the Church. The medieval Church insisted on individual consent for marriage, but also recommended parental advice and guidance. From the twelfth century onward, canon law viewed the consent of both sides as the crucial core of a valid marriage. The Church supported the right of individuals to renounce marriages, which were made before the ages of consent (12 for girls, 14 for boys). Consent, not consummation, made a marriage. As long as no undue force had been exercised to persuade them to marry the Church supported the contract. Besides consent, the Church was concerned that the parties were free to marry. This meant that they were not related within the degrees forbidden by the Church; that they had not previously contracted a legally valid marriage with someone who was alive at the time of the second marriage; and that they were not ordained in major orders or professed in final vows. In the eleventh century, the Church had developed a rule forbidding marriage within seven degrees of consanguinity, or the close relations by blood or marriage of the intended parties. That proved to be unworkable in medieval society, so at the Fourth Lateran Council in 1215, that was narrowed to four degrees of consanguinity. This still meant that many of the nobility and gentry, who were highly interrelated, had to secure a papal dispensation before contracting marriage.

Throughout the Middle Ages there was no singular wedding rite for Christians. Because of the sociopolitical importance of marriage, especially among the upper classes, this came to involve pledges in front of witnesses. However, consent was not the binding force of marriage—sexual consummation was. By contrast, in order to limit the opportunities for fraud and self-deception, and to minimize the uncertainty about the validity of unions, the Church tried to ensure that marriages were made publicly and with ecclesiastical blessing—and consent was the binding factor. Despite not having a singular ritual, then, because of the legal and moral importance of recognizing valid marriages, public declarations became commonplace. By the late Middle Ages, standard practices for marriage had developed, although none were precisely required. These steps began with official betrothal, often including marriage contracts and the formal consents. This was followed by the publication of the banns of marriage (public announcements of the upcoming wedding), usually for three weeks in the home parish of the participants. This allowed time for any public objections to the marriage as well as the discovery of any potential obstacles. The final step was that the couple publicly exchanged consent to the union at the church door in front of witnesses and a priest. However, the exchange was not required to take place in church until after the Council of Trent. The exchange would often be followed by mass, and then the marriage was consummated privately.

Marriage was considered a contract for the life of the parties, and technically divorce did not exist, at least according to the Church. However, there were ways to end an unhappy or unproductive marriage. Most chronicles use the term *divortium*, which literally means "divorce" in Latin, but in practice means "nullity." Annulments meant that the marriage had, in essence, never occurred, not that it had ended. They took place before ecclesiastical courts, and were often quite expensive, but they were necessary for valid remarriage. The most common reason for granting an annulment was consanguinity. Marrying within these degrees was viewed as being similar to incest. Sexual dysfunction was also a valid reason for an annulment. Impotence, particularly if it resulted in the non-consummation of the marriage (*divortium a vinculo*), was the most serious of these. Tests for male impotence were both thorough and public, and usually involved a panel of female members of the community, usually older, established married women, who manually manipulated the man's genitals seeking a reaction. Another common annulment cause was refusal to tender the conjugal debt. In fact, it was generally considered more serious for the husband to refuse his wife since it was believed to be medically important for women to participate in regular orgasmic release in order to remain healthy. Occasional grounds for annulment included flagrant adultery, leprosy, and malicious abandonment. Other possible impediments to a valid marriage included the parties not being of legal age, the parties being under previous oath or vow, the parties being of different faiths, and the parties unwillingly being coerced through "force or fear" into wedlock. Once one of these reasons had been sufficiently proved before an ecclesiastical court, the Church could agree to grant an annulment rendering both parties free to remarry, although any children from the marriage became illegitimate.

Although actual divorce suits were very rare, and annulments were expensive, legal separation was rather common. This was termed *divortium a mensa et thoro* (divorce from bed-and-board). The husband and wife physically separated and were forbidden to live or cohabit together; however, their marital relationship did not fully terminate since civil courts did not have the power to declare a marriage null and void. This form of separation was supposed to be used in cases of adultery, heresy, apostasy, and cruelty, thereby making the grounds both secular and spiritual in nature. Seemingly, however, it was more common than those grounds would allow. Finally, court cases and vernacular literature of the time both make mention of numerous husbands and wives who simply separated. Many of these people found other partners; however, upon death, the legal spouse, if he or she could be found, would still be held accountable for debts or be the recipient of benefits.

Marriage supposedly reaped the fewest rewards in heaven for its participants. Still, it was the only institution that allowed for relatively sin-free sexual intercourse. Thomas Aquinas considered marital relations in the context of "natural law." Nature, he believed supported not just the generation of the species, but also the preservation, education, and advancement of children; therefore, the marital structure was best disposed to provide for such development. Moreover, Creation dictated that man and woman were complementary by nature, and owed each other mutual service, both sexual and nonsexual, since life outside Paradise challenging.

In Thomistic thought, then, the root relationship in the body politic is the "community" of husband and wife in "mutual service." Out of this relationship grows that between parents and children, out of which in turn grow the complex relationships that constitute society at large. Thus, in terms of modern gender theory, both Church and state underscore the basic fundamental patriarchal structure of the nuclear family with the man as head of house, and wife and children under his control. As far as actual sex went, Aquinas suggested that the inherent shame in it stems from Original Sin, which gave rise to excessive passion. It is too much pleasure that damages virtue, not the act of intercourse itself. While there is a place for pleasure in carnal relations, it should not supersede reason, and satisfaction must not be the only motive for the act. The moral manuals of the thirteenth and fourteenth centuries uphold this position, and consider marriage a form of chastity. For example, the *Book of Vices and Virtues* reads: "The third branch [of chastity] is the state and the bond of marriage, for they [husband and wife] shall keep themselves entirely for each other, cleanly and truly, without any wrong-doing the one to the other."[39] Of course sex within marriage could also be an occasion of sin if exercised improperly. However, marital sex, when undertaken with proper restraint and purpose, within the proscribed terms was the only nondeviant form of sexuality approved of by the medieval Christian Church.

CHAPTER THREE

The unexpected actuality: "Deviance" and transgression

"Deviance" is a loaded term, often tied to sexual aberrations. The *Oxford English Dictionary* defines deviants as those who "diverge," and who "deviate from normal social standards," with this emphasis coming from twentieth-century sociology in particular. However, the word "deviance" is taken from the Latin verb *devio*, meaning "to turn from the straight road, or to go aside." The *Middle English Dictionary* defines "deviaunt" as "different," but also, "one who goes astray." One of the first recorded instances of its usage is in the late Middle English translation of the *Romance of the Rose* (ca. 1400 CE) usually attributed to Chaucer, "From youre scole so devyaunt I am" (l. 4789). Here the lover is emphatically insisting to Lady Reason that he has not been helped by her lesson, though he is not one of those who "wrongly werke ageyn nature" (l. 4769). As well, Thomas Usk (d. 1388 CE) describes the world before Christ as "deviacion, that is to say, goyng out of trewe way" in *The Testament of Love* (ca. 1485 CE).[1] From this perspective, "deviant" can be errant behavior of numerous sorts. It can be unnatural ("against kynde" in Middle English) or heretical. In short, anything that is not the ideal is by default deviant. If the medieval ideal is virginity, then anything that challenges virginity—even marriage—is deviant to some degree. The inherent sinfulness in sex, even married procreative sex, upholds this stance. It thus stands to reason that anything that is nonprocreative in nature would fall into the category of deviant. Similarly, if the ideal body is male, then anything not-male would be considered deviant. Alastair Minnis succinctly sums up this position: "half of the human race was deemed fallible because its members lived in the wrong kind of material body, the inferior female rather than the superior male form."[2] Women, hermaphrodites, and eunuchs are all deviants because of who they are; adulteresses, prostitutes, seduced women, and emasculated men because of what they do.

The *Middle English Dictionary* goes on to connect "deviaunt" to the word "contrarie." The second definition contains a reference to the same passage from *Romance of the Rose* as deviant: "From youre scole so devyaunt I am . . . To me so contrarie . . . Is every thing that ye me ler," which also cites *The Imitation of Christ* (ca. 1500 CE): "Suche þinges as we loue or desire, or suche þinges as are contrary to us."[3] While a number of the meanings of contrary coincide with deviant (e.g. differing, inappropriate, unnatural, immoral, variance), these two passages are specifically connected with the final definition, "repugnant or distasteful to." Not only are deviants straying from the path of goodness and averse to society, but they are also offensive in general. Deviance can be viewed as a form of social conflict. After deviance is recognized, what follows is repudiation (the attempt to maintain that nothing unusual is happening within the society), which can be further broken down into four parts: bracketing (denying deviance is occurring by completely avoiding the topic), normalization (declaring to yourself that the deviant behavior is no different than that of accepted behavior), attenuation (deviance is acknowledged, but mitigated as not serious), and balancing (deviance is acknowledged, but the good and bad aspects on an individual are weighed). Individuals are then labeled and stigmatized by those in power.[4] Although this is a process identified by modern sociologists, it certainly occurred in medieval society. Power is central to this view—the power of deviants to engage in nonnormative behaviors undetected, or the power of some groups in society to create rules for and to label others. Studying deviance is therefore crucial to the study of gender. If we understand deviance as a concept of difference, we can also look at how deviance has been related to important social problems and institutional responses to treat and control them, and how these responses have affected the gender roles and power (im)balances. Just as nothing is naturally gendered, so, too, is nothing inherently deviant—there always has to be some social comparison.

Therefore, anything that is against the ideal practice can be classified as deviant. As discussed earlier, the medieval ideal was untouched virginity, for both women and men, with chaste marriage, and monogamous procreative marriage as acceptable options. Anything contrary to these practices would have been viewed as deviant in the sense of working against the purposes of both Church and Nature. Heterosexual adultery, for instance, is termed by Chaucer's Parson "agayns nature" in his declaration: "Al that is enemy and destruccioun to nature is agayns nature" (*Parson's Tale*, l. 864). Here he is referring to a wide range of lecherous activities, working from, as Carolyn Dinshaw terms it, "an assumption that whatever hinders the proper end of coitus [procreation] is against nature."[5] Adultery is at its very core nonprocreative, despite the fact that procreation can, and certainly did, result. It is, however, not a publicly recognizable procreation, except in certain instances, and certainly not for female adulterers. According to medieval cosmology, humans were meant to establish monogamous pairings. The patriarchal underpinnings of society also relied on the nuclear family as the basis for building and maintaining male control. Therefore, adultery is deviant because it both disrupts the social order and violates religious law. As in today's society, men seemingly committed more adulterous acts than women overall, making them participants in deviancy, even if not fundamentally deviant.

On the other hand, menstruation, a natural function of female biology, served as a way of rendering women as deviant bodies, incapable of continence like the pure, sealed male form. The physiological processes specific to woman (i.e. menstruation and lactation) are described as "modes of seepage" so that the female body is always deviant.[6] Menstruation is a natural sign of woman's inability to control the workings of her own body, but also a natural sign of her eternal lack of control and perfection. Medieval medical views believed that menstruation was necessary in order to maintain humoral balance, and, as Caroline Walker Bynum points out, "all human exudations—menstruation, sweating, lactation, emission of semen and so on—were seen as bleedings; and bleedings—lactation, menstruation, nosebleeds, hemorrhoidal bleeding and so on—were taken to be analogous."[7] Still, menstruation was particularly noxious, and according to most popular lore, was unclean, impure, and even poisonous. Pseudo-Albertus warned men to look for watery eyes, changes in complexion, and loss of appetite in women, and then avoid them so as to evade their venom. Theology generally viewed menstruation as a consequence of the Original Sin of Adam and Eve, albeit one that provided health benefits. Mary's purity and perhaps lack of menstruation emphasizes "the extent to which the Fall and the stain of womanhood haunted that physiological process."[8] Menstruation was an outwardly visible sign of the permanent deviance of the female body.

These examples of deviance demonstrate that anything outside the prescribed ideal and the perfect male form is deviant merely by existence. For instance, masturbation was considered a sinful and deviant practice. Under this umbrella, nocturnal emissions were also subjected to scrutiny by the medieval Church. Other more radical and obvious forms of deviance are also important to the study of gender. Castration and eunuchization were practices that existed within many societies throughout the premodern world, and were deeply embedded in constructions of medieval masculinity and male sexuality. Cross-dressers, once called transvestites, violated social and gender roles. Sex workers, especially prostitutes, were a particularly strong challenge to medieval chaste ideals. Same-sex sexual relations and relationships are central to the study of gender and sexuality in any society, especially one as homosocial as the European Middle Ages. Recovering this "lost" history has occupied modern scholars for the past several decades, although more work remains to be done. The study of "hermaphrodites," those individuals we now recognize as intersexed, provide a valuable opportunity to explore the tension between nature and nurture in gender identity. In closing, a look at monsters provides both a theoretical perspective of deviance, and a real-life fear of medieval people.

Under medieval ecclesiastical and secular law, all of these so-called deviances can also be defined as sodomy. Late medieval definitions of sexual sin, and of sodomy in particular, tend to be so all-encompassing as to nearly obscure the topic altogether—sodomy could be any unnatural behavior; sodomy was deviance. Sodomy was a category covering a wide range of transgressive acts that was any activity that challenged the "Nature" of the church-state authority:

> Theoretically, sodomy was a fairly general term for most types of crimes that were deemed to be "against nature." In effect, this meant sexual relations that were nonprocreative. By the middle ages, most jurists and theologians had subdivided sodomy into four general categories: sex between men, sex with animals, nonprocreative sex between men and women, and masturbation. However, in practice even procreative sex could be considered unnatural if it was any position other than the missionary (face-to-face, man on top, woman on her back).[9]

However, despite the term's flexibility, from the twelfth century on, "sodomy" was increasingly associated with sex acts between men.[10] Still, as defined by both religion and law, sodomy included a range of condemned practices, including a great many heterosexual ones. Broadly, these acts were all considered "sins" with varying degrees of punishments involved. Like other acts of deviance, these sodomitic acts are described in terms such as "unnatural," "destructive," and "spreading." In fact, the spreading of vice is directly connected to working "against nature" and the stability of social order. With that in mind, let's first look at a type of deviance that is present in almost every world culture, prostitution.

Prostitution

As noted earlier, deviance includes transgressive forms of heterosexuality as well as other nonstandard sexual activities. In studying the practice of exchanging money for sex, we encounter a transgressive sexuality that is situated within multiple contexts—legal, economic, social, moral, and gendered. The majority of prostitutes in recorded history are female; however, there were also male sex workers who catered to men and women. Nevertheless, regulations and discussions of prostitution in the Middle Ages assume female practitioners and male clients for the most part.

Historically, prostitution was an accepted part of the Roman Empire. Practically, it was seen as a way to sexually satisfy young men and keep them away from married women. Although brothels were generally tolerated, the owners were reviled and had no social or civic status. Prostitutes were supposed to be registered, and the stigma of such a registry remained with a woman her entire life. This general tolerance of the practice carried over into the early Church, except the Church was more forgiving toward the prostitute herself. Augustine (354–430 CE) warned that the abolition of prostitution, were it possible, would have disastrous consequences for society; the practice, he believed, was a necessary evil in an inevitably imperfect world. Moreover, all humans were sinners in need of saving, so prostitutes were no different than other sinners in that regard. Furthermore, Jesus was said to have dined with prostitutes in the Bible, clearly demonstrating their redemptive possibilities. Finally, since all women were considered to be lustful creatures at heart, the demonstration of compassion and forgiveness toward prostitutes served as a reminder to all women that any who strayed from the path of complete chastity had the opportunity to be saved. Unlike the secular empire, the Church also did not support permanent stigmatization of former prostitutes, believing that everyone has the possibility of redemption.

In fact, there were a number of saints who were (supposedly) former prostitutes. One such group was the Desert Harlots, or holy prostitutes, Patristic-era saints who turned from a life of debauchery to an ascetic existence.[11] The Desert Harlots fled into the desert as the ultimate sign of renouncing their body and the fornication that they craved. Their sins were supposedly greater, and thus their repentance more difficult, because they were women. The best-known of these included Mary of Egypt, Pelagia the actress of Antioch, Thaïs the harlot, Maria the niece of Abraham, Paesia, and Theodora. The Biblical archetype of such repentance is Mary Magdalene, companion of Jesus of Nazareth. Several "Marys" in the Gospels were conflated into one, and Mary Magdalene became not only the disciple of Christ, but also the repentant prostitute who washed his feet with her tears and anointed his feet with alabaster. She provided the standard for the Desert Harlots, who, in turn, provided models for converting pagans, for backsliding clerics, and for other sinful women. Modern scholarship has demonstrated that there is no real basis for this conflation other than to provide a template for (sexual) sin and redemption.[12] Medieval Christians, particularly women, who sinned through the body, were expected to repent through bodily punishment and/or renunciation in order to achieve salvation. The depths of carnal filth with which the Desert Harlots soiled their bodies, and, consequently, their souls, was matched only by the ascetic extremes to which they subjected their bodies in their search for repentance. Similarly, just as prostitutes in general represented all that was sinful about medieval women, they also demonstrated the power of redemption.

Overall, "the Church's position on prostitution, crystallized by the fourth century, consisted of these three elements: acceptance of prostitution as an inevitable social fact, condemnation of those profiting from this commerce, and encouragement for the prostitute to repent."[13] Augustine, as noted earlier, advocated controlled acceptance. Subsequently, the period from the twelfth to the sixteenth century witnessed a considerable evolution in public policies on prostitution. Tolerance evolved into a policy of institutionalization in the late Middle Ages, only to be replaced in the sixteenth century by an active repression of prostitution. Of course there was no single medieval attitude governing prostitution, nor a singular approach to dealing with it. Commercial prostitution tended to be an urban development. City life provided anonymity for provider and consumer as well as a larger pool of customers. Town governments in later medieval England took responsibility for the regulation of various occupations and pastimes, and prostitution was one of the matters with which they concerned themselves. Smaller villages may have largely ignored it, or considered it an open secret. Some municipalities did attempt to outlaw the practice, but the success of such an approach was limited. Throughout these attempts, the Church maintained a fairly steady policy of resigned forbearance. Aquinas (1225–74 CE) paraphrased Augustine when he declared that prostitution was a "lesser evil" argument. Controlled, regulated, and confined, the lesser evil of prostitution could be used effectively to contain a number of greater evils, including rampant homosexual acts, the pollution of sexual desires, and the corruption of honest women. That he includes this discussion in the same section where he discusses tolerance for the Jews says a great deal. Outsiders must be incorporated into society as much as possible in order to mitigate their threat.[14]

Instead of condemning prostitution holistically, the Church instead denounced procuring. The individuals who profited from commerce of the flesh were held in the lowest of esteem, seen as greedy extortionists who encouraged vice, akin to Satan in the Garden of Eden. Beyond that, localities took it upon themselves to regulate the trade. Towns with formal brothels generally sought to suppress "free lancers" who worked outside the houses. Towns without brothels often attempted to restrict whores to certain streets or locations. Many places adopted sumptuary laws that governed what prostitutes were allowed to wear, thus neatly separating the good women from the bad. However, as both Karras and Otis note, it is not entirely fair to classify the medieval prostitute as marginalized, even if she does embody deviance. She was incorporated into gossip circles, testified in court, participated in the economy, assisted in rituals, and, most importantly, helped preserve other women's souls. Prostitutes protected women by directing the (natural) male lasciviousness toward them and away from virtuous women; therefore, it was important that whores be attractive. Not only would this inflame desire more rapidly causing it to burn out fiercely, but also it was less sinful for a man to couple with a beautiful woman than with an ugly one—just as raping a beautiful woman was less of an egregious crime, as was noted earlier. As well, prostitutes could redeem men. The Church considered marrying a former prostitute to be a good work, and as such offered some remission of sin to the man who married such a woman. Furthermore, a former prostitute might bring with her money and movable goods acquired during her working days.

Male prostitution is more difficult to track down in medieval Europe.[15] Karras points out that the "lesser evil" argument should, if followed through to its logical conclusion, have also applied to houses of male prostitution, since women, the "weaker sex," should not have been able to withstand sexual pressure.[16] However, despite the acknowledgement of the female sex drive, the traceable instances of male prostitution are almost exclusively same-sex in nature. In his examination of Alan of Lille's (1128–1202 CE) *The Complaint of Nature* (ca. 1165 CE), Jordan notes the equation of the sodomite with the male prostitute: "And many other young men, dressed by my grace in the honor of beauty, drunk with the thirst of money, exchanged their hammers of Venus for the roles of anvils."[17] Aldhelm (ca. 639–709 CE) had made similar associations in the eighth century between "harlots and molles (effeminate men), filthy catamites who performed the act of Sodom in an abominable way [for money]."[18] The connection continues throughout Continental Europe. There is "evidence of male prostitution in Italian cities and references to male brothels in Chartres, Orleans, Sens, and Paris. Some Italian cities, particularly Venice and Florence, became notorious homosexual centers, so much so that in Germany pederasts were known as Florenzer (Florentines)."[19] However, whereas for Italy and France the evidence points to male brothels, in medieval England male prostitution is scarce and tends to be focused on individuals. Later in this chapter, we will look at the case of John Rykener, a male cross-dressing prostitute who serviced both men and women. Although he was not a member of a brothel, he clearly worked in tandem with several women who trained him and found him clients. William II, known as William Rufus (ca. 1056–1100 CE; r. 1087–1100 CE), son of William the Conqueror (ca. 1028–87 CE), was said to have populated his courts with "a band of effeminates and a flock of harlots," and was said to have died in the company of "parasites," usually glossed as "male prostitutes."[20] The chronicler William of Malmesbury (ca. 1195/96–ca. 1143 CE) in discussing these incidents very distinctly connects effeminacy and prostitution with the nonnatural. Perhaps it is this perception of demasculinization that contributed to the lack of male prostitutes in medieval England.

Despite the relatively commonplace existence of public prostitution, the fifteenth and sixteenth centuries brought a great many legislative attempts to close down brothels and ban the sex-for-money trade. Although this indicates some growing concern about vice in general, as Karras notes, it is most specifically directed at uncontrolled feminine lust, not necessarily restricted to commercialized sex. She cites a City of London ordinance in support:

> For to eschew the stinking and horrible sin of lechery, the which daily grows and is practiced more than it has been in days past, by the means of strumpets, misguided and idle women daily vagrant and walking about by the streets and lanes of this city of London and suburbs of the same and also repairing to taverns and other private places of the said city, provoking many other persons unto the said sin of lechery . . .[21]

The problem here clearly lies with the women who revel in lechery and seek out sexual encounters. As with other sins, whoredom is connected with idleness and drinking. Taverns became particularly unsavory places for women, as will be discussed later, and men knew that they could find sex partners, whether for pay or not, at them. A tavern was also a good place for a casual prostitute to meet potential customers since most had rooms for rent as well. Casual prostitution became the standard as regulations against bawdy houses grew in number. In fact, the mid-sixteenth century witnessed the closing of brothels for the most part. Some historians have suggested that concerns about venereal diseases, which were discussed earlier, triggered this action. However, it is more complicated than a simple cause–effect relationship would belie. The rise of syphilis started in the late fifteenth century, yet the brothels remained open. More likely is the connection between general moral decay and the rise of the plague. In fact, prostitutes had been specifically accused of bringing on the plague, since it was often claimed to be God's punishment for the sin of fornication.[22] Many municipalities closed bathhouses and prohibited dances during the plague, and eliminating houses of prostitution are an obvious next step. Just as other outsiders such as Jews and lepers were blamed for calamities, so, too, were women held responsible for the rise of the plague and the general decline of morality.

Masturbation and nocturnal emission

In the medieval church's quest to categorize sexual sins, there are two that occasionally overlap: nocturnal emissions and masturbation. Nocturnal emissions would seem to be the sole province of men, although attempts were made to transfer the blame to women. Theologians struggled with classifying nocturnal emissions as sin. On one hand, they were "visible evidence of [men's] innate sexual longings . . . frequently, if not always, an expression of lust."[23] On the other hand, they weren't the direct result of sexual activity. This in itself is troubling, since it demonstrates a bodily rebellion of sorts, and, particularly disturbing for the medieval moral physiology of the human body, the male body is where reason, virtue, and strength were supposed to dwell. Yet, in this instance, the body seemingly disobeys its owner; therefore, body, male sexuality, and ascetic discipline meet in the theological discussion about nocturnal emissions. Even more troubling was their potential effect on male virginity—if a man had a nocturnal emission stimulated by lustful thoughts, was he then still virginal? Did stimulation and orgasm "count" as a sexual experience? Basil of Caesarea (d. 379 CE) believed it did. Athanasius (d. 373 CE) did not, holding that it was a completely natural phenomenon, involuntary and, therefore, devoid of any sin. Most theologians, including Cassian (ca. 360–435 CE) and Augustine, had a more nuanced view, considering the source before naming it sin. If the emission was the result of a lustful encounter or pleasurable recollection, then it was both willful and sinful; otherwise, it was a physical function.[24] Gregory the Great (ca. 540–604 CE) went so far as to declare that a nocturnal emission should not prevent a man, priest or parishioner, from participating in the Eucharist.[25]

Of greater concern in regard to nocturnal emissions, however, is their connection to demonology. According to medieval tradition, the devil cannot create life, yet constantly seeks ways to infiltrate the human race. A succubus is a demon that takes the form of a woman in order to have intercourse with a man in his dreams, or at least to bewitch him into having intercourse with "her." The demon would then switch to the male sex while retaining the stolen semen. The newly shaped incubus would then seduce a human woman in order to impregnate her with the by-now-demonically altered semen. The magician Merlin was supposedly born from such an unholy union, as was the protagonist of the fifteenth century romance *Sir Gowther*. While this may seem unbelievable to us today, the possibility of demonic sexual encounters was a very real part of medieval life. Certainly, the likelihood was that these fears were an externalization of repressed (erotic) thoughts, or at the very least served as yet another excuse to keep women under "protection" so as to assure their safety from demonic sexual assault.[26] However, ultimately, controlling nocturnal emissions not only kept the male body pure, but also kept the human race pure, since without stolen semen to alter, incubi and succubi could not create monstrous hybrids.

Bodily purity is also the overarching concern in regard to masturbation. Quite controversially, Thomas Aquinas seems to argue that masturbation is a greater sin than rape or fornication. In *Summa Theologica* II II §153 and §154, he addresses the sin of lust. More specifically, in §154.12, he posits that among the unnatural vices, the hierarchy of sins progresses from most to least offensive as follows: masturbation, bestiality, sodomy, and copulation in strange manners. As Louis Crompton notes, "the four nonprocreative forms of sex are worse [than rape and fornication], since—though not harmful to others—they are sins directly against God himself as the creator of nature."[27] This is not quite the case, although admittedly

Aquinas does revile masturbation (while exonerating nocturnal emissions). Rather, in this section of the *Summa*, Aquinas is only addressing how sexual sins offend the virtue of chastity, not their overall gravity. Thus, as a sin and a violation of justice, rape is much more serious than masturbation, but as an offense to nature, masturbation ranks as worse. Masturbation deliberately thwarts procreation and wastes male essence. "Onanism," an antiquated term for masturbation, is derived from the Biblical story of Onan who withdrew during sex with his new wife, who was his brother's widow.[28] Onan was punished for two things: for wasting his seed, that is his procreative potential, and for denying his brother an heir. Masturbation also requires, and in most cases involves, a much less deliberate act of will than fornication does, and therefore the sin is subjectively lesser on intent alone. Intent, after all, is what Aquinas uses to negate the potential of sin from nocturnal emissions. As he writes in §5: "Hence it is manifest that nocturnal pollution is never a sin, but is sometimes the result of a previous sin." Intent creates sin in a way that simple bodily function does not. Because of this, medical treatments involving genital manipulation, discussed in Chapter One, such as for greensickness, were not considered sinful, since the intent was curative, not pleasurable.

The question of masturbation did occupy medieval theology to some extent, although it was considered a sin almost exclusively attributable to men rather than to women. Masturbation did not cause harm to another person, but it was distinctly categorized as an unnatural vice, and regulated under sodomy laws. Of course sodomy was a fluid term, as we have seen, and even occasionally had no overt sexual connotations. However, Peter Damian's (ca. 1007–ca. 1072/73 CE) influential text *Liber Gomorrhianus (Book of Gomorrah*, ca. 1050 CE) numbered four acts as distinctively sodomitical: self-pollution (masturbation), mutual masturbation, interfemoral intercourse, and anal intercourse. Clearly, as Kim Phillips points out, Damian is "primarily interested in the vice as an expression of desire between men," and subsequently a challenge to the purity of the priesthood.[29] What role did desire and solo sex have in the life of an individual dedicated to chastity? For that matter, medieval Christians as a whole were expected to be chaste—to fulfill the sexual role designed for them by God—and masturbation tests all of those options. All the major and minor penitential codes address it in some manner, often distinguishing between clergy and laymen. Quite often, as in Damian's work, it is conflated with same-sex acts between men. The seventh-century Irish Penitential of Cummean, for instance, reads like a ledger for Damian's hierarchy, complete with differentiations between laymen and priests:

> He who sins with a beast shall do penance for a year; if by himself, for three forty-day periods, [or] if he has [clerical] rank, a year; a boy of fifteen years, forty days.... Those who befoul their lips shall do penance

for four years; if accustomed to the habit they shall do penance for seven years. So shall those who commit sodomy do penance for seven years. For femoral masturbation, two years.[30]

Here the various forms of sodomy are linked together, and masturbation is noted twice—once as a solitary activity, and once as part of a same-sex experience. Both sins and penances are also very clearly directed toward men. Occasionally masturbation is denounced as even more serious than sodomy. Leah DeVun notes that both Peter of Poitiers and Peter the Chanter specifically claim that hermaphrodites masturbating is the most monstrous of acts, primarily because they combine active and passive roles, conflating sodomy and masturbation into one grossly sinful act against nature.[31] Heterosexual motivation for masturbation was also sinful. Theodulf's *Second Diocesan Statues*, an eighth-century priest's manual explains: "'masturbation' is called uncleanness either on account of the touch or sight or memory of a woman."[32] The real problem here is pleasure, illicitly gained and illicitly taken. This is aptly demonstrated within the seventh-century Anglo Saxon Penitential of Theodore, wherein the penalties for a presbyter who kisses a woman out of desire and one who pollutes himself through ejaculatory masturbation are the same three weeks.[33]

The majority of concerns about masturbation address men and even more often monks and clerics. However, at least one penitential, the ninth-century Old English compilation now known as the *Scriftboc*, directly addresses female masturbation: "If a woman in any way touch herself sexually so that she knows herself (she does it), she is too fast for two years, because that is a defilement to her."[34] Interestingly, the penances for solitary male masturbation tend to be much lighter. The Penitential of Theodore, for example, dictates that men who defile themselves receive 40 days penance, although boys who mutually engage in vice should be whipped. However, if a woman practices solitary vice, she shall do penance for three years— which is the same penance as practicing vice with another woman.[35] It may be that the author is basing his punishment on the idea that women who masturbate "must" do so using a dildo. The original includes the phrase *coitum habet* ("have sexual intercourse"), and in the medieval world, sexual intercourse and penetration are often inseparable concepts. The disparity in penalties can also be linked to contemporary concerns about female desire. Although a female masturbator would not waste seed or essence, a woman should also not have had any reason to feel desire without male stimulation; therefore, her desire is a dangerous attempt to gain control over herself and her passions. Anchoritic literature warns against this type of misplaced female desire. The thirteenth-century English work *Ancrene Wisse* (*Guide for Anchoresses*), speaks against such arousal gone astray, warning: "For herself to behold her own white hands does harm to many an anchoress, who has them too fair, as those which are ruined by idleness."[36] The anchoress's white hands were clearly unused to honest work, but also tempted her.

Later in the text, the connection between idleness and fleshly temptations, particularly sodomitical ones, is made clear.[37] It is also interesting that the anchoress' own body arouses her rather than someone else's body, be that person male or female. This concern is reiterated by the penitential, as "the confessor apparently asked not only if the woman touched herself but if she excited herself deliberately ('so that she knows herself')."[38] Once again, desire and deliberate excitement appear more problematic than the autoerotic action. In fact, the overall problem with masturbation, whether undertaken by a man or a woman, is improper desire that grows beyond the perpetrator's control. The Penitential of Columban makes this clear by specifying that married men who masturbate deserve stricter penances than unmarried men.[39] The implication is that the sin is greater because married men should not fall prey to random acts of lust when they have the ability to enjoy a proper (and potentially procreative) sexual outlet where desire can be correctly contained.

Castration

I trowe he were a geldyng or a mare.[40]

The famous description of the Pardoner by Chaucer's narrator in *The Canterbury Tales* points to two possible, and troubling, aspects of the Pardoner's sexual status—is he a woman (a mare), or is he a eunuch (a gelding)? In either case, he is not a man. Castration posed an interesting dilemma for the Patristic and medieval Church and society. In a world where biology and genitals were the most fundamental proof of male superiority, what happens to a man who no longer possesses the equipment, the functionality, or both? Were medieval castrated men able to position themselves as masculine subjects in a world where castrates were feminized and marked by an irrecoverable lack?

Castration in the Classical world was fairly commonplace. There were three types of eunuchs, complete ("shaved," with both penis and testicles removed) and partial (only the testicles removed or rendered inactive) being most common, with the removal of the penis alone a third option. Eunuchs served a number of different functions, often as personal servants, especially for noblewomen. Harem guards in the Muslim world were rather famously castrated at a very young age. Eunuchs often served court functions as well, especially in China and Byzantium. Several eunuchs are mentioned in the Bible.[41] Because the eunuch typically did not have a family of his own, his loyalty was considered to be absolute. Nevertheless, some eunuchs were simply slave labor without special signification. Still others were castrated as prisoners of war, thereby eliminating their family line completely. A few religious sects in Classical Antiquity encouraged or required castration. The best-known of these were the Roman followers of Cybele (Magna Mater), the Galli, who ritually autocastrated themselves.⁴² It is against this long, varied, and widespread tradition that medieval castration is set.

Medieval castration was often the result of punishment. For example, numerous rape laws, which will be discussed in more detail later, suggest castration as an appropriate punishment, although historical evidence points to scant few, if any, enactments of such. One famous exception to this rule was Peter Abelard (1079–1142 CE), although his punishment was conducted by his lover's family, not by the law. Abelard began an affair with his young student, Héloïse d'Argenteuil (1090/1100–1164 CE) who lived in the household of her wealthy uncle, Fulbert. Héloïse became pregnant, they secretly married, and then Abelard sent Héloïse off to a convent. Enraged, Fulbert arranged for a band of men to break into Abelard's room one night and castrate him. Abelard records these events, rather bitterly, in his *Historia Calamitatum*.⁴³ Because of its very public nature, the unlawful castration of Abelard creates a framework for discussing the taboo of male genital mutilation. Larissa Tracy notes that the most common type of medieval castration involves "only the testicles, and concerns regarding removal had less to do with sexual identity or ability, and more to do with the ability to propagate and sire children."⁴⁴ Since charges of rape were negated by conception, and to some extent by marriage, this conjecture holds true. Aside from heterosexual rape, other serious deviances from accepted sexual practices could result in punishment by castration. One such deviance was miscegenation, such as a Christian man marrying a Saracen woman—or the reverse, a Saracen man who seized a Christian woman. Violating a nun, even with consent, could be punished in a similar manner. Aelred of Rievaulx (1110–67 CE) reports an incident where a monk who impregnates a nun is punished via castration at his own lover's hands.⁴⁵ Finally, homosexual acts were often penalized by castration, or the threat thereof, and such laws are found in the codes of many different European cultures. Rather infamously, both Piers Gaveston (ca. 1284–1312 CE) and Hugh le Despenser the younger (ca. 1286–1386 CE), purported lovers of Edward II (1284–1387; r. 1307–27 CE), were punished in this manner, although Roger Mortimer (1287–1330 CE), Queen Isabella's (1295–1328 CE) lover, was also castrated. In all of these cases, sexual indiscretion played a part, but so did treason and political disruption.⁴⁶

Castration was also the result of war, persecution, or trickery. Narratives of emasculating mutilation abound in accounts of the crusades, local wars, and revenge in the twelfth and thirteenth centuries. For example, Guibert of Nogent (ca. 1055–1124 CE) relates castration anxiety nightmares in his autobiographical memoirs, and tells war stories with graphic descriptions of genital mutilation, such as the account of Thomas of Coucy (1073–1130 CE), who often hung his enemies up by their testicles and penises until the organs were ripped from their bodies.⁴⁷ Furthermore, one of the most popular tales of the *De miraculis Sancti Jacobi* section of the twelfth-century *Codex*

Calixtinus recounts how a devil impersonated St James and persuaded an unchaste pilgrim to castrate himself.[48] Castration as punishment for capital crimes falls under this categorization as well. Traitors and outlaws were frequently subjected to emasculation before being hanged, drawn, and quartered—all done in a very public space as well. For instance, in 1305 CE, William Wallace (ca. 1270–1305 CE) was hanged, strangled, castrated, eviscerated, and beheaded, and then his corpse was quartered and sent to Scotland as a visible reminder of what rebellion brings. Wallace's literal castration became Scotland's metaphorical emasculation.

Aside from calumnious events, castration could also be seen as curative, both of overwhelming sexual desire and disease. Leprosy was one of the diseases for which castration was a suggested cure. For example, Hugh of Orival (d. 1085 CE), bishop of London, sought out castration as a (supposed) cure for his leprosy, which at the time was seen as a type of venereal disease, as will be discussed later. Other diseases treated by castration included satyriasis, hernias, and epilepsy. Otherwise, the most positive effect of castration was the quelling of sexual desire—a major concern for premodern Christians. Although the practice was never encouraged by the Church, a number of enthusiastic men chose either to be castrated or to castrate themselves in an effort to become more holy. Perhaps most famously, the theologian Origen of Alexandria (ca. 185–ca. 254 CE) supposedly castrated himself so he could tutor women without suspicion. His hagiographer, Eusebius, attributed this action not only to Origen's desire to avoid scandal, but also to his wish to live a Biblical life by literally interpreting Matthew 19:12 as a sign of his faith and self control.[49] These acts of castration were still imparted by human means, however. More fascinating is the phenomenon of what I call "divine castration," that is the miraculous removal (or binding) of the male genitals via God, often in the form of an angelic assistant. This was viewed as a gift. Hugh of Lincoln (1135/40–1200 CE), one of the best-known English saints, received the gift of divine castration as a relief for his intense sexual desire. One night an angel appeared to him and seemingly cut off his genitals. In the morning, Hugh awoke intact, but his burning lust was calmed.[50] William of Tocco, one of Thomas Aquinas's hagiographers, relates a similar scenario. During a time of imprisonment at Monte San Giovanni, Thomas was tormented by a pretty girl who was repeatedly sent into his room. He prayed fervently for assistance, so that no carnal impurity would corrupt him. That night, as he slept, two angels attended him by binding his loins and gifting him with resistant chastity, the pain of which woke the saint.[51] Similarly, John Cassian reports that a monk named Serenus had an angel appear to him in a vision, whereupon his belly was opened, a blazing tumor was removed from his bowels, and the angel informed him that his purity of body was assured. Upon waking, with all his entrails and genitals intact, Serenus noted that he no longer possessed any sexual desire. Palladius tells the story of his companion Elias, who has three angels appear to him in a dream and castrate him before he took up a ministerial post in a convent. All in all, Mathew Kuefler notes that this mystical castration was a trope found across countries, naming Pachon of Scetis, Equitius of Valeria, and Hildefonsus of Toledo as additional recipients.[52]

No matter how it happened or for what purposes, however, castration was a thorny subject in the Middle Ages. The Church took a wholly contradictory position on it. On one hand, it was rebuked; on the other hand, numerous monasteries counted castrated monks among their numbers. Tracy identifies another paradox as well—the male body is at once considered "strong and resilient, yet fragile and vulnerable," and castration calls both of these positions to mind.[53] Politics and religion are dependent upon virility. As Kuefler argues, every one of the Church Fathers who spoke on self-castration spoke to condemn it because they were attempting to demonstrate the manliness of Christianity within a traditional Roman framework, primarily so as to attract converts from the male aristocracy. Castration, self-induced or otherwise, did not support that agenda; nonetheless, there was a begrudging admiration for men who believed so deeply in sexual renunciation that they undertook such a radical act. The result, removal of sexual desire, was acceptable, but the means were questionable. Even the so-called divine castration experiences were dangerous to condone, and their recorders did so only reluctantly. Cassian, for example, notes that the most praiseworthy thing about Serenus's experience is that he did not undertake the action on his own, but rather endured it as an action of God's grace. Apparently, autocastration was a real concern in the early Church. The *Traditio Apostolica*, a third-century treatise attributed to Hippolytus of Rome, mentions men who castrated themselves, and were then banned from the Christian community. Moreover, at the ecumenical council of Nicaea in 325 CE, the first official declaration ordered the removal from clerical office of men who castrated themselves. However, those who had undergone medical castration or were victims of war or enslavement were exempt from the restriction. Just as in the cases of divine castration, the effect—lack of sexual desire—is not as crucial as the cause. Weakness of spirit is not considered a good enough reason for mutilation of masculinity. Instead, a man worthy of clerical office should be able to control his urges without external assistance, unless it comes directly from God.

This idea of worthiness points out yet another major concern with castration, the problematic diminishing of masculinity. It seems rather apparent that castration posed a challenge to medieval notions of gender. Castration both strengthens and imperils masculinity. It gives power to the wielder of the knife; it weakens the recipient of the action. Abelard's case aptly demonstrates this effect, which is especially highlighted by one of his contemporaries, Roscelin of Compiegne (ca. 1050–ca. 1125 CE). Abelard has no identity in Roscelin's view; he is neither monk nor cleric (nor layman), and he has no name, not even his own given name, Peter, since a masculine proper name loses its signification once its subject changes gender. In a dramatic letter dating to 1120 CE, Roscelin writes:

> I'm certain that a noun (*nomen*) of masculine gender, if it falls away from its own gender, will refuse to signify its usual thing (*rem*). For proper nouns usually lose their signification when the things signified fall back from their own completion. A house is not called a house but an imperfect house when its walls and roof are removed. Therefore since the part that makes a man has been removed, you are to be called not "Petrus" but "imperfect Petrus."[54]

Abelard is, according to Roscelin at least, unable to be represented in language. His own name is meaningless, and he is a masculine proper noun without a referent. He is also rudderless in a world where homosocial relationships are the central ones. Castration makes men "not men," thereby removing them from the male sphere, and subsequently inviting speculation as to whether or not "he" is now a "she"—like the Pardoner, a "geldying or a mare." In turn, their rights, privileges, and even actions are questionable. Castration also challenges the natural order of biology. A fourteenth-century manuscript of the *Romance of the Rose* contains a miniature illumination that ties both these aspects together. This drawing shows Origen castrating himself in front of a nun.[55] It is found at the point where Nature lists Origen among a group of men who thought they could defy the destinies she created for them. His autocastration violated his (natural) maleness and the masculine role Nature had constructed for him. Likewise, the *Romance* denounces Abelard and Heloise as equally foolish. Abelard, in an attempt to remasculinize himself and create an image of spiritual martyrdom, compared his own castration to Origen's, thus aligning himself with sexual continence, despite evidence to the contrary. What all these efforts reveal is "gender trouble." If castration can so easily remake male sexuality, then the practice "invite[s] questions on what the input of socialization was in making a man a man and whether beliefs in biological determinism were tenable."[56] The body is a readable text, written and interpreted by the community.

Castration both as punishment and as purification is an exercise in authority. The eunuch is reduced to a feminized position. Biology and gender seem to be coherently aligned; a man without functioning genitalia is not a man. The business of prosthetics speaks to this fear of lack. French surgeon Ambroise Paré (ca. 1510–90 CE) wrote extensively on reconstruction of the (primarily male) body, suggesting the use of a prosthetic penis for those whose member was injured or missing, often a result of advanced syphilis.[57] It is clear from his writing that the main concern is not comfort or even functionality, but rather avoiding "womanly" behavior, namely urinating by squatting rather than standing:

> Those that have their yards cut off close to their bellies are greatly troubled in making of urine so that they are constrained to sit downe like women for their ease. I have devised this pipe or conduit . . . serving instead of the yard in making of water, which therefore wee may call an artificiall yard.[58]

Paré was especially concerned that without a penis, a man's essential maleness would be challenged both because of the missing organ(s) and because of the missing activity. In *On Monsters and Marvels* (1573), he wrote extensively on hermaphrodites, insisting that any presence of a functional penis made "the creature" male.[59] Thus, being a man was defined by the state of an individual's genitals. Without a (functioning) penis, a man was not a "real" man, and violated social norms and expectations. Similarly, Christianity demanded bodily purity, but it also demanded resistance to temptation, not avoidance thereof. Somehow the two positions had to be reconciled, since fear over an inability to control sexual impulses is not an expression of either masculinity or saintliness. Jacqueline Murray suggests the act of autocastration, whether actual or symbolic, became a demonstration of such extreme self-denial that even without their sexual organs the religious communities could view these men as true men. Their strength of will superseded the strength of their body in proving and performing manhood. In this way, castrates could be recognized even if the process could not be condoned.[60]

Cross-dressing

Cross-dressing carried with it serious ramifications in the medieval world. Although there were several famous "transvestite saints," the average cross-dresser did not do so with religious intent or salvation. The hostility toward cross-dressing can be attributed both to religious and to social conventions. A passage in Deuteronomy labels cross-dressers abominations.[61] Socially, cross-dressing women were seen as encroachers on male territory, an understandable, if lamentable, undertaking. In certain cases, the behavior even contributed to their sanctity. Cross-dressing men, on the other hand, were not to be tolerated since they willingly gave up their masculine superiority.

Cross-dressing for religious purposes was the most acceptable form. Among the lives of the saints, there are a number of legends, primarily from the early Desert tradition, that have been dubbed "transvestite hagiographies."[62] About 35 legends of cross-dressing saints survive, all of which depict women who dressed as men full-time.⁶³ There are a few hagiographies, including the life of St Jerome, that mention isolated incidents wherein the male saint (temporarily) dressed in women's garb; however, these incidents are relatively few, and did not involve permanent cross-dressing. While it is problematic to use modern labels for premodern people, and it is true that we know very little about the psychology of these women, in some cases at least, it might be possible to view them as "transgender," especially since it was a deliberate choice on their part to live as men for many years, although it is challenging to determine whether or not they saw themselves as male, or simply involved in a permanent masquerade. Without the distraction of "being a woman," these saints could pursue holiness. Parents, husbands, and children were all removed from their existence so that they could devote themselves to God. For instance, in Matrona's case, the *vita* states explicitly that God "called her daughter home," so that Matrona could continue pursuing her religious life without distraction, and she is "joyful" that her daughter died. Suzanne Kessler and Wendy McKenna argue that gender attribution is fundamentally "an interaction between displayer and attributor, but concrete displays are not informative unless interpreted in light of the rules which the attributor has for deciding what it means to be a female or male."⁶⁴ The rules are shared among all members of a sociocultural group, and constitute knowledge of the socially constructed signs of gender. Moreover, beyond the presence or absence of biological genitals, it is the constructions of "attributed genitals" envisioned to have always existed that dictate the process of gender identification. Men usually have both a literal penis and a cultural one; women have neither, but can gain a cultural one. In instances of cross-dressing, by externally conforming to male standards, these women essentially became men in a more literal sense than the one meant by Saints Jerome (347–420 CE) and Ambrose (337–97 CE).

The majority of cross-dressing legends roughly follow a similar pattern and can be divided into a tripartite structure: (1) flight from the world, (2) disguise and seclusion, and (3) discovery and recognition. Often the story involves a young woman fleeing some sort of sexual involvement, who then dresses like a man to escape and finds herself living a male life for at least a short period. Often the woman will reveal her own identity, although sometimes it is discovered unintentionally, and occasionally after her death. Of course there are variations in this pattern as well. For instance, a surprising number of these lives contain incidents where the cross-dressed woman is accused of sexually importuning a woman. In each of these cases, once the saint's biological sex is revealed, her sexual purity is confirmed. This provides an interesting perspective on the potential for woman–woman relations in the medieval world.

These legends of gender-bending saints are found throughout Church history, and at least seven of them were included in the *Golden Legend*, an extremely popular collection of short hagiographies and the most printed book in Europe until the Reformation. Indeed, many of them remain on the calendar of saints today. The seven lives from the *Golden Legend* were: Eugenia/Eugenius, Margareta/Pelagius, Pelagia of Antioch/Pelagius, Natalia, Thecla, Theodora/Theodorus, and Marina/Marinus of Alexandria. Other cross-dressing saints included: Anastasia the Patrician [of Constantinople], Anna/Euphemianos of Constantinople, Apollinaria/Dorotheos, Athanasia of Antioch, Euphrosyne/Smaragdus, Matrona/Babylas of Perge, Marina of Sicily, Marina/Marinos of Antioch, Callisthene, Euphrosyne Jr, Papula of Gaul, and Susanna, all of whom are Patristic-era saints. There are a few other hagiographies of this sort, and there are also a number of lives of holy women who cross-dressed, but were never canonized, such as Christina of Markyate (d. after 1155 CE).

The most famous cross-dressed saint is Joan of Arc (Jeanne d'Arc; 1412–31 CE). Her story differs from the standard hagiographic trope in several ways. Joan only dressed like a man; she did not "pass" for one. Everyone knew that "The Maid of Orléans" was a virginal woman who donned soldier's clothes to assume the male role of leading an army. In fact, the investigation of her orthodoxy, conducted at Poitiers before she took to the battlefield, indicates that the clerics approved her practice of wearing male clothing and cutting her hair short. Since she had a mission to do a man's work, it was fitting that she dress the part. In every other way, Joan was female. Nevertheless, when she was captured by the English, she was convicted of and executed for supposedly practicing witchcraft, with the major evidence being her cross-dressing. This was compounded by the very real possibility of rape in prison. Although both the English bishop and commander (Richard, Earl of Warwick) were supposed to ensure that she remained unmolested while under their protection, the reality was that Joan's male clothing made her less vulnerable to rape, as she herself repeated on numerous occasions.[65] As Valerie Hotchkiss notes in regard to the "transvestite" saints, "male disguise becomes a natural expression of the renunciation of sex because it effectively shields the female body from sexual union with men."[66] This perspective reflects the heteronormative stance of sexuality in the Middle Ages as well as the prevalence of sexual violence and women's vulnerability and blame. Since women supposedly incited lust in men simply by allowing themselves to be seen, dressing as a man is seemingly a good precaution, assuming only heterosexual lust motivates the man in question.

Outside of hagiographies, female cross-dressing is found in fiction, particularly romances. Three such examples can be found in *Roman de Silence*, a thirteenth-century French romance, and two fourteenth-century French *chanson de geste*, *Tristan de Nanteuil* and *Yde et Olive*. Princess Silence is deliberately raised as a boy by her parents in order to circumvent a restriction on female inheritance. She grows up excelling at all pastimes, both masculine and feminine. She is an accomplished hunter and warrior, but also reads, writes, and sings. She becomes a famous knight, and her secret is inadvertently revealed when the lustful queen, Eufeme, attempts to seduce her. Silence rebuffs the queen, who in retaliation accuses her of rape. To punish Silence for her refusal, Eufeme sends her off on the impossible task of catching Merlin, who can only be snared by a woman. The captured magician reveals Silence's secret as well as Eufeme's affair with a priest disguised as a nun. Eufeme is killed for her wanton sexuality, and Silence marries the king, thus inheriting a kingdom by marriage even though she could not claim her own kingdom by birth. In *Yde et Olive*, Princess Yde flees the incestuous desire of her father, Florence, by disguising herself as a man and traveling to Rome. There she enters the service of the emperor, wins renown, and is given the emperor's daughter, Olive, in marriage. On their wedding night, Yde attempts evasion, but eventually confesses her secret to Olive, who proves sympathetic and swears to keep the secret. Unfortunately, they are overhead and reported to the emperor, but they are saved from executing when Yde is miraculously turned into an "actual man." Yde is crowned emperor, the couple has a child, and they live happily ever after. In *Tristan de Nanteuil*, Tristan captures Blanchandine, daughter of the king of Armenia, with whom he has a son. However, she is compelled to dress as a knight, and while she is in disguise, she is forced to marry the sultan's daughter, Clarinde. Before the wedding night, Blanchandine is changed into a man by an angel because she believes Tristan to be dead. He and Clarinde go on to have a son together and rule her father's territory. In a similar manner to the cross-dressing saints, Silence, Blanchandine, and Yde are the exceptions to the rule rather than pattern cards for potential female behavior. In each instance, the natural order is ultimately preserved. None of the women chooses to cross-dress or perform masculinity but is constrained by circumstances; all refuse unlawful sexual activity with men and women; each is safely subsumed into the heterosexual/patriarchal order at the end by either reasserting femininity or literally becoming male. Moreover, each story acknowledges the importance of biology to the definition of masculinity, and of procreation to the role of the aristocracy—men, especially upper class men, have a generational imperative unless they are devoted to chastity for religious reasons.

Although female cross-dressing is transgressive behavior, it can be contained or redirected, and hegemonic patriarchy can be restored. It is male cross-dressing that presents a challenge to authority structures as well as gender configurations. The hostility to such a possibility is palpable. It makes sense that women might strive to dress as men because they would gain advantages; it makes no sense, to the medieval mind, anyway, for a man to give up his privileged position in order to dress as a woman, except in limited circumstances. Women were, for the most part, not allowed to act in plays; therefore, men and boys played female roles.[67] However, even this carried a penalty, since men who played female roles were generally of lower social standing and received less money than their counterparts who played male roles.[68] Otherwise, it was also occasionally acceptable for men to dress in female clothing as part of a farce or comedy performance. And, while not "acceptable" so much as done for expediency's sake, there was also the tradition of male disguise for martial advantage. Most of these situations had the advantage of not being permanent lifestyles, even in fictional accounts: dressing like a woman might make the male character, linguistically at least, a woman, but this instability only suggests that gender categories are "not as fixed as one might think" rather than causing an actual gender shift.[69] The cross-dressed man could not be the protagonist of the story. Male cross-dressing is essentially superficial and transitory because otherwise it does not make sense. Even the tradition of a warrior disguised as a woman, such as Achilles being hidden by Thetis, presents a challenge because the man's inherent masculinity will not remain suppressed. The active sense of "maleness" cannot be permanently overcome, whereas innate "femaleness" is by nature passive, and can therefore be overcome.[70] The results of male disguise can be comedic and farcical, but in the end, they will revert to stereotypical masculine action. Beyond these socially acceptable exceptions, however, men who dressed as women were deeply concerning to medieval Church and society.

Not too surprisingly, few records of male cross-dressers exist. In what may be the only legal process document from late medieval England on same-sex intercourse, we find the brief story of "John Rykener, calling [himself] Eleanor," a male prostitute in fourteenth-century London.[71] Rykener was detained wearing women's clothing. During his interrogation, he confessed to having sexual relations for money with both men and women, including a fair number of priests, while dressed in female clothing. He also assumed both male and female roles during sexual encounters, and worked as a seamstress on occasion, a female profession. However, he seemingly did not think of himself as a woman, and identified as a man. Another case involves a man clothed as a woman who was housed in a French nunnery. Gregory of Tours (ca. 538–594 CE) provided a detailed account of this incident in his report on the rebellion at St Radegund's in Poitiers in 590 CE. The abbess was accused of keeping a man dressed as a woman in her chamber to sleep with whenever she desired. The man was brought before the tribunal, at which time he confessed that he was impotent, and that is why he dressed in female garb.[72] Gregory's story emphasizes the sexual overtones of the situation, although the man's "confession" of being impotent also calls into question his gender identity. Without a functioning penis, the individual became a "not-man," akin to being a woman. Fear that cross-dressing led to other unnatural behavior was evident, not only through these incidents, but also by indication within penitentials. The penitential of Silos assigned penance for one year and Frankish penitentials for three years to men who "in the dance wear women's clothes,"[73] perhaps indicating a connection to paganism or even witchcraft. Clearly, male cross-dressers were deeply suspect. Overall, however, cross-dressing incidents become the site of intense cultural and ideological negotiations involving the testing and contesting of conventional social roles and the cultural category that is gender. They do point to the idea that gender categories were less fixed and determinate in the Middle Ages than is often thought to be the case, although performance and biology remained intertwined. The male role as well as the male body was preferable and desirable, while the female counterparts were not; nevertheless, cross-dressing results in queer moments that cannot be entirely undone by the ultimate return of culturally sanctioned sexual and status arrangements.

Homosexuality[74]

Same-sex relations between men were common and acceptable in ancient Greek society. Young men were sponsored by older men who were responsible for introducing them to the ways of citizenship. Roman society had a more complicated approach to same-sex relationships. Marriage ceremonies held to unite two men were not an uncommon practice in Rome.[75] Men who penetrated other men were accepted, at least to some degree, but men who were penetrated were shamed because they were feminized. By the end of the Empire, homosexual acts, particularly those between men, became outlawed and supposedly published by castration and/or death.

This sense of shame is the attitude that carried over to medieval society. The great fear of male–male sexual encounters was loss of masculinity, and thus loss of power. Generally, it was not thought that homosexual encounters would be an exclusive sexual expression. In other words, presumptive heterosexuality assumed that all individuals were fundamentally heterosexual. Same-sex encounters would not have been expected to affect any other aspect of a man's life, including marriage and reproduction. Indeed, as we have seen earlier, marriage was not necessarily conducive to romantic attachment, nor was a wife expected to be her husband's preferred companion. Patristic Church Fathers and early penitentials address male same-sex activities, assigning penances and denouncing practices; however, the penances usually involved fines and fasting, bodily renunciation, and ascetic discipline. Same-sex activities were just one of many species of lust that needed to be stamped out, especially since male humans were prone to sins of the flesh. Occasionally harsher penalties such as excommunication surfaced, or long periods of fasting (up to 20 years). This forgiving attitude, however, would soon be altered.

In the eleventh century, Peter Damian's *Book of Gomorrah* roundly condemns homosexuality as being illicit, unnatural, and immoral. Assuming that men "leap upon" other men in a mad fit of lust, Damian asserts that if a male takes a female subject position, then he is neither male nor female, but rather a disruptive force beyond definition who threatens the social order. Throughout the text, he discusses sodomy in terms of gender or category confusion. For instance, in chapter sixteen, male sodomites, burning in lust for one another, are imagined as having a queen. This feminine desire at the heart of sodomy also figures in Damian's later description of sodomites, as those who choose to "to relinquish the strong deeds of a virile life and to exhibit the seductive weakness of feminine conversation."[76] In chapter seventeen, Damian, clearly frustrated, entreats his audience: "Unmanned man, speak! Respond, effeminate man! . . . Let the vigour of the male appearance terrify you, I beseech you; your mind should abhor virile strength."[77] The use of phrases such as "unmanned man" (*vir evirate*) and "effeminate man" (*homo effeminate*) effectively, if scathingly, conflates gender categories in the body of the sodomite. It also serves to reassert the binary categorization of male/female as the only effective and natural outlet of carnal impulses.

It is the elision of male homosexual practices with unmanliness that made accusations of sodomy such a terrifying political weapon. Several English kings were accused of sodomy by their political enemies, with varying degrees of success on the parts of their accusers. William Rufus was critiqued in such a manner both during and after his life, primarily because of the tensions between Church and state that dominated his reign. In 1102, Anselm of Canterbury (1033–1109 CE) ordered William to hold a council concerning moral reforms, including clerical marriage, male fashion (dress and hair length), hereditary succession, and sodomy. William refused, and thus a protracted battle between archbishop and king ensued. William of Malmesbury, writing in 1125 or thereabouts, equates the court fashions of William's court with the effeminacy of the men who frequented it: "It was in those days that the fashion for flowing locks, luxurious clothes, the wearing of shoes with curved points was launched: to rival women in soft living, to mince with foppish gestures and to flaunt naked flesh, was the example set to young men."[78] Another detractor, Orderic Vitalis (1075–ca. 1142 CE), comments extensively on the length of hair, types of sleeve adornments, and other fashion touches at William's court. He "follows William of Malmesbury's impetus in blurring gender and sexuality, implying that effeminacy is synonymous with the non-natural . . . [and] a taste for sodomy is a manifestation of artifice, only one affectation among many which are thought to demasculinize and denaturalize."[79] To Vitalis, the court fashions were outward symbols of moral decay under William's rule, made worse by the effeminacy, which in turn prevented men from doing anything vital or useful. Several chroniclers identify William as a sodomite himself, not just a supporter of such, and that he died without being married or producing an heir supported their case, if only obliquely.

Edward II faced similar problems, although his opponents were his own nobles, not Church officials. In fact, several years after his death, canonization procedures were begun on his behalf, although they did not come to fruition. Edward's main fault lay in not living up to his father's reputation. Edward I (1239–1307; r. 1272–1307 CE) was a strong and powerful king, who annexed Wales and fought successfully against Scotland to expand English territory. Edward II, on the other hand, was not a particularly capable military leader. His reign was marked instead by political infighting and squabbles. He contributed to this disaster by markedly favoring close personal friends, first Piers Gaveston, and later Hugh le Despenser the younger. In each case, the favorite received honors, lands, and monies ostensibly reserved for others, and each was eventually executed. Chroniclers reported on his disporting with Gaveston in "wicked and immodest manners" to the shame and embarrassment of his wife, Isabella, daughter of Philip IV of France (1268–1314 CE). Eventually, she took a lover, Roger Mortimer, and with him plotted rebellion against Edward. The result was the imprisonment and eventual death of Edward II, and the enthronement of his son, Edward III.[80] Again, sodomy was used as a charge to justify political actions, including regicide and civil war.

Philip IV also used sodomy charges to his own advantage in the strident opposition to and violent suppression of the Templar order. On October 13, 1307, members of the Order of the Knights Templar in France were arrested under the orders of King Philip IV, who was "coincidentally" deeply in debt to them. The charges were vast, and included denying Christ, God, the Virgin and the Saints; committing sacrilegious acts against both the Cross and images of Christ (e.g. spitting or urinating on them); denying the sacraments; performing idol worship; absolving fellow Templars of sin; engaging in secret ceremonies; illegally increasing their own wealth; telling novices that unnatural lust was lawful and indulged in commonly; placing obscene kisses on new entrants (on the mouth, naval, and buttocks); and practicing sodomy. Each one of these charges was damning, particularly for a religious order, and each was connected to heresy. Here, sodomy is a personal moral failure, but also a widespread infection within the order, which indicates wholesale corruption and a challenge to religious and secular authority. The evidence was shaky, and the few "confessions" extracted under torture were recanted. Whether this was a true ceremony or concocted testimony does not matter, since the result of the extended accusations was precisely what Philip intended—suppression of the order in France, execution of his opponents, and the infusion of their wealth into his coffers.[81] Additionally, although the papal investigation showed no evidence of heresy outside of France, Clement V (d. 1314) disbanded the order and dispersed the members and lands. The swiftness and completeness of the punishment of a wealthy and powerful order based primarily on accusations of sodomy and unnatural lust demonstrates both the fear of deviance and the authority of heteronormativity.[82]

Finally, Edward III's grandson, Richard II (1367–1400; r. 1377–99 CE), also faced accusations of effeminacy. This was particularly the province of those chroniclers writing after his deposition from the throne in 1399. He was described in a vast array of terms, including foppish (a description also applied to William Rufus), tyrannical, extravagant, mercurial (all descriptions also applied to Edward II), as well as spineless and "beautiful." The language implies that he had unnatural or deviant tastes in sexual congress. His reign was marked by chaos and instability, including the Great Rising of 1382 (Peasants' Revolt) and continued threats of French invasion. His marriage to Anne of Bohemia (1366–94 CE) was decidedly unpopular, and produced no children. He was a firm believer in royal prerogative, ruling with a ruthless grip on the nobility and peasantry alike, making him wildly unpopular across the board, and particularly vulnerable to charges of effeminacy. Coupled with his military defeats and eventual ousting from the throne, contemporary chroniclers made Richard's lack of manly qualities and suspected homosexuality the basis for his incompetency.[83]

The later Middle Ages were particularly harsh toward suspected sodomites both because of the unnatural and deviant qualities of the list involved, and because of the potential disruption of the social and sexual order. In his writings, Aquinas described homosexuality as among the worst of sexual sins, arguing that homosexual sex acts contrary to the natural order of things as ordained by God. Aquinas's position caused this view to be assimilated into Western society. Beginning in the thirteenth century, homosexual acts, especially those between men, became increasingly associated with heresy and apostasy. The demonizing of those involved in homosexual acts moved from Church to state as well, as "penalties ranging from mere fines to castration, exile, and death, enter secular law" and prosecution became public and persistent.[84] More than ever, it was crucial that individuals perform in the manner expected of them by society, fulfilling social and gender expectations without deviance.

Female homosexuality in the Middle Ages is even more challenging to study than male.[85] The presumptive heterosexuality of Western society not only assumes opposite sex relationships, but also defines "real" sex as penetrative in nature, and holds that gender is naturally categorized as masculine and feminine. Where there is no penetration, there is no sex, and therefore little to discuss. Moreover, the history of lesbian studies has been plagued by exclusion. Women who marry and have children are overlooked in studies of woman–woman eroticism, despite the prevailing demands of premodern societies for heterosexual relationships. Even nuns were defined as brides of Christ, leaving little room for alternate identities. Moreover, the evidence that we have of premodern female sexuality—heterosexual, homosexual, or otherwise—is scanty, and as the majority of surviving texts are male-authored, a lot of what we do have has been filtered through the male perspective. We are left with little primary language that demonstrates how premodern women may have expressed their emotions of love and desire for other women. Instead, women are constructed as objects, since they cannot construct themselves as subjects. It is my intent to restore some of this subjectivity.

Perhaps the best-known instance of woman–woman eroticism in the Classical world is the poetry of Sappho of Lesbos (d. ca. 570 BCE) from the late seventh century despite the fact that only fragments of her work survive today. Surviving Greek pottery also depicts scenes of female homoeroticism, with female figures caressing each other, kneeling before one another, and touching vaginal areas. Various other vases, amphorae, wine jugs, and drinking vessels have female homoerotic implications: drunk nude women hugging; women kissing; women bathing together; women masturbating alone and mutually, with and without dildos. In none of these instances are the women masculinized, nor are the relationships heteronormatized.[86] Roman society, however, openly condemned female homoeroticism. Seneca the Younger (4 BCE–65 CE) writes: "Today women equal men in regard to lust, although born to take the passive role . . . So perverse is their new species of invented immodesty: they actually penetrate men!"[87] The lack of female passivity is the real trouble here. Not only are the women in question desiring subjects, but also they are assuming an active sexual role. In doing so, they are usurping the natural male-dominated order and acting against their defined gender role, becoming "perverse."

Early Christianity contains only a few notations about lesbianism, although enough evidence remains to prove its existence. Augustine of Hippo, for example, wrote that nuns should restrict the love between them to "spiritual love," eschewing carnal love, and that married women and virgins should refrain from "shameless playing with each other."[88] That he cites such behavior as commonplace indicates the extent to which lesbianism was known within the Hellenistic world. Similarly, John Chrysostom (ca. 349–407 CE) notes, "God gave them [Romans] up unto vile affections: for even their women did change the natural use into that which is against nature."[89] Although Chrysostom is clearly repulsed by the unnatural situation, he does not suggest harsh penalties. Another venomous description is found in the sixth-century *Liber monstrorum* (*Book of Monsters*). At the bottom of the catalogue of passive male homosexuals and intersexed individuals, the anonymous author includes a crude poem about lesbians, and sums up the "pointlessness" of their existence as follows: "You do not give what you get, though you service a cunt."[90] Medieval lesbians are pointless monsters enslaved only to lust and uselessness. Again, however, though monstrous, the women are not severely punished for their behavior.

A few penitentials mention female homoerotic practices, though the penalties are usually light.[91] The Penitential of Theodore, simply states, "If a woman practices vice with a woman, she shall do penance for three years," and Bede's Penitential requires only three years for "fornication between women," with the same sentence later handed down by Egbert, too.[92] In a later passage, however, Bede (672–735 CE) adds another dimension: women who fornicate *per machina*, that is by means of a device, must complete 7 years of penance. It is the unnaturalness of female penetration that upsets Bede's sensibilities more than the thought of lesbian activity itself. Hincmar of Reims (806–82 CE) takes it one step further, specifically describing a "hideous" lesbian encounter: "They do not put flesh to flesh as in the fleshly genital member of one into the body of the other, since nature precludes this, but they do transform the use of that part of their body into an unnatural one: it is said they use instruments of diabolical operations to excite desire."[93] Here, Hincmar insists not only that woman–woman sex is unnatural, but also that it cannot produce desire without a (false) phallus. Like Chrysostom, Hincmar worries about the disruption of socially established gender roles, but also fears female sexual appetite. There was no such thing as a "natural" phallic woman.[94]

Thus, within the medieval religious world, the most severe penalties for lesbian activities were reserved for those women who resorted to unnatural devices. Such a device, a dildo of some sort, created at least two separate problems. The first was a disruption of the natural sexual hierarchy—man as penetrator and woman as penetrated—not to mention the disruption of standard medieval biology, since these devices were assumed to be deliberate ploys to acquire and to imitate male genitalia. Bernd-Ulrich Hergemoller notes: "Woman was without exception regarded as a being who was sexually intended exclusively for man. . . . If, in the view of medieval man, women enjoyed themselves with one another, they could only do this if they worked on themselves with a dummy penis they made themselves."[95] Women who penetrated other women assumed a masculine role, thus displacing men and appropriating masculine power, at least temporarily, but possibly longer. The historical case of Katherine Hetzeldorfer demonstrates this complication. In 1477, Hetzeldorfer was drowned in the Rhine near the imperial city of Speyer for her crime of committing heinous acts of sodomy with another woman. During the course of her interrogation, Hetzeldorfer revealed that she has had sexual relations with at least three other women, and made advances toward numerous others. Intriguingly, the jurists are not concerned with Hetzeldorfer's apparel—though she is clearly dressed in male attire—but are rather deeply concerned with her "instrument" and the manner of her sexual intimacies:

> She says that she did it at first with one finger, thereafter with two, and then with three, and at last with the piece of wood that she held between her legs . . . And she also says thereafter that she made an instrument with a red piece of leather, at the front filled with cotton, and a wooden stick stuck into it, and made a hole through the wooden stick, put a string through, and tied it round . . .[96]

The all-male judicial audience is concerned with Hetzeldorfer's phallic appropriation, and the other female witnesses play into their preconceived notions. However, what is consistently overlooked about this case is that it is one of the very few recorded references to digital penetration in female homoeroticism. Perhaps because it was usually connected to medical treatments the male jurors failed to recognize the potential.

All of these reactions to female–female sexual encounters point to the underlying "performative essentialism" noted earlier. When women act against nature, they are monstrous, they are sinful, and they are penalized; however, when they act as men, they are ruthlessly suppressed. Moreover, the underlying assumption is that women who choose to be with other women are also choosing to "be men." There is little understanding outside the encoded binary system of male/female. Women were not encouraged to act as individuals, or even as a female collective. For instance, "almost none of this writing [edifying literature for anchoresses or nuns] deals specifically with relationships between sisters in a convent. 'Brotherhood' was a major theme of twelfth-century writing, but 'sisterhood' decidedly was not."[97] The formation of the female self was always done in connection to the male. Forging an identity through connections with another female was both unnatural and dangerous.

Hermaphrodites[98]

The idea of the hermaphrodite dates back to the Classical world. According to the myth, the nymph Salmacis fell in love with Hermaphroditus, son of Hermes and Aphrodite, and prayed to be united with him. The result was a fused being. Plato (428/27 or 424/23–348/47 BCE) also posited hermaphroditic origins for the human race. In his *Symposium*, he writes that humanity was one, androgynous race, but the gods could not stand the perfection and divided the bodies into male and female.[99] In medieval belief, however, hermaphrodism was tied to the theories of generation, being a condition determined before birth.

As several scholars have noted, and as discussed earlier, the Middle Ages inherited two different theories of generation, the Hippocratic/Galenic model and the Aristotelian model. In return, this led to differing views of hermaphrodism. Leah DeVun describes the Galenic contribution as a blending of biology: "originated by the writers of the Greek Hippocratic corpus and popularized in the Middle Ages by the Pseudo-Galenic tract *De spermate*, hermaphrodites were neither male nor female, but an intermediary sex that combined male and female characteristics in equilibrium."[100] Hippocrates assumed that sex existed along a continuum from the extreme male to the extreme female, with hermaphrodites centrally located, and therefore indeterminate and regarded as neither male nor female.

The Aristotelian model instead argued that hermaphrodites were not an intermediate sex, but rather the result of doubled genitals. Primarily this was the fault of the mother, because her contributed matter (menstrual blood) had exceeded the amount needed to produce and nurture one fetus. However, Aristotle also believed that there was an underlying "true sex" that could be determined "by the complexion of the body (that is, the combination of heat, cold, dryness, and moisture within it), which always indicated either male (hot and dry) or female (cold and wet) sex."[101] This viewpoint is connected with the one-sex model, in which there was no such thing as the female body; instead, there was just one body, which if it was cold, weak, and passive was female and if it was hot, strong, and active was male. Sex was therefore a manifestation of heat, and not necessarily fixed at birth; rather, it was unstable and could be changed during a person's life. These categories were based on gender distinctions—active/passive, hot/cold, formed/unformed, informing/formable—of which an external or an internal penis was only the diagnostic sign. Maleness and femaleness did not reside in anything particular. Thus for hermaphrodites the question was not "what sex are they really," but rather to which gender the architecture of their bodies most readily lent itself.[102] Albert the Great (ca. 1200–80 CE) writes in *De animalibus* (ca. 1258–63): "Sometimes the form of each member is so complete that it is impossible, either by sight or by touch, to decide which sex prevails . . . But the prevailing sex should definitely be the one governed by the heart."[103] There can never be perfect overlap or doubling in this view; one sex will always be prevalent, and it is up to society to help determine which one that is.[104]

This view makes the body dangerously mutable, a source of constant anxiety that could collapse into chaos. As Dreger points out, "Hermaphroditism causes a great deal of confusion, more than one might at first appreciate, because—as we will see again and again—the discovery of a 'hermaphroditic' body raises doubts not just about the particular body in question, but about all bodies.[105] Even in cases in which the body is meant to be a stable, unalterable construct, there is a disturbing amount of slippage. Specifically, the body cannot be counted on to produce gender, and, in fact, can betray it. For instance, facial hair is considered, both in medieval and modern societies, to be a masculine characteristic: "þe hi ʒtnes and þe ornament of mannes face . . . [and] token of vertue . . . [a beard develops because] a man is kyndeliche more hoote þan a womman, [and is thus] a certeyn assay to knowe differens bytwene men and wymmen."[106] In this schema, a beard proves masculinity, and is caused through heat. However, that does not necessarily explain the phenomenon of bearded women, several of whom are saints, including Wilgefortis and Galla. Galla, whose story appears in the *Golden Legend*, is described as a chaste widow who nevertheless was "very hot-blooded." She was informed by her doctors "unless she gave herself again to the embraces of a husband, the excessive internal heat would cause her to grow a beard, unnatural as that would be. This actually happened . . ."[107] Troublingly, bodily proofs of masculinity do not necessarily seem to bring bodily stability. These must be backed up by social and spiritual actions.

Presumably, then, if the primary difference between males and females is their temperature (men are hot and women are cold), if a woman became too hot, she could transform into a man. Thus, "according to premodern theories of medicine, the transformation from female was not in itself contrary to nature," yet the existence in between genders as a hermaphrodite was.[108] Historical examples support this contention. Miri Rubin reports such a case from fourteenth-century Alsace. An individual, presumed female, was married to a man for ten years, but physically unable to have sexual intercourse. The ecclesiastical court intervened, the marriage dissolved, and the individual sent on pilgrimage. On the way to Rome, she stopped in Bologna, and a physician cut open her vagina, whereupon a penis and testicles popped out. These being functional, she returned home, married a woman, and "did hard physical labor."[109] The person in question here was not scorned by society, but rather allowed to marry and contribute economically. As with beards, the individual's capability to perform hard physical labor, the traditional realm of masculinity, was as important to his redefinition as a man as was the appearance of his penis and testicles. Ambroise Paré's *On Monsters and Marvels* reports the story of a girl named Marie who became a man named Germain. One day, Marie was chasing pigs, thereby becoming overheated, and when she jumped across a ditch, male genitals popped out between his legs. From that moment on, the individual lived as a man. Although clearly both exercise and raised bodily temperature that contribute to this sex change, Paré also advises that physicians examine a wide range of corporeal features including the tone of the person's voice, the length and texture of the hair, the shape of the breasts, and the presence or absence of hair around the anus before determining an individual's "true" sex. Even more striking is the fact that Paré recommends considering other, noncorporeal, characteristics such boldness or meekness and other such gendered stereotypes.

The status of hermpahrodites was considered by the Church, the law, and the social order. In the Alsace case, the individual simply returned to society and was treated as a man. This was not unusual. Around 1235 CE, English jurist Henry of Bracton (ca. 1210–68 CE) wrote a treatise called *De legibus et consuetudinibus Angliae* (*On the Laws and Customs of England*). In it, he identified the legal rights of individuals by first defining "persons" into three groups: "Mankind may also be classified in another way: male, female or hermaphrodite. Women differ from men in many respects, for their position is inferior to that of men."[110] Bracton goes on to note, "A hermaphrodite is classed with male or female according to the predominance of the sexual organs." Thus, under this system, it is possible for a hermaphrodite with a visible penis to have more legal status than a biological female. Similarly, Peter the Chanter (d. 1197 CE), suggested that the hermaphrodite choose a sex and remain bound by that choice, with the choice being determined by relative body heat. Once chosen, however, the individual effectively became that sex, and was bound by its dictates.[111] Hugh of Pisa (d. 1210 CE), a canon lawyer, provided some practical hints on how to decide on the "prevailing sex": a beard, the performance of manly tasks, and preferring the company of men. Again, a combination of secondary sex characteristics, combined with social roles, served as gendered markers. Since medieval society generally prioritized the male body and the male social function, hermaphroditism and sexual ambiguity threaten the hierarchialization upon which the society rested. The male form was paradigmatic, and anything that fell short of it was lesser. The response to the threat posed by deviant unsexed bodies resulted in extinction by erasing ambiguity. Deviant bodies were heteronormalized according to their gonads, their body heat, their secondary characteristics, or their social dispositions.

In the Middle Ages, hermaphroditism was viewed as miraculous and supernatural. As such, despite legal and scientific provisions, these "monstrous beings" were often put to death because "the monster" was surely a portent, perhaps a messenger of evil, and at the very least, "a demonstration . . . of bad happenings, and as such it deserved and even required prompt annihilation."[112] Hermaphrodites were just one such monster discussed in these texts. For instance, *De secretis mulierum* (*On the Secrets of Women*, attributed to Albert the Great, but likely written by one of his followers), a thirteenth-century medical tract, places them firmly in the category of monster. He notes that while a hermaphrodite participates in both male and female natures, "he should always be called 'male' simply because the male is the worthier sex. While the author views hermaphrodites as a combination of masculine and feminine qualities, he nevertheless determines the hermaphrodite's sex according to the value of men and women within a binary gender system."[113] The ability to potentially participate in more than one sex category speaks to the capacity for monstrosity. Monsters were the truly deviant in medieval society. If all the other deviances we have explored are redeemable in some way through prayer and legislation, the monstrous hybrid was practically irredeemable. By their very nature, monsters embodied deviance in its fullest. With that in mind, let us conclude this exploration of "turning astray" by looking at medieval monstrosity.

Monsters

According to Bettina Bildhauer and Robert Mills, medieval monsters were "a means of circumscribing bodies and producing grids of intelligibility within which particular identities might be perceived." Monsters, "like periods of history, can be subject to linguistic and cultural resignification," and thus embody "cultural tensions that go beyond the idea of monster as uninhabitable, unintelligible 'Other.'"[114] Overall, however, monsters were seen as the most deviant of beings who often strove to cause harm to humanity merely for the sake of being disruptive or vicious. In Christianity, this complexity was compounded by questions of salvation:

if monsters were descended from Adam, wouldn't they have a soul and the possibility of redemption?

In general, the Middle Ages based its concepts of monsters on Pliny's taxonomy as found in his *Natural History* (ca. 77–79 CE). In this work, he obsessively catalogued an astonishing variety of mysterious creatures, many of whom were roughly human in form, but with odd alterations to their bodies. For instance, the *Blemmyae* had eyes on their chests instead of their faces, and the *Sciapodae* had only one large, muscular foot and leg. Augustine continues this tradition in his *City of God*, chapter sixteen, as does Isidore of Seville (d. 636) in his encyclopedic *Etymologiae*. Isidore is the first to explicitly link monstrosity as a deviation from the norm, that is the human body. In the Middle Ages, the body was regarded as an instance of the sacred whole, a register of the cosmological order. Every being was considered to have a place in the logic of the world. The body was essentially seen as a rational one, which replicated the larger cosmology and was both sacred and universal. David Williams argues that this view originates in Neoplatonic thought. The body in the Middle Ages was "related to the allegorical concept of microcosm in which the cosmos is contained in the 'little cosmos' of the world and both are represented in miniature in the human body."[115] The body is thus seen as harmonious and symmetrical, a reflection of God creating order. Isidore imagines the monstrous body as disharmonious. This disharmony will eventually become a reminder to the reader of his/her own sinfulness and potential disorder.

Monster literature and catalogues continued to be popular throughout the Middle Ages. Two such examples include the *Wonders of the East*, a book written in two versions, Latin and Anglo-Saxon, between ca. 970 and 1150 CE, and the eighth-century *Liber monstrorum* (*Book of Monsters*). Both describe strange places and monstrous races, terrifying animals, and amazing hybrids. All of these monsters lived on the outskirts of real civilization however, banished to the edges of human society. Like the most spiritual of the ascetics, the monstrous races lived in hostile and desolate environments such as deserts, caves, and fens. As John Block Friedman notes, "Men who lived outside cities, since their lives were guided by no law, were not really human."[116] Monsters were at least social, if not physical, Others.

The greatest fear of monstrosity is not simply the corruption or destruction of humans; rather, it is the potential for interbreeding. Once Augustine raised the specter of rationality and ensoulment, the fear of miscegenation became manifest. The offspring of a monster and a human would be a dangerous sort of hybrid, able to "pass" in human society, entitled to human rights and privileges, but never being truly human. This is the literal embodiment of deviance—a creature whose very existence is "agayns kynde" and completely unnatural. The reproductive potential of monsters causes human anxiety because of its alien product, but even more because the reproduction wouldn't be possible without some sort of underlying similarity: "A creature that exceeds the rule of 'kind' in terms of physicality threatens the boundaries of humanity, but one that does so and is capable of propagation is far worse."[117] These hybrid creatures could both encroach upon true human communities and create their own society that would inevitably challenge humanity for control of the earth. Fearfully, the hybrid "is a subject of difference that is almost the same, but not quite."[118] To the medieval person, that sameness was a reflection of the otherness within the self, the potential imperfection that lurked within humanity.

Monstrosity does not always come from without. It can also be produced within the body, manifesting at birth. Many medical texts refer to "monstrous" deliveries of dead children, molebirths, babies with physical defects, hermaphrodites, two-headed beings, creatures that are half-human and half-animal (hybrids), and creatures with rotted flesh, blaming such births on the parents' sinful behavior such as sexual deviancy or drunkenness.[119] Thus, monstrous births were tangible, visible signs of parents' subversion of natural law. More specifically, the fault of monstrous offspring generally lay with the mother. Since women contributed matter and men form, which provided both soul and personality, monstrous progeny would clearly have to be the result of inferior (female-provided) matter. Bad wombs, unnatural sexual positions, the mother's internal thoughts, the food she ingested, the temperature she maintained, and the sights she saw could all affect a child's shape, size, and normality.

This teratological view is deeply gendered considering that even female emotions can cause disarray to corporeal boundaries. Some commentators even went so far as to say, "woman is not human [*homo*], but a monster [*monstrum*] in nature."[120] Miller succinctly notes that monsters not only "issue from within the boundaries of the female body, [but also] they materialize the disordered interior of the female body."[121] Because the female body is conflicted and chaotic, it can easily produce another such if proper care is not taken. This possibility caused Bracton to consider the question of "Who may and may not be called children and reckoned as such" in his law code, specifying: "Those born of unlawful intercourse, as out of adultery and the like, are not reckoned among children, nor those procreated perversely, against the way of human kind, as where a woman brings forth a monster or a prodigy. But an offspring who has a larger number of members, as one who has six fingers, or if he has but four, [or only one,] will be included among children."[122] Interestingly, bastards are aligned with monsters under these provisions, having fewer rights than any human being, including women.

Finally, we can conclude with a brief mention of the monstrous woman in medieval society. By this, I mean both the female body as indicative of monstrosity, and the potential for women to violate social boundaries and thus become an outcast, akin to a monster. A monstrous body is constituted through lack or hybridity; it is a body of excess and porousness; it is a body that varies from the norm.[123] All of these descriptors fit the female body as conceived in the Middle Ages. The female body lacked heat and an external penis; it is a body of excess fluids and permeable boundaries; it is a body that is continually measured against the male form. The female body was dark and secretive, full of caverns and crevices, "tantalizingly full of apertures, from the privileged mouth to the wild and terrifying anus . . . [creating a desire for] entry, penetration, and discovery."[124] Women were inherently monstrous beings since the criteria defining the (male) normative body do not apply to them. Like all monsters, women were simultaneously attractive and frightening. The fact that every female body has the potential to be monstrous makes even the most contained virgin body problematic. Even more problematic is the incorporation of women into general society. Unlike other monstrous beings, they are not marginalized to the outskirts of civilization; instead, they are keepers of the home and hearth, and the bearers of young. Therefore, it became a cultural imperative that all female bodies had to be controlled by men in order to preserve basic and fundamental humanity.[125] As Cohen notes, medieval monsters transgress cultural boundaries and break social rules. Women who violated the roles proscribed for them by Church and state were labeled as "monstrous." This included women who spoke in public, who claimed their own sexual desire, and who earned an income. One of the most famous literary examples of this is Chaucer's Wife of Bath, who is loud, brash, bold, sexually aggressive, and wealthy. She is traveling by herself, has been married numerous times, and is a member of a guild. She monopolizes conversations and tells ribald stories. In short, she is every medieval man's greatest fear in one character, and the embodiment of deviance.

CHAPTER FOUR

The gendered Christ: Sexuality and religion

Throughout this book so far, the language has encompassed the ideas of masculinity and femininity out of necessity, rather than the reinforcement of binaries, and here, I will employ the ideas of masculinity and femininity as they would have been understood by the texts' authors and their different audiences. Gender roles, as noted previously, were tied to the essential physical body. For instance, the male body was thought to be hot and dry and the female body was cold and wet. As Joan Cadden states, "many of the differences which defined the two sexes in relation to each other were directly related to warmth and coolness: male strength and hardness contrasted with female weakness and softness."[1] Along with this idea, because women were thought to be weaker and softer than men, they were also considered more susceptible to weakness and passions of the flesh. In general, women were associated with the body and the flesh while men were thought to be more spiritual and rational; therefore, "male sexuality involved not unbridled lust, but carefully measured behavior."[2] These two positions encompass what I earlier called "performative essentialism," that is, while male and female may be tied to the genetic body, masculinity and femininity are created through a combination of the physical self and physical activity. We have already seen that Thomas Laqueur has traced the historical one-sex model, wherein the male and female bodies were essentially the same, with either internal or external genitals. Church leaders believed and taught that the inferior, female placement of the sexual organs thus emphasized a divine order in which the male form of the human body mirrored the perfection of God and the female form reflected the inherently flawed and imperfect nature of women. And, while Cadden has critiqued Laqueur's narrow focus, she does not disagree with the idea of a fluid one-sex/one-flesh model. Both agree that medieval society believed that performing certain gendered actions could change a person's perceived sex. Individuals and societies did not ascribe manhood to men or femininity to women simply because they were born with particular anatomy; rather, they required men and women to perform gendered actions and assume gendered roles after which they would be described as male or female. Both men and women operated and moved along this continuum. Women could become men, and men could become women. Gender is always under construction, and this construction relies upon a combination of personal biology, individual choices, and cultural concepts of socially and religiously acceptable behaviors.

This position can be further extrapolated from the importance that was placed on the paradigm of natural/unnatural. Certain behaviors were not seen as abnormal but instead as "agayns kynde" (contrary to nature). In the previous chapter, this concept was connected specifically to sexual acts. Even heterosexual acts within marriage could potentially fall into this category, as Karma Lochrie explains, "the natural form of sexual relations was vaginal intercourse, while the natural position was what is called the missionary position, with the woman on her back and the man on top."[3] It is through this belief in certain behaviors being natural or unnatural that gendered expectations arise. For example, in most circumstances it would have been unnatural for a man to be submissive to a woman, sexually or otherwise, or for a woman to assume a dominant role. Manliness, masculinity, was dependent upon his ability to "be active in the world and the active partner in sexual relationships."[4] Since there is no innate gender and it is instead a creation that constantly regenerates itself through behaviors, seemingly gendered behaviors are continually being repeated, to the extent that they become seen as natural. Arguably, then, men are constructed as masculine when they are in a heroic or powerful role, but are emasculated when they are lovesick or deviant. Similarly, women are presented as feminine when they perform traditional familial roles (wife, sister, daughter), but are problematized if they assume more active functions—including promoting Christianity. It is necessary to observe masculinity and femininity in action as performance as neither is a clearly definable entity, and as biology because it is closely related. Since there is only one human body, the possibility of gender swap resides in every person. However, since gender is a cultural process, not a set model, it is also actions. These gender performances "mark not only private but also cultural constructs of power and powerlessness, frequently reveal individual and collective anxieties about identity boundaries, about the Other in terms of sex, status, race, and religion."[5] Many exceptions to standard perceptions of the natural order were tied into religious experience. Men and women were active in religious vocations, passive in worldly endeavors, and active in pursuing a sexualized relationship with Christ. Because of the gendered associations with such actions, a certain amount of gender fluidity is constructed both through characteristics and through actions. Gender is always being negotiated. In the interaction between normal and other masculinities—or between normal and other femininities, there is "a space wherein subjectivity is rearticulated and reconfigured" and this reveals the anxieties in medieval society concerning what it means to be male or female.[6]

(Religious) masculinity

Masculinity can be defined as the normative performance of maleness. As an ideal, masculinity serves as a measuring stick against which the behavior of any particular male (and to some extent a female) is judged. Given that medieval society bestowed power, authority, and privileges to those considered appropriately masculine, it is important to think about how the content of "masculinity" is determined and how its performance is regulated. To think about masculinity, then, is to think about the cultural organization of power. It is also significant to note that the masculine ideal was not necessarily the same in the secular and sacred worlds.

Traditional scholarship suggests that medieval society equated male biological supremacy over women with superior social and cultural power. Furthermore, a man's ability to prove his manhood rested in his capacity to demonstrate dominance over women and weaker men; to lead his family, country, or army; to confirm his virility by procuring a wife and creating children; to provide food and shelter for his offspring.[7] Although this is to some extent true, and supported by the biological views of the time, it is also a reductive position. Men who did not demonstrate virility through physical prowess, production of offspring, and domination over those weaker than he, failed to receive social acceptance as true men. By these standards, virtually no one in a religious vocation would have qualified as a "true man." Reducing masculinity to a mode of secular production also potentially weakens the power of the Church. So, after twelfth-century reforms instituted clerical celibacy, clerical masculinity was redefined in opposition to secular masculinity. Since the clergy were denied outward markers of lay masculinity, such as weapons and offspring, the focus turned inward toward control. Rather than negating their masculinity, clerics' distance from women helps them define "an extreme masculinity," one more powerful than lay masculinity because "it was not weakened by association with the weaker sex."[8] In other words, rejection of sexuality became defined as a masculinizing action. As we shall see, while this rehabilitated male religious masculinity, it also effectively masculinized female virgins.

One aspect that remained at the core of masculine behavior, inclusive or exclusive of sexual intercourse, was dominance. In the case of monks and eventually of priests, because they were not supposed to demonstrate virility and dominance sexually, another outlet had to be found. Early Christianity refined the Classical understanding of biology, sex, and gender, retaining the earlier emphasis on male perfection, which in turn elevated sexual abstinence as a form of piety. Within the religious realm, the ability to prove righteous devotion to God defined true masculinity. The Church praised men who displayed the ability to resist the temptations of the flesh. This became especially important after clerical celibacy became the standard. The absence of women compelled men to define their masculinity without using women to perform demonstrations of dominance, virility, or physical strength, and forced some men to assume both male and female gender roles. Jo Ann McNamara argues that by filling both masculine and feminine roles, religious men constructed a masculine identity that emphasized verbal dominance and mental prowess, rather than sexual virility and procreation, and incorporated feminine attributes into this different version of masculinity.[9]

Without ready and legitimate access to women, religious men redefined masculinity by shifting emphasis away from physical force and sexual dominance and toward other aspects of the body, spirit, and mind. Acts of dominance remained important components of proving manhood; however, religious men created different means of performing them. McNamara suggested that mental prowess was one key component. Men were naturally more intelligent and reasonable than women, so without women to distract them, clerics would be even more advanced in scholarship. Certainly a great many medical and scientific achievements were accomplished by members of the clergy, although it is perhaps the level of education they received and the time they were allowed to devote to such pursuits that assisted the endeavors, not the lack of sexual congress. Some scholars have suggested that a "discursive competition" also resulted, with religious men turning to intense vilification of women as an attempt to construct a more powerful, virile masculine identity.[10] A different sort of bodily control has also been suggested. Lynda L. Coon proffered the possession of a "public voice" that conveyed authority and was a marker of the speaker's masculinity. Chant was "audible proof" of a monk's masculinity as well as being a mark of his status within the monastery.[11] Of course voice control was coupled with self-control in order to perfect the monk's masculine performance. He controlled his voice as he controlled the rest of his body, and in doing so earned a public masculine position.

In fact, as clerical celibacy took hold across Europe, religious individuals and communities came to perceive acts of self-mastery and self-denial, particularly over sexuality, but also over the body in general, as indicators of true manhood. This view has been identified as "Gregorian masculinity," which emphasized the importance of constant spiritual contemplation and rigid self-control over the body and mind.

True men did not experience idle thoughts, which lead to lust, and in turn lead to the pollution of body and mind, and, eventually, soul.[12] The ability to control—to dominate—is still the central tenet in the definition and performance of masculinity. Mastery is achieved through ruthless suppression of desire, just as secular masculinity demanded suppression of emotion. This domination is often presented as part of a spiritual war. By law and practice, clerics were, for the most part, prohibited from carrying weapons, and were thus denied a visibly gendered token as well as an instrument of protection and power. Lacking the ability to prove their sexual and military prowess, "celibate men came to redefine masculinity in such a way that they could *be* masculine without having to *act* masculine."[13] By using military metaphors (wars, battles, struggles) to describe spiritual achievements—particularly their triumphs over the temptations of the flesh—clerics integrated secular and spiritual values, thus shifting the parameters enough to enhance their masculinity.

Another way religious men tried to conform to traditional secular definitions of manhood was to adapt narratives of fatherhood into religious scripted activity.[14] Religious leaders, such as priests, bishops, and abbots, acted as spiritual fathers. Furthermore, performing sacramental ceremonies, particularly baptisms, marked a cleric's parishioners as his spiritual "children." Like physical fathers, spiritual fathers were expected to guide and discipline their children. Clerics nourished parishioners spiritually and physically, since medieval charity came from within. The discourses surrounding masculinity remain relatively stable in this model, with the focus being on adaptation for the chosen vocation (marriage or Holy Orders). A similar adaptation of a secular narrative of masculinity can be seen in some confessor-mystic relationships. Perhaps the best-known of these is Raymond of Capua (ca. 1330–99 CE) and Catherine of Siena (1347–80 CE). Although Catherine experienced a mystical marriage with Jesus, even receiving a ring made of the Blessed foreskin as a token, the relationship between Raymond and Catherine can also be scripted as a chaste marriage of sorts. He was her friend, biographer, confidante, guide, confessor, supporter, and partner. Together they even had "spiritual children." Finally, while male reproductive organs played an important role in determining manhood for the general, secular population, they did so for clerical masculinity as well. As discussed in the previous chapter, the Church prohibited eunuchs from being ordained; thus, functional male genitals were still central to the religious definition of masculinity even though control over their use was the required performance. In fact, control over their genitals was expected of clerics at all times. Even bodily functions such as nocturnal emissions posed a threat to clerical masculinity, as the uncontrollable body was a feminized body.[15]

The threat of feminization was prominent within clerical masculinity. Despite adaptations of ideal masculinity for the peculiarities of the religious life, the fact remains that a great many of the parts of the code of religious masculine identities resembled feminine virtues. For example, passivity, submission, and chastity broadly defined femininity in the Middle Ages, and each of these virtues was asked of religious men. To some extent, this had the appearance of making religious men lesser men. Clerical clothing also had a feminizing effect. Priests were barred from wearing spurs and armor, which were obvious visible signs of gender. Aside from these restrictions however the actual everyday vestments worn by clerics resembled female clothing more than male. Although medieval clothing was somewhat androgynous—surcoats, cloaks, and tunics all had similarities across both sexes—women's clothing was commonly longer than men's clothing. Other than the length of clothing, the main difference between men and women's attire was found in the accessories. Women wore their belts high, while men wore the belt around the hips. Women also wore their sleeves loose, and men often wore them buttoned.[16] Religious vestments were often long, belted high on the waist, and loose-sleeved—all feminine characteristics. Clerics were also barred from wearing spurs, bearing arms, owning hunting dogs or falcons, and frequenting taverns. Each of these practices is strongly associated with secular masculinity and virility; therefore, each activity in which clerics could not participate veered them closer to emasculation.

The other side of the coin is the assumption that clerical celibacy was practiced in the manner in which it was intended; that is, clerical celibacy assumes no sexual intercourse of any kind, heterosexual or homosexual, with or without a partner. Masturbation, nocturnal emissions, sodomy of any kind, and fornication all broke the vow of chastity (and obedience). Priests often deviated from church rules by engaging in behavior that signaled secular manhood: they frequented taverns, brawled, gamed, carried weapons, and failed to wear clerical dress. In doing so, these priests rebelled against a clerical model of masculinity and "behaved and appeared as secular men through their participation in masculine activities and with their clothing."[17] If clerics were directed to eschew precisely those practices that society defined as "manly," then notions of clerical masculinity had to be (re)structured to incorporate characteristics of lay masculinity.

The definition of manhood is fluid and polymorphic, and masculine identities often fall into various and often conflicting categories. In this way, a level of flexibility existed in religious masculinity that allowed both men and women to become masculine. Because these religious understandings of masculinity emphasized self-control and purity over virility and dominance over oneself rather than the dominance of others, they thus removed the importance of the male body in defining masculinity. In other words, a physical woman could become a social man, and a physical man could become a social woman. Coupled with the blessing of at least some of the Church Doctors, religious women were able to free themselves from the more rigid gendered system of the secular world if they positioned themselves favorably within religious life.

(Religious) femininity

Femininity can be defined as the normative performance of femaleness. As an ideal, femininity serves as a measuring stick against which the behavior of any particular female (and to some extent a male) is judged. Given that medieval society subordinated women, rendering them without power or privilege except for what was given to them by men, it is important to consider how femininity is defined, and by whom. To consider the construction of femininity is to examine the limits of marginalization and suppression. Unlike the definitions of masculinity, there is more congruence between the secular feminine ideal and the religious one; however, the embodiment of chastity on a permanent basis also had the effect of, if not the recognition of, regendering women.

The ideal medieval woman was passive, submissive, and obedient. She was chaste, courteous, and humble. These idealized expectations were reinforced by male medieval writers of all sorts, and religiously by the preeminence of the Virgin Mary. Mary was the ideal women: obedient to God and to her spouse, a loving and nurturing mother, chaste and virtuous, and humble and kind. On the other hand, the fear was that women were grasping, greedy gossips, and sexually lascivious temptresses that required male control. Religiously, this view was reinforced by Eve, who disobeyed God, tricked her spouse, condemned humanity, and necessitated patriarchal control of the world. Much anxiety was generated by the perceived weaknesses of the female body. While this did firmly place men in charge, it also provided an excuse for unruly women. They were often excused from their behavior, because as the overly emotional inferior sex it was expected that women could not control their "lower passions."[18] Women were therefore considered naturally predisposed to carnal transgressions; thus, women who managed to control these passions were exceptional, and to some extent, not female.

All of this cultural anxiety about the female body and its inherent sexuality led to the insistence that female sexuality had to be firmly controlled by the Church. This meant a number of things for medieval women. Legitimate marriage provided the only acceptable sexual outlet, and once widowed, women were encouraged to remain free from sexual duties by not remarrying. In both cases, the woman (and her unruly body) was firmly under male control. In fact, female education entrenched in women a mindset of submission to their husband and his family. Often, young girls from upper class families were sent to their future husbands' courts and raised there, wholly immersed in the culture of their future kingdom even before they were of marriageable age. This practice not only assured the husband's family that she would be properly educated, but also that their lands would be protected from "foreign ideas."[19] Women were therefore ideally submissive, requiring subjugation as facilitated by marriage for patriarchy to function properly. Unruly, deviant, and single women threatened the idealized patriarchal order of medieval society as they exhibited female agency outside of accepted behavioral norms.

Women who did not marry were problematic if they remained outside the patriarchal system; therefore, those who did not, or could not, marry were encouraged to enter the religious life. From the fourth century on, convent life was the accepted form of female spirituality. Monasticism as a whole developed out of individuals who left their community to seek a better spiritual life through fasting, prayer, and isolation. Men and women both fled to the desert or other remote locations in order to pursue an ascetic life. Gradually, some formed communities, and from there, these communities were organized into monastic orders. This was especially crucial for women, who were seen as unable to guide themselves properly. Since women were inferior to men in every way possible, it stood to reason that they could not be trusted to look after their own spiritual welfare. Therefore, men regulated female convents. They drew up the rules, they determined the locations, and they controlled the sacraments. Convents became substitutes for marriage in the secular world. Postulants had dowries, they went through a "marriage ceremony" upon entering, and they received a new title: Bride of Christ.

Making Christ a nun's husband provided the security of a male "head." Religious women took vows of poverty, obedience, and chastity. These vows resemble marriage vows, in that women in the secular world ideally were impoverished (their spouse regulated all monies and properties), obedient (their spouse legally and morally controlled them), and chaste (their spouse owned their body and was owed sexual intercourse). The term Bride of Christ had long-standing authority within the Church. In his famous Letter 22 to the virgin Eustochium, Jerome (347–420 CE) refers to her as "my Lord's bride." Ambrose, in his treatise *On Virginity*, recognizes all consecrated virgins as Christ's brides. By the fourth century, the same century that saw the development of female monasteries, exhortations to virginity and guides to female comportment regularly drew from the erotic language of the *Song of Songs*, and the ceremony for consecrating virgins closely modeled contemporary marriage rites.

This Patristic literature for virgins became the main source of medieval formational literature for religious women, and sanctified virgins were regularly praised as Brides of Christ. This tradition grew, taking a turn in the twelfth century. Bernard of Clairvaux (1090–1153 CE) popularized the understanding that the bride was an individual's soul, not necessarily just a specifically consecrate virgin (although such women still had claim to the title). By the late twelfth century, women, and even men, were no longer passive recipients of bridal status, but instead were actively recognized as (or, in some cases, proclaimed themselves to be) individual and living brides of Christ. These Brides of Christ wore wedding rings, bridal gowns, and bridal veils, either in their souls or on their bodies. These women claimed

Jesus as their lover and spouse. They visited him in bedchambers and castles, or even in vineyards and cellars as the bride in *Song of Songs* had done. Many underwent formal marriage ceremonies, in their monastic profession certainly, but others in more elaborate mystical marriages, complete with exchanges of rings and tokens, and the donning of wedding clothes.

Before exploring this idea further, we should take a moment to examine the exegetical basis for this view of humanity as Christ's spouse. The tradition stems directly from the *Song of Songs*, though medieval conceptions of the bride of Christ were also influenced by women's religious movements and medieval mysticism. In the predominant bridal tradition, Christ the Bridegroom would be drawn to a particularly enticing soul, and then redeem and transform her with tender love. This transformation derived from exegetic understandings of the *Song of Songs*. Perhaps the most influential writer on this subject was Origen (182–254 CE). He took the Jewish understanding that God had enacted a marriage with Israel and adapted this reading of the *Song of Songs* by casting Christ, rather than God the Father, as Bridegroom. Origen also introduced and popularized the two most common allegorical identities for the bride: the Church and the Virgin Mary. By encouraging the using the *Song of Songs* for liturgies of the Virgin Mary, he reinforced the association of the bride with the Virgin, and with virgins in general. Around this same time, John Chrysostom (ca. 349–407 CE), in his *First Baptismal Instruction*, characterizes the sacrament of baptism as the union of the soul to Christ through "marriage." He recognizes the joyous and beautiful moment when the bride is separated from her family and united with her new spouse. Later exegetes built on this foundation, and encouraged Christians reading the *Song of Songs* to imagine themselves as brides—sinners who, despite their sins, are still beautiful in Christ's eyes, and are thus still worthy of his love. By stepping into the role of bride, and casting Christ as Bridegroom, medieval interpreters were actively placing themselves into an erotic and physical relationship with God. Men and women could become brides of Christ during their lifetimes, winning divine love through virtuous living, especially through chastity and purity.[20]

The extreme emphasis on virginity does become problematic when it is practiced to the exclusion of other good works. Heroic chastity is one thing; haughty virgins are another. Overall, active pursuit of virtue is more important than passive protection of virginity. One such text that deals with this quandary is the twelfth-century dialogue, *Speculum Virginum* (*Mirror of Virgins*), which was composed for the spiritual education of young nuns. *Speculum Virginum* was widely disseminated and translated into several vernacular languages. It was explicitly designed to be an exemplary model for female emulation, and was actively used by later generations of women as a way for them to engage in their own spiritual development. It includes the idea of marrying Jesus, relying upon standard bridal imagery (e.g. crowns, flowers, gardens, and bridal gown), but this religious goal is achieved—earned—by actively cultivating virtue.²¹ A similar aspect can be found in the *Speculum Inclusorum* (*Mirror for Recluses*), a fifteenth-century anchoritic guide. Anchorites lived a life of complete vocational withdrawal and isolation from the outside world, to the point of being walled up in their cells and taking a vow never to leave. In *Speculum Inclusorum*, the anchorite is explicitly warned to pursue this rather extreme life only if he or she is actively devoted to it, and not as a passive escape from the world and its temptations. Once again, practicing virtue is more important than avoidance for "protection."²²

Still, practicing virtue alone was also not enough, and women had to be especially vigilant against bodily lusts. One manner of dealing with such became rigorous self-mortification. Ascetic practices and common penances normally included fasting, abstaining from meat, and extended periods of prayer; however, more extreme devotions became increasingly popular in the late Middle Ages. Some of these ascetic practices included thrusting nettles into one's breasts, wearing hair shirts, binding one's flesh tightly with twisted ropes, enduring extreme sleep and food deprivation, performing thousands of genuflections, and praying barefoot in winter. Among the more bizarre manifestations were rolling in broken glass, jumping into ovens, hanging oneself from a gibbet, and praying while standing on one's head.²³ Asceticism became especially crucial for women because sex, sexuality, and women in general were seen as the downfall of men. By exerting control over the body, and by choosing spirit over desire, even a woman could achieve an exalted level of sanctity.²⁴ In this way, asceticism became an active choice and a pursuit of one's desire (Christ and spiritual perfection), not simply a passive escape from the world. Despite this effort to control the body, the main problem with female spirituality still lay within the belief that women were particularly vulnerable to desire, whether or not they had experienced carnal pleasures.

Enclosing women in a convent provided a physical barrier from the world.²⁵ Walls provided the physical and spiritual protection needed by vulnerable women—even one's attitude could be seen as a cultural barrier of protection. The papal bull *Periculoso* (1298 CE) required enclosure for all female religious, citing sexual respectability and temptation as the causes:

> Wishing to provide for the dangerous and abominable situation of certain nuns, who, casting off the reins of respectability and impudently abandoning nunnish modesty and the natural bashfulness of their sex ... we do firmly decree ... that nuns collectively and individually, both at present and in future, of whatsoever community or order, in whatever part of the world they may be, ought henceforth to remain perpetually cloistered in their monasteries ... so that [the nuns] be able to serve God more freely, wholly separated from the public and worldly gaze and, occasions for lasciviousness having been removed, may most diligently safeguard their hearts and bodies in complete chastity.²⁶

Boniface VIII (r. 1294–1303 CE) clearly felt that nuns needed to be protected from their own weak female nature as much as from the world full of danger and temptation. Similarly, tracts on virginity stressed the horrors of marriage and childbirth in an effort to use fear as a weapon against lust. One such treatise, *Holy Maidenhood*, a late twelfth-century work, explicitly details the horrors of marriage and childbirth, complete with pain, beatings, starvation, death, and deprivation. Such works provided mental containment to accompany the physical isolation, in order to solidify the benefits of enclosure. Enclosure assured the purity of women who were dedicated not only to serving God, but also to marrying him.

The Bride of Christ metaphor also grew stronger among religious women after clerical celibacy was mandated in the eleventh century. It stands in contrast to the rhetoric used to describe priests' wives. Medieval attitudes toward clerical wives drew on notions of female corruptness and lust, characterizing the figure of the priest's wife as a woman whose greediness drained church finances and whose promiscuity defiled priestly purity. Because they demanded sex, clerical wives detracted from the holiness of their husbands. A wife tarnished a cleric's soul even as she despoiled his body. She brought potentially harmful impurity to the sacred space of the Church as well, through her menstruation and other bodily fluids, through her lustful and impure thoughts, through her venality and general disorder. Clerical wives and children were perceived as siphoning money and resources from the church. Steps were taken to guard against special favors and inheritance issues, primarily in the form of edicts issued by Church councils and synods. For instance, both the councils of Bourges (1031 CE) and Clermont (1095 CE) stipulated that priest's sons could not be ordained or inherit their father's benefices, and referred to such offspring as "cursed seed," and potentially "abominable."[27] Clerical wives were at the center of complex fears about pollution, and the language of contagion was often assigned to them. Virginal Brides of Christ, on the other hand, provided hope of purification.

Thus, while good works and virtuous living were certainly encouraged, especially as models for the laity, the most important aspect of religious femininity was always virginity. In *On Virginity*, Ambrose (337–97 CE) declares, "where chastity dwells such griefs [of worldly happenings] disappear because there religion will flourish and fidelity be safeguarded."[28] Jerome concurs, comparing the prayer and fasting of virgins to the "painted flattery" of married women. Most important is Jerome's position on what this does for virgins: "while a woman serves for birth and children, she is different from man as body is from soul. But when she wants to serve Christ more than the world, then she shall cease to be called a woman and shall be called man."[29] These early Church fathers believed that, for women, a life of marriage and family was incompatible with and a hindrance to a life focused on God.[30] Beyond merely raising herself above the temporal concerns of the typical medieval woman, however, a female religious was also, in theory anyway, no longer seen as being flawed in the same way that other women were. Through the renunciation of worldly concerns a woman could become something more spiritual and rational and something less corporeal. In short, a virgin could become a man. Centuries later, Thomas Aquinas (1225–74 CE) upheld this position: "By taking the vow of virginity or of consecrated widowhood and thus being betrothed to Christ, they are raised to the dignity of men, through which they are freed from subordination to men and are immediately united with Christ."[31] Aquinas here expands the potential regendering to include consecrated widows—women who were once sexually active but presumably are no longer so—making spiritual virginity, not simply physical virginity, the telling factor. Clearly women who chose a life of chastity and religious devotion were elevated above those who chose the more traditional, and secular, route of marriage and children.

Examinations of virginity and single status are complicated by medieval people's comprehension of "maidenhood." Maidens might not actually be virgins, but they were pious and submissive, and while generally never-married, they could also be widowed or chastely married.[32] Similarly, the definition of a virgin, a state that would appear to be dependent wholly upon the essential body, is in early Christianity a site of performance. In other words, the concept of performative essentialism drives both these definitions. Maidens were maidens perhaps because of their never-married status or supposed physical virginity, but could also be considered thus by their actions (or lack thereof), such as modesty, blushing, and sweet dispositions. Virginity, already a fluid state encompassing both physical and spiritual definitions, is even more complicated. This troublesome aspect is highlighted by Patristic opinions about virginity tests, which demonstrate a problematic relationship between corporeal and spiritual signs of virginity. Physical tests, dependent upon inspection of the genitals, were condemned—not as invasive or even potentially erotic, but rather as inconclusive and unreliable. For instance, Ambrose exhorts, "the virgin of the Lord is weighed on her own scales in giving proof of herself . . . And no inspection of hidden and secret parts, but modesty, evident to all, gives proof of her integrity."[33] The virgin's genitals do not provide evidence; rather, her dress and comportment (actions, performances, roles) suffice.

Even more complicated is the set of role models for holy women beyond the Virgin Mary, the virgin martyrs. Unlike the Blessed Virgin, these women were neither passive nor particularly humble. They were not victims; they were "fearsome opponents of men and defiant resisters of the *status quo*."[34] The martyrs were opinionated, strong-willed, and contrary. With their bodies, the early martyr-saints visually communicated the Christian faith, and female saints gained extra spiritual credit for their stoical endurance of martyrdom owing to the prevalent belief that because they were women, God had created them physically weak. As they underwent trials for their faith, the virgin martyrs were spiritually masculinized. The notion of "becoming male" is a spiritual and mental shift, an internal development, as pointed out by Jerome and Ambrose, not an external transformation such as that of the transvestite saints discussed in the previous chapter. Most importantly, "'Becoming male' removed the female body from the realm of secular social and sexual arrangements and made it the ally of the religious self, no longer to be defined by, or associated with, the biological or social functions of women's bodies."[35] "Becoming male" implies that through internal (for the most part, anyway) masculinization, a woman combats foes or overcomes situations, which she would otherwise be unable to defeat so handily. Only in modeling male behavior is the woman able to succeed and achieve a complete victory (salvation), yet, it is important for them to be seen as female-bodied, since these battles double for struggles with temptation and lust. Thus the virgin martyr also embodies the basic dichotomy of the Middle Ages—she is male in spirit, but female in body. By performing in a masculine manner, she transcends her essential female nature, which is tied to the flesh.

The virgin martyrs were a specific group of Christian holy women who died for their faith and for defending their chastity. The archetypal life can be divided into three parts: renunciation (of family and paganism), testing (of faith and chastity), and consummation (death and union with Christ).[36] The majority of these accounts focus largely on the women's sexual or socially perceived feminine attributes. Typically in these stories, a young, beautiful, and noble virgin is betrothed to a lecherous pagan lord who, upon being refused by the virtuous maiden, orders her to be viciously and publicly tortured in sadomasochistic ways. The rejected suitors more or less exchange lustful desires for murderous ones; nevertheless, they still crave power and control over the virginal body in question, and because of the rejection, they must prove that their masculinity is still intact by publicly restoring their reputation through dominance.

These torture scenes are highly sexualized, with the saint's attractive, naked body stretched out, put on display, and then beaten and battered with an assortment of (phallic) torture instruments, and/or mutilated in sexualized manners including breast removal and eye gouging. Seemingly less sexualized punishments, such as burning and whipping, are also inflicted upon the women's bodies. The virgins' femaleness is usually highlighted either by repeated acclamations of her beauty or praise for her fierce protection of her virginity, especially in the face of fierce opposition. During the course of the torture, some of these women battle demons, some are objects of incestuous affections, some have body parts removed, some enter into chaste marriages, some are skilled in verbal battle, and some are self-proclaimed brides of Christ. Eventually the martyr is killed, publicly, and usually after she has converted a number of pagans. She is never, ever raped, although the threat of sexual violation is always present. Some are even sent to brothels, both for the implicit threat involved, and for a type of "sex education." All of the women are very active and very public in their denouncement of paganism and sexuality, and all are ecstatic and enthusiastic in the face of death.

Virgins and virgin martyrs exist outside the norm and do not follow strict gender-defined rules, often refusing to participate in traditionally assigned roles for women (e.g. marriage and childbearing). As such, they are unable to be defined by (negative) "female" terms, and are therefore labeled with (positive) "male" terms. Occasionally this also includes the assumption of physical male characteristics, although not in the same manner as the "transvestite" saints. Some of these female saints suffer not only spiritual struggles, but also physical assaults upon their female body parts, especially breasts and wombs. For instance, Allen Frantzen asserts that when Agatha's breast is removed, "she has transcended the female body and become, however briefly, like a man."[37] She is spared death by burning because of an earthquake, but then dies in prison after being healed by St Peter—all events faced with equanimity supposedly because she has absorbed some masculine strength of character. It was also important that even as these martyrs were "becoming male" that they did not look male; in fact, they were represented in above-standard terms of beauty. These women possessed the ideal female forms. Perhaps their external beauty was meant to resemble mirror their inner, spiritual perfection; however, it also serves to reinforce the sexualized plots that underlay the male performance. The simple fact is that the virgin martyrs are renowned for being virgins even though men clearly desired them sexually, and because they refused sexual ownership, they were tortured in sexual ways. They performed masculinity by refusing to submit in a feminine manner, but their performance was triggered by their essential femaleness. Although these hagiographies do focus on the femininity of the martyrs, they also illustrate that underneath that piety, their concern is directed toward maintaining control over their physical body in order to also have command over their spirit, rather than simply to preserve an intact hymen. So, for example, in regard to St Margaret, "the corporeal rendering of Margaret's suffering allows her body to become a visible sign of the divine, rendered in physical terms in order to serve as an observable object to the spectators who witness her pain and her tortured body."[38] In this manner, the virgin martyrs are regendered as male in the sense meant by both Jerome and Ambrose. These women ceased to concern themselves with female things—not only did they reject family and suitor, but also they rejected being tied to the body, which is a female concern, and instead focus entirely on the salvation of souls (theirs and others'), which is a male concern. Moreover, as Ruth Mazo Karras points out, and as discussed earlier in this chapter, "one core feature of medieval masculinity ... is the need to prove oneself in competition with other men and to dominate others."[39] These martyrs do precisely that: they engage in a competition for possession and control of their body, and in claiming victory also proclaim dominance over their captor(s), thereby performing masculinity while displaying femininity.

Despite seemingly fixed expectations of proper feminine behavior, it is evident that femininity in the Middle Ages was a cultural construct that both inhibited and enabled female agency. From a modern theoretical perspective, Judith Halberstam's discussion of female masculinity makes clear the performative aspect of gender characteristics. For Halberstam, masculinity can be consciously shaped, and by examining female masculinity the ostensible stability of masculine maleness is confirmed as a social construct. Discourses about sexuality, such as the assumption that all sex is penetrative in nature, marked the heterosexual masculine identity linked to the male body as the normative and seemingly fixed ideal of masculinity; therefore, the assumption that women wanted to mimic men or that they desired to somehow "become men" fits this pattern.[40] Halberstam's polemic work was an effort to move away from the hegemonic patriarchal framework and consider female masculinity legitimately and separately, as its own framework instead of an inversion of the male. Since medieval conceptualizations of sexual behavior relied upon an idealized heterosexual and phallocentric model, where sex was an act between a male/active giver, and a female/passive receiver, any practice that involved submission also involved surrender of masculinity. Effeminacy, not necessarily (legitimate) femininity, was viewed negatively. Power and control were closely linked to masculinity throughout the medieval European world, so enacting masculinity could provide women with a measure of agency. Conversely, if those same women began performing within their expected gender roles, their natural femininity would reassert itself, and they would lose power. This is why guarding their virginity was so crucial for the virgin saints, who were extraordinary individuals. In cases where women transgressed the normal limits of womanhood by proving themselves not only stronger but also more "masculine," they were deemed "exceptional" individuals and their actions were applauded rather than condemned.[41] Particularly within the framework of medieval Christianity, female masculinity was an acceptable status as long as it was not used to subvert the overall hegemonic dominance of the patriarchy. Saints and virgins upheld the hierarchy of the Church, and were thus acceptable exceptions.

The fluidity of Christ

Religious expression of gender flexibility did not confine itself merely to human men and women. The godhead, that is all of the members of the Trinity, was also subject to (re)gendering. Pre-Reformation theology, as well as today's Roman Catholic Church, explicitly states that God is neither man nor woman—he is God. God has no sex because He has no body, and in medieval thought, a body is a requirement for a sexed (or gendered) existence. Therefore, God is officially masculine only by analogy. Both

Biblically and traditionally, God the Father is presented as a masculine figure primarily because of his authority and activity. He is the begetter and the lawgiver, not the vessel; thus, he is active, not passive. This reasoning upholds what we have already seen within medieval society, especially in religious vocations—it is the body in action that determines a gendered experience. God is constructed as God the Father because of his position in the universe, despite displaying "maternal" tendencies, such as compassion and tenderness. In fact, throughout the Hebrew Bible, God is variously configured as a mother giving birth to her people, a woman in labor, and a nursing mother, alongside images of him fulfilling traditionally feminine occupations, such as baking, weaving, and sewing. The Holy Spirit, or Holy Ghost, presented more of a challenge. Often figured as a tongue of flame or a dove, the idea of the Holy Spirit almost defied a gendered existence. However, grammatical gender issues have affected how different cultures traditionally depict the Holy Spirit. In a number of Eastern Rite churches, for instance, the Holy Spirit is gendered female because in languages such as Syrian the word for "spirit" is grammatically feminine. Otherwise, the gender of the Holy Spirit continues to be a troubled issue primarily because of the lack of embodiment, as well as the fluidity of function. The Holy Spirit is both comforter and prophet, roles that have been occupied by both men and women throughout Church history.

It is in the person of God the Son, Jesus Christ, that gender performance and gendered embodiment come into contest and create room for a wide range of sexual and gender metaphors and presentations. The later Middle Ages saw an increased emphasis on Incarnational theology—on the humanness of Jesus. The First Council of Ephesus (431 CE) recognized and affirmed the doctrine of the hypostatic union. That is, the person of Jesus Christ is at once both fully human and fully divine; nature and divinity become one in hypostasis. Hypostasis is a term that comes from Greek Stoicism, and conceptually is the shared existence of spiritual or corporal entities. As a human, Christ was biologically male. He is God the Son, the second Person of the Trinity. However, as a divine being, Christ is technically a genderless spirit. He amply demonstrates fluidity of gender despite his having a physical male corpus.

This focus on Christ incarnated resulted in an increasing emphasis on the Passion and its accompanying pain and suffering. The image of the Man of Sorrows (*vir doloris*) is one such tradition that reflects this shift. These images often depict Christ stripped from at least the waist up, wounded and bleeding, usually crowned with thorns, and sometimes attended by angels and accompanied by the instruments of the Passion (*arma Christi*) and/or a chalice catching the holy blood. The bleeding and suffering emphasize redemption through Christ as well as the Eucharist. Furthermore, the image represented the two natures of Christ, dead as a man, but alive as God.[42] In such images, he often appears almost genderless, with fair, unblemished skin, a neatly trimmed short beard (if any), hairless underarms, and few signs of genitalia. Although the viewer understands that Christ is a man, it is the sense of his being a "man"—a human—that is important, rather than his male virility. In fact, his "defeat," being beaten and crucified, is his strength and his victory. His wounded body is heroic and masculine, but it is also bleeding and feminized. The wound in Christ's side is especially feminized. It is referred to as a refuge, a hiding place, and a chamber. It is an eroticized bower and a divine womb. Irigaray describes it as a "glorious slit" into which the mystic enters, wherein she is covered in "hot and purifying blood."[43] The correlation between Christ's side wound and the vagina suggested by Irigaray becomes most apparent in devotional images produced in the later Middle Ages. Fluids pour from it into open, eager mouths or chalices, and saints and the Church emerge from it as if being born.

While the tortured body of Christ became the dominant image of later medieval piety as a demonstration of the essence of Christ's humanity, it was not the only one. Jesus as mother is an interesting example of male usurpation and assimilation of a uniquely female circumstance. The image of Jesus as mother was tied to the increase in both affective spirituality and Incarnational theology, since in both instances "feminine" characteristics expressed the human nature of Christ. In particular, motherhood was reconstructed in terms of sacrifice, which has a natural and direct connection to Christ. In the Middle Ages, mothers were thought of as having a tripartite nature: "the female is generative (the fetus is made of her very matter) and sacrificial in her generation (birth pangs); the female is loving and tender (a mother cannot help loving her own child); the female is nurturing (she feeds the child with her own bodily fluid)."[44] Jesus shares all of these characteristics. As will be discussed in the next chapter, according to medieval medical theories, the female provided the "matter" for conception, while the male provided the "spirit." Thus, Jesus is literally part of Mary's flesh, just as humanity is part of his body. The spirit of God is conceived in humans through the Word made Flesh, Jesus. Moreover, Christ's wounds are often depicted in womb-like terms, providing a shelter in which Christians could hide. The matter of Christ's sacrifice is obvious in the crucifixion. More than that, however, Christ is often depicted as having given birth to the Church on the cross, and therefore experiencing "birth pangs" along with his sacrificial and redemptive suffering. Similarly, Jesus's loving nature is emphasized not only through his redemptive sacrifice, but also through his forgiving and gentle nature. He also disciplines because he loves, just as a mother tenderly chastises her children in order to instruct. Finally, Jesus feeds humanity his blood, just as he was fed Mary's. In medieval medicine, all bodily fluids are conflated, and breast milk in particular is processed blood. Thus, Jesus's blood from his side wound is the equivalent of female breast milk: "In medieval devotions . . . milk and blood are often interchangeable, as are Christ's breasts and the wound in his side"; therefore, the image of Christ and his salvific blood "was precisely and concisely said in the image of the nursing mother whose milk *is* her blood, offered to the child."[45] The result is an accessible deity who generously doles out love even as he requests it, and a Jesus who is maternal even as he is also a man and deity.

While there were a few allusions to this idea in Patristic spirituality, the concept was especially embraced by Bernard of Clairvaux and other twelfth-century Cistercians and the anchoress Julian of Norwich (ca. 1342–ca. 1416 CE). Bernard wrote a number of sermons and treatises in which he highlights the maternal aspects of Jesus. Bynum notes that Bernard's use of "maternal imagery for male figures is more extensive and complex than that of any other twelfth-century figure, [and he] uses 'mother' to describe Jesus."[46] In particular, Bernard emphasizes the nurturing and generative aspects of Jesus; furthermore, he also connects those same characteristics with abbots (often, more specifically, himself). Abbots, like Jesus, pour out affection and instruction through their "breasts" from which their children suckle. Other Cistercian writers followed Bernard's lead, referring to nursing their charges at their breasts, the soul hiding in the heart/womb of Christ, and so forth. Julian of Norwich emphasizes different aspects of divine motherhood in her mystical narrative, *Revelations of Divine Love*.[47] While she does emphasize Christ's tender and loving nature, she also spends a great deal of time discussing maternal enclosing and protection. Enclosure was central to the anchoritic vocation, in which the practitioners took vows of "stability of abode" and were subsequently permanently enclosed in small cells (anchorholds), usually located/attached to churches or in churchyards. Often anchorholds were compared to wombs. Another aspect Julian emphasizes is unification between Jesus and each person, conveyed in her text through the terms "knittyng" and "onyng," both of which express oneness and connection. Julian further differentiates between "moder substantial" and "moder sensual," that is mother in grace and mother in nature, both of which are embodied in Jesus, but the "substantial" comes from the Father and Holy Spirit as well, while the "sensual" comes only from Christ. These individuals were certainly not alone in developing Jesus's maternal aspects, however. Valerie Lagorio, for example, has examined the extent of divine motherhood in Latin and vernacular works of the eleventh through fifteenth centuries, which she attributes to multiple family relationships, the iconic motherhood of the Virgin and of the Church, and the ancient image of Wisdom (*Sophia*) as mother. She notes that many maternal images convey Christ's role as nurturer and disciplinarian.[48] Hildegard of Bingen (1098–1179 CE) used two "strategies of validation" to overcome feminine weakness when promoting divine motherhood, reformulating it as humility and "chosenness," thus providing empowerment through positive feminine features.[49]

On the other end of the spectrum, instead of feminizing Jesus and presenting him as a maternal figure, some writers, theologians, and artists presented him as a courtly lover-knight, which is connected to the

Bride of Christ role. Mystics often describe in intimate and compelling detail their marriage ceremony with Jesus. He is presented in standard chivalric terms: handsome, brave, wealthy, generous, loyal, strong, wise, and kind. Every quality of both a perfect knight and a perfect husband is embodied in Jesus. In some texts, Christ pursues the shy, reluctant virgin, who feels herself unworthy of his special attention. In others, the woman becomes the pursuer. One such example of this is *The Wooing of Our Lord*, a thirteenth-century devotional treatise intended for anchoresses. In this lyrical prose piece, courtly love imagery of Christ as the perfect lover-knight is combined with passionate eroticism. Nuptial metaphors and crucifixion imagery overlap, blending divine marriage with shared divine pain. All the qualities that Christ has that make him the perfect spouse are defined in human terms. The anchoress herself, although she is merely human, pursues Jesus, calling him her "lemman" (sweetheart) among other endearments. Although *The Wooing* is unusual in that the woman is the ardent pursuer of Christ, he is still presented as a distinctly male figure, a man and lover worth giving up all other earthly connections to possess. Similarly, Mechthild defined three possible roles for herself: virile man in battle; well-dressed virgin in God's palace; joyous bride in bed with a beautiful God. She is multiply gendered, fluidly switching from male to female, but her Christ is a virile male companion both on the battlefield and in the bedchamber. In many of these texts, physical union with Christ is described in images of marriage and sexual consummation, and the imagery grows explicit, erotic, and even orgasmic.[50]

Related to the idea of Jesus as a courtly lover who espoused the pure virgin, the twelfth century also saw an increase in pious legends involving the Virgin Mary and members of the clergy in a similar spousal relationship. The most popular archetype of these legends involved canons or deacons, lower clergy who were still grudgingly permitted marriage. On the eve of their marriage, these men would be visited by the Virgin Mary who would reproach them asking why, if she was so beautiful and so perfect, would he reject her in favor of another woman. When the man reassured Mary of his continued devotion, she would then tell him that if he put aside his sin-filled carnal wife and clung only unto her, she would then become his spouse in heaven. The motif of Mary as substitute wife and antidote to clerical incontinence increased as the Middle Ages progressed, as emphasized by the steady stream of miracles in which Mary intervened to save the priesthood from sexual transgressions. Indeed, by the twelfth century there was a growing popularity among clerical men to seal their chastity through a symbolic marriage to the Virgin. Some of these celestial marriages went so far as to be performed by another cleric, uniting Mary, in the form of a statue, and the chosen priest, in the standard matrimonial ceremony, complete with an exchange of rings.

The more common mystical marriages, however, involved the union of Christ and holy person (*sponsa Christi*). *Sponsa Christi* was a trans-gender role, because within affective spirituality, perpetual celibacy became a way to erase all traces of gender and sexuality.[51] Just as virginity was a way for women to shed their cultural gender and become more like men, it was equally conceivable that men could temporarily assume femaleness. The term for soul, *anima*, was gendered feminine; thus, the holy man could unite with Christ in a similar manner as the wedded bliss female mystics shared. For instance, in Bernard of Clairvaux's early twelfth-century sermons on the *Song of Songs*, he instructed his monks, "they [the bridegroom and bride, Christ/Word and soul/monk] share the same inheritance, the same home, the same marriage-bed, they are flesh of each other's flesh."[52] He establishes his vocabulary as one of amorous craving and domestic harmony. The bride and bridegroom blissfully move through their daily activities and anxiously await fulfilling their desires in bed. In deliberately choosing this language, Bernard denies neither the existence nor the power of carnality; instead, he reworks earthly desire into spiritual love, where the female soul is harmoniously subordinated, through consummation, to her spouse (Christ). Bernard was certainly not the only theologian to explore the *Song of Songs*, nor was he the only one to advocate affective spirituality, but his writings had a far-reaching effect.

Finally, some mystics and nuns imagined Jesus as an infant. Miniature cradles, containing doll-like figures of the baby Jesus, were common in the Middle Ages, especially in convents in the Low Countries. In some convents, it became customary for each nun to rock the cradle present before the altar as she entered to pray. Many nuns had personal sculptures of the infant, which they would then take pains to dress and carry. This so-called devotional play blurred the lines between sacred and secular. Young women were socialized into the role of wife and mother even in the convent, and were encouraged to cultivate a contemplative piety that would encourage a personal relationship with their spouse, Jesus. A number of mystics experienced visions wherein they kissed, cuddled, and played with Baby Jesus. Some, like Margaretha Ebner (1291–1351 CE), even suckled him, or, like Margery Kempe (d. after 1438 CE), acted as the Virgin's midwife and companion. In fact, many of these same women who fed, diapered, and embraced the infant also enjoyed a spousal relationship with Jesus. Multiple roles such as this clearly demonstrate the polyvalent and gender-fluid nature of Christ.

A third gender? Possibilities and conclusions

Medieval Christianity was deeply connected to the body. The Incarnation signaled the importance of the divine body, and increasingly fervent devotion to the Eucharist as well as a rise in mystical connections with Jesus demonstrated the centrality of corporeality. Perhaps more than any other contemporary cultural institution, the medieval cult of relics revealed the desire to have intimate contact with a precious, sacred body. Bits of saints (or their possessions) were carefully and expensively enshrined, and put on display for public veneration and consumption. Concern with the body was connected to anxiety over what would happen after death; however, the possession of relics was also important to religious institutions as a method of maintaining economic control. During the Middle Ages, relics were a vital source of revenue. They attracted pilgrims, donations, and bequests. They also firmly cemented the relationship between the material and the spiritual worlds.

Clothing and other material artifacts whether worn in life or death were vital to establishing not only gender, but also other types of social, ethnic, or moral status, even as the regulation of space marked individuals' religious, political, and gendered status. All of these markers and their accompanying status were negotiable in practice, no matter how rigid the theory and rhetoric behind them. For example, despite the ideal binary of a masculine public sphere and a feminine private sphere, medieval practice did not always involve such a neat division: "Markets, streets, and guildhalls provided common spaces and public spheres; designs of late medieval castles, townhouses, and cottages promoted the privatization and engendering of domestic spaces; and housewifery, challenged by the abounding possessions of late medieval households, was redefined to better accommodate to an emerging consumer economy."[53] Similarly, sexual practices and lack thereof contributed to the gendered perception and presentation of medieval people. Both spatial and sexual activities, especially in conjunction with religious vocation, and viewed through the lens of recent scholarship, has brought into focus the complicated connections among the sexed human body, the discourses and ideologies that "make sex," and the construction of gender identities. The Middle Ages were an era of heightened anxiety about the body and its sexuality. Discourse about the body, the marks or signs of sexual and gender identity, the soul/body dichotomy, and the correspondences between the material or physical condition of the body and the mind and soul proliferated. Foucault's claim that each era simultaneously produces the means to represent, manage, and control sexuality in the discourses that circulate around bodies is borne out in these texts.[54] From this control of sexuality, fluidity of gender developed.

Some medieval historians have drawn attention to the complexity of medieval gender by identifying distinct groups which did not conform to conventional roles, from late Roman and Byzantine court eunuchs to thirteenth-century dowagers, as third genders.[55] To some extent, eunuchs, virile women (*viragos*), and virginal males were treated as separate genders in a variety of medieval societies. For instance, Jo Ann McNamara has argued that in the early Middle Ages, "monastic theorists tended to conceptualize a third gender, apart from the two sexually active genders."[56] Similarly, Jacqueline Murray contends that "chastity was a distinct sexual orientation" shared by male and female religious.[57] If anything, in medieval literature, a virgin's speech and actions often bring her gender into question, stemming primarily from her failure to coincide with social expectations for appropriate femininity. Both Sarah Salih and Stacey Schlau argue that nuns and other virgins became a sort of third gender. Salih suggests, "virgins can be said to be distinct from women, and quite possibly to escape the inferiority of women."[58] Schlau similarly claims that female virgins were not thought of as either distinct gender, but instead "transcended their womanness," and became something else.[59] Because virgins remove themselves from the economy that fixes them as wives and mothers, they essentially also remove themselves from womanhood and, thus, from the binary of gender, becoming something outside of gender, or at least creating a new category. If gender is a role one performs—as it is at least some of the time in the Middle Ages—then in this perspective, virgins enacted a third gender, the performance of which was intended to demonstrate their bodies were impenetrable. This corresponds with at least some Patristic Theology. Tertullian (ca. 160–235 CE) addresses the confusion caused by unveiled virgins who allow themselves to be seen. Such a virgin "wholly ceases to be a virgin to herself; she has been made something else!" A virgin without a veil destabilized and defied categorization. There was no way to refer to her, "unless a virgin is some monstrous third sex [*tertium genus monstruosum*] without a head."[60] Exposure to the unfiltered gaze of other people fundamentally changes the virgin, if not physically, then at least metaphorically. She becomes monstrous because she no longer fits neatly into the natural category "woman," but neither is she a man.

Religious men were also sometimes redirected into a "third gender" designation. Monks and clerics participated in nurturing, feminine activities, such as singing and caring for the poor and infirm, despite their role in masculine activities such as celebrating the mass and writing religious treatises.[61] However, rather than feminizing clerics completely, Cullum posits that they existed as a third gender, rather than as an alternative to secular masculinity. There was a fundamental conflict between lay and clerical masculinities, as even in a redefined system, clerics could never fully become socially adult men. In this perspective, clerics were *male*, but they were not *men*. R. N. Swanson concurs, and suggests the term "emasculine" be used to describe them.[62] Having renounced masculinity, he purports, clerics achieved a quasi-genderless status, but were still not women or without (suppressed) desire, so they were not "amasculine." Clerical chastity challenged normal social patterns, potentially disrupting the patriarchal relationships of male-headed households, certainly; however, there is little evidence that medieval people understood religious men as a third gender, rather than just a different sort of man.

Of course, not all critics agree on a liminal gendered space. Ruth Mazo Karras argues, "genders should not be multiplied beyond necessity."[63] Moreover, the fact remains that men enjoyed the ideal position of both body and soul in the Middle Ages. Thus, "despite all the flexibilities of medieval genders, the pervasive notion of a God-given hierarchical gender binary—'man' as more perfectly human than 'woman'—constrained medieval ideas about both sexual difference and the agency of women."[64] If medieval female virgins destabilize the gender binary by not fitting neatly into the category of "woman," they could, perhaps, be seen as androgynous or transgender instead of a unique category. Bennett notes that the framework for the construction of a third gender is evident in the Middle Ages; however, the cultural production of a consistent category would likely have been too destabilizing to the social and political functions of the state, and eventually to the Church hierarchy as well. It would have been less troubling to think of a few special women as able to transcend their true nature and acquire a different, masculinized self, since through God anything is possible, even a woman suppressing her female nature in order to become spiritually purified. Similarly, it would be easier to conceptually redefine masculinity to encompass other forms of dominance and control rather than to dispute male supremacy. We need only look at the flexibility and polyvalency of Christ, the only aspect of the godhead to have a physical (male) body, to understand that medieval religion saw gender as a complicated issue, not only one that produced fluid and nuanced individuals, but also one that did not permanently alter the binary status quo in which performance added to or detracted from gendered identity, but was superseded, eventually, by biology.

CHAPTER FIVE

The political sphere: Power, labor, and economics

"One of the greatest constraints upon medieval women was economic," write the editors of *Sisters and Workers in the Middle Ages*.[1] Indeed, economic issues shaped the lives of women in the religious life as well as the secular, and men benefited from women's lack of economic power. Feminist historians face some daunting challenges when looking into how economics affected gender roles. Barbara A. Hanawalt succinctly sums up the main issue—there are simply not very many records that reflect women's involvement, both because of the time periods under study, and because women did not "count" under the law.[2] By shifting the focus from "masculinist studies" of economic institutions to looking at actual production structures, such as guilds, and consumption issues, Theresa Earenfight suggests that we can deepen and expand our understanding of gendered power relationships and "social and cultural capital."[3] Moreover, we can shift our perspective of what it is we are looking for, as Christopher Cannon recommends, if we look at "the difficult process of the recording the life [of a medieval woman] . . . *as* the difficult process of living."[4] Thus legal theory about women, coupled with the lack of direct testimony can reveal another space in which we can address issues of gender. Similarly, lack of regulations regarding victualling and ale brewing may have provided easier access to women's entrance into those economies.

Working women challenged both gender roles and gender assumptions. Certainly, in any agrarian-based society, as medieval Europe decidedly was, all members of the household participate in the economic maintenance of the family unit. Wives were generally expected to oversee the daily aspects of living. On farms, this primarily meant housekeeping, food preparation and preservation, and household maintenance. Of these, food preparation and preservation was the most time-consuming. Cows had to be milked before cheese and butter could be made. Harvested grain was ground at the common mill, but bread needed to be prepared and baked daily. Animals had to be fed and watered. Eggs were gathered. Gardens were planted and weeded. Foods were dried, salted, or smoked for preservation. Flax and wool were soaked and spun into yarn and cloth. Village living was similar, except with fewer animal husbandry duties. In each of these cases, the women and men both toiled as a means of survival, and each was interdependent upon the other for success. Yet, despite the necessity of her contributions, the peasant woman was still subject to male control and ownership.

Symbolizing both economic importance and rightful subjugation, peasant women were often symbolized in medieval art by a distaff—the staff used to hold raw wool for spinning into thread. In fact, Eve is often (anachronistically) pictured with a distaff in order to illustrate her alignment with manual labor in the postlapsarian world. Because she brought about the expulsion from Paradise, it was only right that all descendants of Eve—women—be expected to cheerfully accept labor as their just lot. All of these labors, particularly the spinning of wool and animal husbandry, generated income for the family unit; in fact, female labor often accounted for overall success. Even if a peasant woman did not marry, the domestic arts often provided income for her as a household servant. The majority of servants performed similar tasks as wives (e.g. assisting with various crafts, caring for children, maintaining the household, etc.).[5] Moreover, the majority of townswomen were expected not only to maintain their household, but also to assist their spouse in whatever business he pursued. In fact, she could assist in his craft or pursue her own. In London, according to a 1363 regulation, men were only allowed to pursue one trade while women had no restrictions. Some pursued as many as three different trades in order to generate income.[6]

Similarly, upper class women were responsible for the overseeing of the estate in her husband's absence, and in certain cases, in her own right, although she did not have legal standing. The aristocratic woman was "a competent woman who often ran manors, farms and castles single-handedly. She was an influential person who had to deal with the management of acres of land, crops, animals and property; hundreds of employees and their homes; legal arguments, fights, riots and even armed attacks."[7] Although the duties of an upper class woman were more supervisory in nature, that did not mean that they were few in number. When wives were called upon to act in their husband's stead, she assumed not only the mantle of lord, but also the guise of manhood. For instance, Christine de Pizan (1364–ca. 1430 CE), explains this regendering in *Le Livre des trois vertus à l'enseignement des dames* (*Treasure of the City of Ladies*; ca. 1405 CE): "The lady who lives on her estates must be wise and must have the courage of a man . . . She should know everything pertaining to her husband's business affairs so that she can act as his agent in his absence or for herself if she should become a widow . . . for the wise housekeeper can sometimes bring in more profit than the revenue from the land."[8] Here it is acknowledged that women are essential to the economy, not only as producers of goods, but also as managers of resources. Since proper management was considered a trait of medieval proper masculine identity, it is a measure of masculine performance for a woman to competently husband resources.[9] Moreover, the woman is expected to perform masculinity for the sake of the land and its populace, but relinquish this performance upon her husband's return. The expectation remained, however, that the upper class wife would be able to perform adequately as a man. A clear example of this can be found in the letters of Margaret Paston (d. 1484 CE), a wealthy heiress in Norfolk, England who was married to the lawyer, Sir John Paston (1412–66 CE). She left behind a series of letters written between 1441 and 1447 that detail her duties when she was left in charge of the vast estates. In over 100 letters, Margaret addresses everything from repairing tenant housing to settling disputes to organizing defenses. Additionally, she was still expected to brew medicine, supervise cooking and cleaning, and complete other such "female" activities.[10] Despite this amount of work and responsibility, the upper class woman neither owned land nor had right over it. She worked for the profit and security of her husband. In the meantime, men were free to pursue politics, trade, and warfare without worry.

Unskilled laborers of the lower classes, sometimes called the urban poor, were not citizens of the towns in which they dwelled. Some worked in the lesser crafts, such as cloth manufacturing, which were related to domestic skills. Many plied their actual domestic skills as servants, washerwomen, wet nurses, or food-preparers. A number of these women were street vendors, who differed from the artisans in that they resold products that had been purchased wholesale. Numerous products were sold in this manner, including fish, poultry, dairy products, charcoal, oats, salt, and flour.[11] These women were often the only members of the family to bring in actual money, yet research has shown that women in this class of laborer earned substantially less than men did. In fact, "women as day laborers by contract . . . earned salaries usually about half of what men earned."[12] This inequity was evident in every trade, especially as the later Middle Ages witnessed an increase in women who worked outside the home, as we would term it today, in skilled professions. These women were members of guilds and medical practitioners among other professions, and early in the medieval era, brewing ale was almost the exclusive province of women. Each of these professions contributed to the construction of medieval gender, medieval sexuality, and gender roles, and will be examined more closely. However, as economic historian Joan Thirsk reminds us, "if a venture prospers, women fade from the scene."[13] Male dominance comes at the expense of female success, or even at the expense of female participation. We must continue to investigate the reasons behind this silencing and interrogate the historical entrenchment of patriarchy.

Outside of craft and trade professions, there were some women who exercised political and economic power, providing a challenge to the stereotypical image of medieval women as oppressed and subservient. In the Church, women could hold positions of great responsibility as abbesses of convents. The abbess, who was elected by her peers, exercised considerable power over the sisters in her care and held her office for life, unless it was taken from her for misconduct.[14] In double monasteries, where foundations existed for both men and women, the abbess had seniority over monks, too. Double monasteries were fairly common in the early Middle Ages, as the centuries progressed, the number declined, perhaps because of a growing distaste for a female-led political structure, but also due to potential sexual indiscretion. Officially, they were banned in 787 CE at the Second Council of Nicaea, but it took centuries for this edict to be enforced—and in the twelfth century, the practice was officially revived. While England had the most double monasteries, they were also found in France, Germany, and Sweden. The English Gilbertine Order and the Swedish Bridgettines were both founded under this revival. Some of the most famous and learned abbesses were leaders of these houses. St Hilda (ca. 614–80 CE) of Whitby Abbey is one of the better known, as she was instrumental in the Christianization of England and supervised the institution of the Synod of Whitby (664 CE) at which it was decided that Christians in Britain would follow Roman standards, not Celtic ones. Another double monastery, Fontevrault Abbey, founded in 1099 CE, was a large and wealthy establishment that boasted almost three thousand monks and nuns by the first-half of the twelfth century. The position of abbess at Fontevrault was coveted, and over the years a number of noblewomen, including members of the Capetian and Bourbon royal families, served in that capacity.

Aside from ruling double monasteries, some abbesses of large and important houses were equal with lords of the realm. In Germany, for example, under the Holy Roman Empire, a number of Ecclesiastical Territories were ruled by an abbess who also held the title "Princess-Abbess" (Fürstäbtissin or Reichsäbtissin). Those in the Imperial Immediacies ruled directly, without any intermediary liege lord, and therefore had the right to collect taxes and tolls themselves. They also held seats in the College of Prelates of Swabia or the Rhine as well as the Imperial Diet (the legislative body for the Holy Roman Empire). A number of abbesses of minor convents also functioned as landowners and exercised lower court rights. In England, Cynethryth (d. after 798 CE), Queen of Mercia, was the only Anglo-Saxon Queen consort who had coinage issued in her name and image. After Offa's death in 796, Cynethryth entered the religious life and became abbess at Cookham monastery. The coins were issued until after her death, and were a popular form of donation. Coins issued in the image of women who ruled as queens in their own right were, of course, more common. Just in general, however, an abbess also exercised power that was normally reserved solely for men. They were responsible for hearing their charges' confessions—and, in turn, for issuing absolution and penance, and in extreme cases, for excommunicating an intransigent. Abbesses had access to the altar in a manner forbidden not only to most women, but also to most men. For instance, they were able to present the offering of bread and wine to the priest.[15] Still, they were only borrowing a mantle of masculine authority from their spouse, Christ, as designated by the patriarchal authority of the Church.

Despite their vast contributions to the economy, however, women across medieval Europe were generally banned from full citizenship rights, including land ownership and access to education. Citizenship was a late medieval development, of which the central benefit were the "freedoms," or "liberties," meaning exemptions from certain taxes and feudal duties, as well as the enjoyment of certain benefits such as military protection. In return, citizens owed financial and civil loyalty. Citizenship was the only path to full membership in public political life.[16] Women were, as a matter of course, excluded from the political sphere, if not from the public (economic) sphere of medieval Europe.[17] Thus, the "financial acumen, mercantile property, and artisanal skills of medieval urban women never earned them the right to help govern . . . [and] the rule that reserved political space for men alone . . . seems to have been unalterable."[18] Thus, even when they attained full guild membership or other economic independence, women were legally constructed as passive citizens at best, and nonadults at worst. To some extent this disempowerment might also be an extension of the continuing efforts of hereditary monarchs to disenfranchise the growing middle classes. Women's power, such as it was, even for queens, was generally bound up with the family unit, a dangerous challenge to centralized authority.

As with many aspects of medieval life, a study of gender and work becomes a study of the separate spheres of male and female life. This is especially true for the artisan class of the late Middle Ages. Ruth Mazo Karras notes that the goal of artisanal masculinity was "domination of others (including women but mainly men) economically through ownership of an independent workshop."[19] Ownership of a workshop provided men with the opportunity for full citizenship and the assumption of an important place in society. Women and boys were both excluded from these spaces. Thus, both the acquisition of goods and capital and the control of these goods delineate adulthood and masculinity. However, while financial success could secure a man's masculinity, it did not permanently regender women since they could perform masculinity when necessary, such as in the absence of a husband, but never fully achieve adulthood. As Derek G. Neal points out, "being a man meant being present, visible, accepted among and interacting with a community of other males in the formal and informal structures of a man's immediate community: the marketplace, the guild hall, the manor court, the vestry meeting."[20] Masculinity was an enactment of public dominance, and therefore could never be permanently secured by women, who were unable to fully participate in the public sphere. Even the women with political advantage, such as queens and abbesses, were still ultimately bound by the limits of the law and their sex.

Medieval queenship

While sacred and secular power was often aligned, outside monastic walls, women could wield political power, especially as queens and regents who exercised royal authority on behalf of absent husbands or underage sons, thereby gaining power through their family structure. By far the most common medieval queen was the queen consort. Before the twelfth century, it was common across Europe for the queen to be a central figure in royal administration. In particular, queens were often in charge of the royal treasury, since it was a domestic chore that kings could not be bothered with. However, as the Middle Ages waxed, the Church grew increasingly concerned with the image strong queens presented to their female citizens. Ecclesiastical writing began to address what the Church considered the proper role of queens shaping the image for the masses, until "by the end of the twelfth century, the metaphors of peacemaker, mother, nurse, benefactress, and intercessor combined to create a new image for the high-medieval queen."[21] Queens were supposed to be obedient, passive, submissive, chaste, pious, kind, retiring, decorous, and fruitful. Moreover, queens were often in a position to influence policy even if they did not sit on the throne as ruler, and the Church exploited this. For instance, numerous monasteries and hospitals were founded by queens, who were expected to set an example of charitable living.

Aside from the traditional role as queen consort, there were a small number of queens regnant throughout Europe in the Middle Ages, most of whom reigned in Eastern Europe, Italy, and Spain. Several women ruled first as queen consort and then as queen regnant upon widowhood. Queen Jelena of Bosnia (ca. 1345–ca. 1399) was one such woman. Others inherited the throne from their fathers. Perhaps the most visible of these was Melisende (1105–61 CE), Queen of Jerusalem between 1131 and 1153 CE, and regent for her son, Baldwin III, from 1153 to 1161. The eldest daughter of Baldwin II, she was raised as her father's heir presumptive, a common practice in Eastern Frankish society, although a queen regnant's spouse often ruled *jure uxoris* (by right of wife). Mary (1371–95 CE), Queen of Hungary and Croatia, succeeded her father, Louis I, in 1382, with her mother, Elisabeth of Bosnia serving as regent. She was crowned "king of Hungary," not queen, in an effort to impress her role as monarch upon the nobles. After numerous years filled with warfare and strife, she eventually came to share the throne with her husband,

Sigismund of Luxembourg. While Louis had wanted Mary to inherit his Polish throne as well, her sister Hedwig was crowned instead. Margaret I (1353–1412 CE), was Queen of Denmark, Norway, and Sweden, and founded the Kalmar Union, the state that brought together the Scandinavian nations from 1397 to 1523 CE, primarily as a mechanism for preventing German expansion northward.[22] She inherited the throne of Denmark from her father, but became Queen of Norway and Sweden through her marriage to Haakon VI, and, after his death, through her son, Olaf. She was temporarily elected "Sovereign Lady and Ruler," and nobles agreed to accept any king she chose to appoint. It was also common practice in the Spanish and Italian regions for kings and queens to co-rule. Sardinia was an exception, and the thirteenth century saw a number of women serve as *giudicessa* (fem. judge), the most powerful of whom was Eleanor of Arborea (1347–1404 CE).[23] She composed the quite progressive *carta de logu* (code of law) in 1392. After its enforcement in 1395, it remained in place until 1827 CE.

Queens did play an important role in the maintenance of dynastic rule, and some were capable and involved administrators. Still, however, queens were first and foremost women, and therefore bound by medieval conceptions of womanhood. The precarious position of being a woman left a queen particularly economically vulnerable, since she also carried with her the weight of dynastic succession through bearing royal heirs. A practice developed from the twelfth century forward across Europe to set aside particular lands, and their accompanying revenues, for the queen. In this way, she would always have income—but more than that, these lands provided political safeguards and stability for the monarchy itself, even after the death of a king. English queens were given estates at the discretion of their spouse. Central European, Scandinavian, and Scottish queens received specific queens' estates. In Portugal and some regions of what is now Spain, part of the crown's estate was selected to embody the queen's patrimony.[24] Overall, most scholars agree that the queen's financial position and her political power were interdependent, although both were also inextricably intertwined with her familial connections. For instance, in Anglo-Norman England, queens participated in governmental dealings as partners primarily because of their independent incomes and resources. Similarly, medieval Scandinavia valued both the landed property of the queen consort and her political training. Queen consorts in the Holy Roman Empire tended to be chosen more for their political talents and familial networks than for their properties, but certainly their independent incomes did not harm their chances of success.

Both queens consort and regnant could exercise remarkable powers, but the position of queen regnant presented conceptual and legal difficulties. As Theresa Earenfight points out, a queen who rules alone still needs an adjective: she "is called 'female king,' 'sole queen,' or a 'female monarch' who exercised 'kingly power' or 'regnal power,' or an 'autonomous monarch.'"[25] These words both highlight the gendered instability that arises when a woman rules alone, and obscure the exercise of female authority. As scholars have demonstrated, a number of women ruled either alone or as co-ruler during the Middle Ages. These queens are interesting because they occupy a liminal space in terms of gender. Medieval Europe was a patriarchal society, a viewpoint affirmed by both Church and state on a regular basis. However, the unusual combination of their gender and royal authority gave these queens an opportunity to redefine power and gender roles by exploiting the ambiguity involved in the status of being a female king. Moreover, as Earenfight suggests, it may be time to discuss medieval queenship differently than we discuss medieval kingship. For instance, tradition has legitimized power that stems from military prowess. While certainly some queens supported a strong military foundation, others sought power through different channels, such as cultural and religious patronage. Both manners of ruling can be equally as effective. As well, "queens consort could step into these institutional gaps and govern as regent or lieutenant because monarchial power in pre-modern Europe was never isolated in one person."[26] Monarchy is neither "rule by a single person" nor a strict political structure in and of itself; instead, it is dependent upon a network of family and loyal supporters. In this sense, queens could function as the head of a family while still not actually crossing the line into masculinity. This is similar to an upper class wife managing the estate in the absence of her husband, only on a grander scale. Of course queenship was hemmed in by an overarching patriarchal political system, under which queens were "permitted" to rule, rather than expected to. Yet, the many ways women presented as rulers throughout the Middle Ages speaks to an underlying ability to regender the public and political body of the monarch in order to retain economic or dynastic stability. Medieval queens were unusual in their positioning as both masculine and public in function as political leader, and feminine in their function as the reproductive force of dynastic succession. To some extent, this characterizes them as potentially "unruly" women in need of masculine governance and authority. Significantly, "one way that women could challenge the patriarchal order was through the phenomenon of the disorderly or unruly woman."[27] No matter the social class, a woman who stepped outside proscribed bounds, especially by speaking in public, earning income, and challenging (male) authority was dangerous. Examining the history of brewing and alcohol consumption can provide us with an insightful example.

Brewsters[28]

A number of scholars, most significantly Judith A. Bennett, have turned to the history of medieval brewing as a template example of women's economic disenfranchisement, which in turn led to increased sexualization and demonization. Perhaps more than any other occupation, this process is reflected not only in social and economic trends, but also in legal regulations, popular literature, artwork, and religion. Overall, the brewing industry of late medieval England demonstrates the continued marginalization of women and the maintenance of gender inequality.

Women dominated brewing in early post-Conquest England. Water was suspect both in taste and quality, so across medieval Europe, alcohol was the preferred liquid. In France and Italy, the population consumed watered wine, and in the Low Countries, the preferred drink was hopped beer. However, the English population preferred either weak ale or hard cider. Ale spoiled very quickly, and coupled with the high demand, there was a constant need for brewing. By the early 1300s, it was a small-scale, localized business that was mainly the province of women. It could be accomplished within the home and required little initial investment or education. Prior to the commercialization of the industry, it was also less regulated and easier to start up. "Perhaps one of the reasons brewing suited women was that it was difficult to supervise, making it easy to avoid regulations, especially if it was not clear whether the brewing was for domestic use or for sale."[29] Furthermore, since women were barred from so many professions in the Middle Ages, brewing was one way they could contribute to the economic success of their family, or even of themselves, without challenging the public masculine sphere, particularly since it was often a "secondary" economic activity, complementary to whatever the male head of the household contributed.[30] Since women were the primary providers of food and drink for their families, brewing was a natural outgrowth of these duties. Although many brewsters were married, there were a number who were single or widowed. In some ways, the unmarried brewsters enjoyed a better living than the married ones, as she could retain her profits. However, unmarried and widowed brewsters also had less help. Few could afford to hire servants, and they may not have had children to conscript into service. Still, the income was steady as was demand for product. Women were particularly adept at determining local markets since they knew neighbors and resident preferences.

This relative success—a brewster could often live comfortably, if not excessively—began to change in the fourteenth century, and as a result of those changes, women were no longer the primary crafters. This was an extensive alteration:

> One fact emerges very clearly: between 1300 and 1600, the brewing industry was transformed. In 1300, brewing as a small-scale, local industry pursued by women who worked from their homes . . . [it was relatively] unorganized and underdeveloped. By 1600, brewing in many cities, towns, and villages was so large scale and so centralized that it was assuming a leading role . . . It was also largely controlled by men.[31]

There are a number of reasons why this change took place. Most scholars agree that one of the primary reasons was the switch from ale to hopped beer. Hops had been cultivated and used on in Continental Europe for quite some time, but only first came to England around 1400 CE from the Low Countries.[32] Beer kept longer than ale, and thus could be produced in larger quantities in more central locations. It provided higher profits and traveled better. Along with the influx of hops, urbanization assisted this industry change. Larger populations in one area meant larger quantities of product could be produced and sold more quickly for more profit. Marketing was also more effective, and alehouses began to be social centers of smaller neighborhoods within larger urban settings. Finally, the expanding brewing market also meant that the industry became more regulated, leading, in turn, to the organization of brewing guilds.

This shift in brewing technique meant that those who wanted to make beer needed more and different equipment. Additionally, as the demand for beer grew, the grain requirement also increased. Women often did not have the ready capital to invest in new equipment, or access to the grain needed, and they were not able to get credit to invest in such items on their own. With beer brewing working on "a grand scale, with larger capital costs, higher risks, and expanding markets . . . women could quite simply not compete with men: they lacked the necessary capital, they lacked ready access to distant markets, and they lacked managerial authority."[33] Women did not control their own assets, and even if they could gain access to the cash needed, often grain suppliers would not deal directly with female purchasers, and few laborers wanted to take directions from a female supervisor. Even married partnerships carried with them a risk if the woman was involved directly in the actual brewing process, both from worker rebellion and from inheritance issues created by death and remarriage. As well, expanding markets meant both longer distances traveled within the country, and, potentially, overseas markets. Neither of these two selling options was easily negotiable by women, who were restricted in their travel movements, and lacked legal standing to make contracts. Finally, a specific market for beer developed in the late fourteenth century—the military.[34] While troops were technically responsible for their own provisioning, leaders understood the necessity of providing drink, and beer traveled better than ale. Military leaders, however, did not want to deal with women brewsters either in production, or for transport of the goods. To some extent this was due to the male brewers becoming a corollary part of the garrison, billeting with and shipping out with the soldiers; however, at least some of this attitude was due to the widespread association of alewives with disorderly conduct, as we will discuss in more detail later.

Alien beer production in London contributed to the lessening of women's place in the trade, too. Dutch, and to some extent German, brewers flooded the London markets, and they were highly masculinized trades. In their home countries, brewing was a high status, male-dominated profession.

When they came to England, there was no reason for them to change their outlook. Dutch brewers were only male, and hired only male assistants and servants. They also formed their own organizations, worshipped together, and generally excluded even English men from their social circles unless forced to do otherwise by law. By the time the brewing industry reasserted itself as a native English trade, or the immigrant brewers adapted, women had already been forced out.

Regulative action and licensing laws discriminated against female brewers as well. One major change was the incorporation of brewing into the guild structure. In 1438, the Brewer's Guild of London was formally established, although the brewers of London had formed a loose collective several years prior. Barbara A. Hanawalt reveals some intriguing membership statistics. From 1418 to 1425, about one-third of guild members were female, both married and unmarried; however, the unmarried women did not maintain a membership longer than two years running. Moreover, despite guild membership, married brewers had to be registered jointly with their husbands (even if the spouse did not work in the craft), female members were not allowed guild livery or governance, and even those members declared *feme sole* were listed jointly with their spouse in both debits and credits.[35] The vanishing rights of female brewers sped up the pattern of removal.

When the pattern of consumption shifted from ale to hopped beer, there was an accompanying spatial shift from home consumption to tavern consumption. Unlike home brewing establishments, taverns were primarily owned by men and considered public male spaces. They also quickly became seen as unsavory places. Common parlance of late medieval religious tracts called taverns the "devil's schoolhouse," where people learned to dance and sing to the devil's tune (sin) and ignore God's words.[36] Italian and French tracts called taverns the cesspools or cellars of the Devil, and aligned them with the sins of lechery and gluttony, all of which echo the words of the Patristic Fathers in regard to the female body. Moreover, the "unsavory reputation of taverns and alehouses as anti-churches combined with the view that drinking women were sexually permeable to create an assumption that a woman consuming alcohol at a drinking establishment was sexually available."[37] As well, taverns provided places to gather, gossip, and socialize, but they also allowed for more illicit pastimes such as gambling and gamboling. As women were pushed out of the brewing of ale and beer, they were pushed into service in taverns. This, in turn, further sexualized and subjugated them. Sexual imposition was almost invariably high at taverns, taprooms, and inns. Hanawalt suggests that the ambiguous domestic atmosphere contributed to this sense of sexual availability, since they were "both a place of business and a domestic space."[38] Moreover, every female role associated with taverns and inns carried with it some sense of sexual promiscuity, including the owner or owner's wife, who was commonly likened to a procurer, with the tapsters or servers as her bawds. The stereotypical belief was that an alewife who wasn't actually prostituting herself was at minimum flirting with her customers to get them to drink more or pay higher prices, quite likely for substandard product.

Common literature of the day upheld this notion: "in ballads, tracts, popular prints, pamphlets, and other media, ordinary people expressed a fearful dislike of alewives."[39] Perhaps the most famous example in literature is John Skelton's "The Tunning of Elinor Rumming" (ca. 1517), which is likely a reference to real-life alewife Alianora Romyng.[40] The poem's loose structure mirrors the openness of the female bodies it depicts, and lists off a number of somewhat disgusting images of a brazen and slovenly woman and her equally disheveled (female) customers, with unlaced corsets, wrinkled clothes, noses dripping snot, and the like. John Lydgate's "Ballade on an Ale-Seller" (late fifteenth century) portrays an alewife deviously tricking her male customers into overpaying for their ale by flirting. However, the narrator is seemingly "more concerned with the fact that she gets men to fall in love and then casts them off, than that she does this to sell ale."[41] The Chester Mystery Play cycle, William Langland's *Piers Plowman*, and a number of other contemporary literary works represent alewives as unsavory characters that lie, seduce, flatter, and deceive. While all victuallers were suspect to some degree, with rampant accusations about poor quality foodstuffs, female crafters were subject to a double-edged scrutiny, both of the actual wares for sale (her ale), and of the potential ware for sale (her body). In fact, instead of being wary of male brewers, many were the subject of popular songs celebrating their brewing skills, whereas female brewers were recorded as serving weak or salted ale. Because women were by nature less trustworthy than men, the potential for them to cheat customers was high. Because women were by nature more lustful than men, sexual transgression was inevitable. Authors such as Geoffrey Chaucer, in his "The Wife of Bath's Prologue," commonly noted the connection between sexual indulgence and alcohol. Alewives even more so than regular women were viewed as uncontrolled and uncontrollable, driven by lust for money, sex, and alcohol.

Aside from literary depictions, various art forms upheld these stereotypes of alewives as well. The alewife was a frequent artistic subject in Last Judgment paintings, being "included in at least ten English Doom paintings, the alewife is conventionally shown holding an ale mug and often wearing an elaborate and fashionable headdress."[42] Perhaps the most well known of these is found in a wall painting of the Last Judgment at Holy Trinity Church in Coventry, England.[43] In this image, three naked alewives, wearing horned headdresses and carrying tankards, are in chains, being led to their fate by a grinning demon. Miriam Gill suggests that the collaboration among the visual arts, literature, and theology would have meant that simple details such as a fancy headdress and a pot of ale would serve as an effective visual "shorthand" for medieval viewers, quickly conveying a host of negative associations.[44] Similar details are used in the other Doom paintings found in England in order to covey the alewife and her chicanery.[45] The shorthand is not limited to paintings, however. In Norwich Cathedral, a roof boss clearly shows a naked alewife riding on the back of a demon as he wheels a sinful man to hell in a wheelbarrow. In St Laurence Church, Ludlow, Shropshire, a fifteenth-century misericord dubbed the "thieving alewife" has a naked alewife wearing a horned headdress and flourishing a tankard being dragged into the mouth of Hell. The horned headdress is especially evocative of baseness, since it is of the type the Church called a "devil's snare," and was thought to "encourage an unhealthy interest in vanity at the expense of concern for the soul."[46] To return to Gill's idea of shorthand, then, the common images of the alewife conveyed not only fraud and deception, but also gluttony (the ale pots), vanity (the headdress), and, perhaps most of all, lechery (her nudity). Thus, as Bennett aptly observes, "when parishioners gazed up at the walls of their churches to see alewives cavorting happily with devils, their understanding of such images was partly shaped by a wide range of other popular representations of alewives as sinful, tempting, disgusting, and untrustworthy women."[47] In other words, alewives became the extreme version of the potential failings all women had, providing justification for barring women from both brewing and from taverns altogether. The ideological inhibition of female participation in brewing was hastened along by these misogynistic cultural representations of brewsters.

As the trade continued to transform, women's access to it became more and more limited, until finally, they were excluded from the taverns on many levels. This is not to say that women could not enter public houses at all. In fact, women were a frequent presence in the tavern throughout the early modern period; however, unspoken rules of social conduct governed their actions. Women generally no longer entered alehouses unaccompanied, except, perhaps, in larger cities and only then during the day and for brief periods. Women could drink only in same-sex groups, or with a very limited range of opposite sex companions, preferably of close relation. Many establishments provided private as well as public rooms, and these created social spaces for female customers, couples, and mixed parties, as well as individuals of higher rank. When women did break these rules, their behavior, coupled with the drink, was all too likely to lead to a wide range of illicit sexual activity, from consensual fornication and adultery to vicious sexual assaults, including gang rapes.[48] Bennett argues that this exclusion was not simply a deliberate choice on the part of the men; rather, it was a consequence of legal, economic, and social disadvantages that stemmed from the persistence of fundamental assumptions about female roles. One of these assumptions was that women were fundamentally incapable of producing quality products; another was fear that they might produce comparable or even superior goods. Guild control of commodity production also resulted in firmer male control of economic power structures. When brewing came under the province of guild regulations, it was only a matter of time before women were essentially removed from the profession.

Guilds

Guilds were the most significant economic movement in medieval culture.[49] They were central to urban life in England, although distinctly important to society as a whole. Guilds, composed of members who shared a common interest or occupation, were organizations that protected the rights of their members and regulated their behavior. They were social networks that generated a social capital of shared ideals, common information, mutual sanctions, and collective political action. Guilds' social capital affected rival producers, suppliers, employees, consumers, the government, and the wider economy, and guilds and guild regulations had an immense effect on women's economic and political contributions to medieval society.

The two main types of guilds were Merchant Guilds and Craft Guilds.[50] Merchant Guilds had their roots in cooperative organizations that merchants as far back as the tenth century formed for protection while traveling. They grew into organizations that allowed for the negotiation of trade levies and regulation on who traded where and what, and more generally were associations of traders in a particular locality or a particular line of wares. The Merchant Guilds dominated local politics for many years, and although membership for women was not explicitly forbidden, it was virtually nonexistent. For the most part, women were members of the petty merchant guilds, not the major ones.[51] Women could not travel without permission (or, to some extent, without protection), and were not able to negotiate and sign contracts; therefore, a woman merchant would have been close to useless. Furthermore, the Merchant Guilds often placed their highest-ranking members in the position of mayor or alderman, and female members, if such existed, could not have held these offices.

The Craft Guilds have a more varied history in connection to gender politics. Craft Guilds grew out of the increasingly specialized nature of industry, and consisted of a group of artisans engaged in the same occupation. Although they began as societies of shared interest and aid, they grew into monopolies on particular crafts, to the extent that people were not allowed to practice a trade without being a member of the guild. Many women were artisans of sorts, such as brewsters, but these professions were not covered by the guilds, and many of the so-called domestic arts (e.g. cooking, baking, sewing, and so forth) became specialized professions dominated by men in the later Middle Ages. Between the coronation of Edward I (1239–1307; r. 1272–1307 CE) and the demise of Edward VI (1537–53; r. 1547–53 CE), Craft Guilds operated in many sectors of the economy.[52] The Craft Guilds began with victuallers, such as bakers and butchers who converted agricultural commodities into foodstuffs. Another set of crafters sold skills and services, providing everything from Clerks to Goldsmiths, but again taking raw goods (e.g. words or gold) and converting them into finished products. Eventually, the varieties of crafts grew into highly specialized areas, such as cordwainers (fine leather workers), curriers (dressers of tanned leather), girdlers (makers of girdles and belts), and loriners (makers of stirrups for horses) just to name a few. There were three ranks among guild members: masters, journeymen, and apprentices. Masters were guild members who owned their own shops and had sufficiently proved their expertise in the craft to other experts. Apprentices were adolescents in training under long-term contracts called indentures. Journeymen fell between those well-defined roles, although they were subservient to masters. Many were skilled in their own right but had not saved sufficient funds to establish an independent workshop.

Guilds ostensibly worked for the betterment and protection of their members. They were exclusive organizations, requiring fees and skills to belong. In turn, the guilds protected their members' rights. Guilds oversaw the training of apprentices and approving new masters. They provided a type of health insurance for their members, including provisions for the sick, and funeral expenses for poor members. Widows and orphans received financial aid, and poor female children received dowries. Guilds managed labor markets, regulated wages, and advanced their own interests at their subordinates' expense. Guild members acted to increase their incomes, and their efforts required action in concert. Members had to cooperate and coordinate for these goals to be accomplished effectively.

As well, all craft guilds pursued pious goals. Sylvia Thrupp notes that in addition to the regulations governing their craft, guilds were at the same time benevolent and religious societies with rules covering provisions for mutual aid, the arbitration of disputes, and the procuring of spiritual benefits.[53] Almsgiving was encouraged, and many guilds supported local churches, built chapels, and donated windows or church furnishings. Two types of spiritual services for members stand out: participatory activities and actions performed on the behalf of members.[54] In the first case, guilds venerated certain saints collectively, gathered together at church, participated in ceremonial activities such as processions, or supported productions such as mystery plays. Participation in these events was often required as well as encouraged. The second case primarily concerns postmortem activities, such as having masses and prayers said, or building a chantry chapel. Again, these activities required the cooperation of a guild's members for success. The guilds were watchdogs of member morals as well, in particular guarding against gambling and usury, but also watching for other issues such as adultery, excessive drunkenness, and sexual liberties.

Memberships in guilds were restricted not only by the craft, but also by sex. Guilds did not all restrict women to the same extent. The guilds that admitted women in their own right were primarily in the textile industries. Others allowed married women to join as "sisters" within their husband's guild. In this manner, their contributions to their spouse's workshop were acknowledged, and they did receive some privileges of guild membership; however, it was clear that they were "second-rank" guild members, barred from wearing guild livery and from certain guild activities.[55] In fact, it is unlikely that a male artisan would have operated his business on his own. Most did not set up shop until after they were married, thus incorporating the heterosexual domestic partnership, and its offspring, into his personal production system. Middle class women, and to some extent their children, were expected not only to maintain their households, but also to assist their husbands in business. Widows of guild masters could also continue running the family workshop, and these women were granted the most rights within the organizations as they were seen to be quasi-functioning under the auspices of their late spouse. They could take on and supervise apprentices and journeymen both and had the right to participate in most of the ceremonial functions. However, even these women were generally not allowed to participate in guild politics, or to serve as guild office, and upon remarriage to anyone outside of the craft, were usually summarily expelled from guild membership.

Women in France had similar experiences with guilds. As Simone Roux notes, the great Ordinance of Jean le Bon (1350) and the statute of linen-clothing women workers (1485) mark out the history of the Parisian women who earned living in workshops and in shops. Both men and women followed the same rules of professions, no matter if they worked in single-sex or mixed-sex professions. At least three female-only silk production guilds existed. Similar to England, a Guild Master's widow could continue her husband's trade if she did not remarry, or if she married a man of the trade. The Statute of 1350 was especially important because it sought to reorganize the guild system after the Black Death. Because the working population was decimated, access to guilds was widely opened to women. The Statute also set wages for female servants and for women in nonguild professions, such as wet nurses, barbers, and washerwomen. Guilds were concerned with members' morality, too, and regulations note that women who had made "scandal of their body" were excluded from the public meetings of the guild, but they could still work, and keep workshops. Aside from Paris, Rouen and Montpellier both note female and mixed guilds, especially in the textile crafts. However, it does not appear that women were specifically barred from any profession.[56]

The case of guild membership is an interesting one for the study of gender. Many of the traditional professions women took up were not regulated by the guilds, and thus did not enjoy the same protections and privileges. Because women were excluded from positions of authority did not necessarily mean that they were excluded from work, but rather for "valuable" work. This cemented the devaluation of female labor: work performed women was considered less valuable than the same work performed by men. Additionally, the same work did not result in the same respect or political power. Political scientists and economists point to guilds as exemplars of "social networks" which generated "social capital," thereby benefiting the economy at large.[57] Of course, like most medieval social and economic institutions, men dominated them, and scholars have emphasized how guilds generally used their powers to limit women's participation in economic life. By and large, strong guilds meant fewer opportunities for women.[58] Some guilds were willing to include women, but most were not, at least in practice, if not explicitly through regulation. For instance, "male masters displayed no eagerness to train young women, and with few or no women recognized as masters, the guilds did contribute to the narrowing opportunity for women."[59] This likely began early on, since there are virtually no recorded instances of medieval journeywomen. Social control proved just as detrimental as exclusion: "The fact that guilds seldom permitted women to become masters did in the end relegate them to the least-skilled and certainly least-remunerative aspects of the trade."[60] The complicated relationship women had with the guild system led to the downfall of the woman's status as a worker during this time period, and, consequently, to the overall value of women as viable economic contributors to society, firmly reinforcing patriarchal control.

Aside from the obvious suppression of female authority, guilds also served as a way to enact masculinity on a different level. Medieval masculinity was not just dependent on suppression of women or the feminine; it also relied upon dominance over other men. Knightly culture relied on social display, on the battlefield, at the tournament, or in the court, and, the resultant displays of honor, including wealth and reputation, comprised the central aspect of the knight's masculine identity. Clerics and scholars proved their masculine prowess through education and debate, eviscerating opponents with the spoken word. The artisan class demonstrated this control of other men through the subjection of apprentices and journeymen. A young man could only achieve true adult status by pleasing his master—and as Karras notes, there was a disconnect between expectation and economic reality, as every apprentice did not achieve master status or own his own workshop.[61] Instead, many ended up as "skilled laborers," essentially remaining journeymen forever, and thus occupied an intermediary status between boys and men forever. The reality of urban life restricted the possibilities of attaining full adult masculine status. In such circumstances, groups of young men sought solidarity with their fellows in collective action, especially as a way to attempt to prove independence, a major factor in securing masculinity. The guild system, therefore, created and enforced a subservient class of men that reaffirmed and upheld the masculinity of those men at the top of the system.

The link between religion and economics at the local level is also connected to religious and economic trends in the wider world. Both the control over the market and the concerns about salvation point to reasons for the Craft Guilds controlling female membership. If guilds served as mechanisms for organizing, managing, and financing the collective quest for eternal salvation, then incorporating too many women into their structure would make that quest more difficult. From a medieval theological perspective, women were inherently more sinful than men. They more easily succumbed to temptation, especially in areas of lust and greed, both of which the guilds strove to shield their members from. Relying on too many uncontrolled women brought the entire guild into dangerous territory. At the very least, they would have to spend more money to compensate for the additional burden; at the most, they would endanger the souls of the "real" (male) members at the expense of a few female members.

Moreover, reputations played key roles in establishing the prominence of the Guild itself as well as in creating and sustaining markets and profits. A guild selling superior merchandise at a reasonable price could sell as much as it could manufacture. Markets for popular products were extremely elastic.[62] In order to keep up, guilds "advertised" via reputation, so that crafters could sell wares to consumers who did not know them personally, sometimes in distant markets. Guilds that allowed too many women into their ranks risked their reputations for superior work, and thus jeopardized their market dominance. They also imperiled their very continuance, as the guild system depended upon the training of apprentices and journeymen for their continued influence and economic dominance. Both lower ranks of members preferred to work with male masters, leaving the female guild practitioners at risk for slower goods production and fewer profits. There are a number of such recorded cases of "rebellious" apprentices, including several in which the young men turned violent.[63] The elastic markets contributed to both these problems as well, since guilds did not consider it worthwhile to train women into trades that fluctuated depending upon sales, especially of luxury items.

Women were also at risk of being cut from the guild roster despite fulfilling all the membership requirements simply because of economic downturns. Judith M. Bennett and Maryanne Kowaleski note that the "secondary status of women [in guilds] . . . left them particularly vulnerable when trade diminished or competition increased. Gilds often responded to adverse economic developments by placing further restrictions on the employment of women in the craft."[64] Thus, while guilds provided some sort of security for women, overall they ended up limiting women's economic power. Even though guilds of both sorts began to lose their authority in some parts of the Netherlands and England in the sixteenth century, although they survived in France, Italy, Scandinavia, Germany, and Iberia into the late eighteenth century, they left behind an economic legacy that spawned, at least to some political theorists, modern capitalism as well as firmly drawn lines of gender role division.[65] Overall, this commercialization of the European economy fundamentally changed attitudes toward the relationship of women, work, wealth, and power, leaving persistent traces of misogyny that still remain.[66]

Female medical practitioners

Although many medieval working women were involved in crafting or merchandizing of some sort, many were also involved in a wide range of medical fields. This is a particularly interesting development in connection with gender ideals found elsewhere in medieval society. Monica H. Green aptly reflects, "the assumptions we have accepted so uncritically about women's health care and the sexual division of labor in the Middle Ages have masked a reality far more complex than hitherto imagined."[67] Some of these assumptions have concerned the subject of women's study, as primarily being limited to women's health issues and obstetrics. Others have concerned the extent of female medical practitioning in medieval Europe as a whole.

Just as the female head of the household was commonly responsible for providing foodstuffs, she was also generally responsible for minor medical treatments. The general population seemed to have a basic understanding of the prevailing medical theory of the time—the four humors—and would have been at least passingly familiar with some easy treatments for imbalances, illness, and injuries. We would call this today a combination of first aid and folk medicine. A fair number of "receipts" (recipes or formulas) are found in a wide variety of medieval texts, many of which address folk remedies as well as cooking techniques.

The majority of women involved in the practice of medicine outside of their own home during the Middle Ages were midwives. Midwives were women who assisted other women in the process of giving birth. These practitioners were exclusively female, although certainly there were physicians, both male and female, who studied obstetrics and gynecology. The medical expertise of a midwife could vary widely. Midwives were generally taught via practical training and assisting other midwives, although by 1600, in London, a more formal apprenticeship arrangement, modeled after the guild system, was in place where younger midwives served seven years under an older midwife.[68] There were no formal rules associated with midwifery until well into the early modern era, 1560 for England, and for the most part, midwives were on their own until then.[69]

Midwifery often involved not only folk medicine practices, such as bathing the child in salt and honey to dry up the humors, but also older folk "magic." For example, jasper was a gemstone credited with childbirth assisting powers, and may have been placed on the woman's abdomen during birth or at her bedside during labor.[70] There has been a persistent historical myth regarding midwives being increasingly connected to witchcraft as the Middle Ages waned and the early modern witchcraft craze took hold. When there were such accusations, they were tied to so-called birth magic, such as belief that the midwife provided charms either to assist the mother in childbirth or pregnancy, or to encourage conception. As well, the *Malleus*

Maleficarum (*Hammer of Witches*, 1486 CE) contained an entire diatribe against witch-midwives, heightening fears of baby snatching and demonic intervention inside the womb.[71] Nevertheless, despite these incendiary claims, midwives are statistically underrepresented among the women who were ultimately prosecuted for witchcraft.[72]

Aside from midwives, women occasionally practiced in the lesser medical fields of barbery-surgery and the apothecary trade. In the Middle Ages, barber-surgeons, identified by the distinctive red-and-white striped poles on their shops, performed minor surgical procedures, including bloodletting and cupping therapy, as well as extracting teeth, giving enemas, shaving, and haircutting.[73] Like midwives, barber-surgeons learned their trade through apprenticeship, and eventually formed into a craft guild.[74] Similarly, apothecaries began as general tradespeople, but eventually formed into a craft guild as well.[75] Apothecaries prepared and sold medicines, "simples," which consisted of one ingredient, and "compounds," which were mixtures of ingredients, to physicians for distribution and also directly to patients. In addition, they offered medical advice and other products. Like the other craft guilds, the barber-surgeons and the apothecaries occasionally admitted female members, especially women who were related to male guild members. Widows of members were generally allowed to retain their husbands' status in the guild if they so chose, at least until they remarried, and there are some records indicating that daughters of members were allowed to be guild members in their own right, although without all of the accompanying privileges of livery and leadership. The guilds of Lincoln, Norwich, Dublin, and York appear to have accepted female members until quite late in period. There are, similarly, a few recorded instances of female apothecaries, although less is known specifically about them.[76]

Certainly, examining all of these women contributes to the study of gender in medieval culture; however, two more transgressive instances, female physicians and Hospitaller nuns, provide larger gender role divergences. Although female physicians did not exist in much of Western Europe during the early modern period all the way into the nineteenth century, there were a few in the Middle Ages. Moreover, while some of these women focused on areas related to gynecology, "women's practice was limited neither to obstetrical cases nor to female patients."[77] Originally, physicians, like most other professions, trained through a system of apprenticeship, and were generally not controlled that closely. Beginning in the twelfth century, secular authorities began regulating qualifications, so that by the late thirteenth or fourteenth century, many medical practitioners possessed some sort of qualification; however, these took many forms, including "university education in medicine, membership in a guild of medical or surgical practitioners with power to examine candidates for membership, or possession of a license to practice from a public authority."[78] Accordingly, the demise of women's participation in medicine is primarily the result of the restructuring of the medical profession, both into a guild or professional organization, which by their very nature usually excluded women, and by increasing licensure and education requirements.

Prior to this decline, however, there were indeed female physicians. Many of these women were in Italy, where they could both attend the School of Salerno and act as instructors, but there were also female physicians across Europe, including in England.[79] This is not to say that female medical practitioners were not controversial, but this depended more on geographical location within Europe than purely on gender. For example, in Germany there were no general regulations for the practice of medicine. On the other hand, English women practitioners were not admitted to universities, and, therefore, their knowledge was limited to what they could learn through apprenticeship, making them more vulnerable to charges of charlatanship. In France, women practiced quite regularly, and until a general ban on university attendance, were fairly well educated, even attending the University of Paris Medical School.[80] It is important to note, however, that while "women practitioners existed in many different regions of Europe between the thirteenth and the fifteenth centuries, they represent only a very small proportion of the total number of practitioners whose names are recorded ... about 1.5 percent in France and 1.2 percent in England."[81] Of course this may mean that there were more practicing and they were simply not recorded; however, it is doubtful that the number was exceedingly large. Nevertheless, that women practiced as physicians at all is more than can be said for some of the later centuries.[82]

Female practitioners also contributed to the medical literature of the day, the most of famous of whom are "Trotula" of Salerno and Hildegard of Bingen. Contrary to popular historical belief, modern scholarship has demonstrated that there was no singular individual named "Trotula." Instead, "Trotula" refers to a group of three medical texts on women's medicine written in the twelfth century, most likely in Salerno, which is in Southern Italy. There is evidence of female practitioners of medicine there—Green has noted at least five dozen references—and of these three Trotula texts, at least one was authored by a woman, and such attribution has been noted since the time of its composition.[83] "Her" reputation was widespread during the Middle Ages, and she was an especially popular figure in misogynist depictions of women who claimed too much authority and the dangers of education. Perhaps the most famous of these references is found in Geoffrey Chaucer's *Canterbury Tales*, specifically "The Wife of Bath's Prologue," where Trotula is mentioned in Jankyn's "book of wikked wyves" by name.[84] Hildegard's reputation fared better. Hildegard (1098–1179 CE) was a Benedictine abbess, a visionary, a composer, and an author. She began her religious education at age eight, when she studied with the anchoress Jutta (1091–1136 CE).[85] Under her tutelage, Hildegard learned the basics of Latin, and began to record her religious visions. Aside from her mystical treatises, however, Hildegard also authored *Subtililates diversarum naturarum creaturarum* (*The Subtleties of the Diverse Nature of Created Things*, ca. 1151–58 CE), which has been preserved as two texts, the *Physica* (*Natural History*), also known as *Liber simplicis medicinae* (*Book of Simple Medicine*), and the *Causae et Curae* (*Causes and Cures*), also known as *Liber compositae medicinae* (*Book of Compound Medicine*).[86] Both works address natural history and curative powers of various natural objects. Her medical and scientific views rely heavily on the Greek cosmological system of the four elements and the corresponding four humors. She also spends a great deal of time detailing various substances, objects, plants, and trees that have medicinal uses. More surprisingly, especially for an abbess, Hildegard did not denigrate sexual relations, and included positive descriptions of female pleasure and orgasms.[87] Like the women of Salerno, Hildegard was respected during her life. She publicly lectured throughout Germany, corresponded with popes, and inspired a great many followers, and in doing so, transgressed almost every gender boundary of her time.[88]

The study of female physicians in the Middle Ages is a fascinating addendum to gender studies, not only because it is so unexpected, but also because it connects with another marginalized group, Jews.[89] Jewish men, as has been noted earlier, were feminized within Christian culture. Like their female counterparts, Jewish physicians were most prominent in Italy and France. A number of skilled Jewish physicians were teachers at the medical school of Montpellier where they also contributed to the development of the science of medicine by their translations of Arabic medical works into Hebrew and Latin, as well as by writing their own texts. Siraisi notes, "no doubt Jewish practitioners served primarily their own communities, but they were also in great demand among Christian patients."[90] Both ecclesiastical and secular authorities issued bans on Jews treating Christians, but these regulations were readily modified or simply ignored. In fact, the popes employed a number of Jewish physicians during the papal remove to Avignon.[91] Christian communities in Languedoc, Southern Italy, Aragon, and Sicily all regularly admitted Jewish practitioners to their ranks. There are also records of female Jewish physicians, especially in Italy and Southern France. It is intriguing that medieval male Christians who delighted in their inherent superiority over women and non-Christians would allow such individuals to care for their sick or disabled body. Perhaps once a man fell ill he was temporarily devalued and demasculinized so that it did not matter if a subordinate cared for his flesh, since his soul was more secure. However, hospitals, when they did arise, grew out of monastic practices.

Anne Witz suggests that the "historical tensions around the gender of the practitioner seemed to be related more to the general tension between the domestic and market modes of providing healing practices."[92] Like the case of the brewsters and other crafters, it was the rise of medical guilds, coupled with licensing platforms and the evolution of European universities and their professional schools that systematically excluded women, thereby creating a legal male monopoly of the practice of medicine, at least as physicians. To say it was the education alone would be to ignore both the lack of formal education of male practitioners, and the dominance of the increasing economics of the profession by the guild system. Nancy G. Siraisi relates that wealth was "loosely correlated with ranking in the medical hierarchy," meaning that physicians were "normally a good deal better off" than others.[93] Education brought prestige, but a successful practice brought income. Guild membership assured that women had less access to both, and assured male supremacy within the profession. It is fairly clear that this particular working of patriarchy was motivated by fear of female accomplishment: "indeed, if skilled educated women had not competed with various categories of medical men, it is unlikely that the denigration of female practice would constitute such a strong theme in past medical writings, or that female healers in England and elsewhere would have been prosecuted for what were seen as infringements on licensed physicians' and surgeons' practices."[94] Female success could not exist at the expense of male dominance.

Also interesting to the study of gender in medieval culture are Hospitaller sisters. Hospitaller sisters were nuns that were adjacent to the Military Orders for men, who had their origins in caring for Pilgrims, and later Crusaders, but continued beyond the Middle Ages by working in hospitals and occasionally as teachers.[95] The first such order was the Hospitaller Sisters of St John of Jerusalem, which evolved from a hospital into a multifaceted international religious order over the course of the twelfth century. Originally, the Hospital of Saint John of Jerusalem was a congregation of brothers serving the hospital in Jerusalem supported by benefactors in Southern France and Northern Spain. Sisters were added to the hospital sometime in the twelfth century. The hospital in Jerusalem was therefore a mixed-sex community that cared for the sick and the poor. Neither sisters nor brothers did actual nursing; instead, the sisters oversaw the care of children and the running of the household duties, while the brothers supervised the nurses and doctors who were paid for their services.[96]

From the original hospital, other communities were established, all under the auspices of the foundational establishment in Jerusalem. Houses, called commanderies, were established in Spain, France, Italy, Portugal, and England. In order to deal with long-distance communication issues, the Hospitallers relied upon a system that included a middle step, the priory, so communication traveled from headquarters to the priory and then on to the commandery. The original priory was established in St Gilles, Provence, France, but soon others developed for ease of communication, including one in England in 1185. This priory was created at the behest of King Henry II (1133–89; r. 1154–89 CE), and seemingly governed 22 commanderies, a rather surprisingly large number. While Henry supposedly desired all Hospitaller sisters to dwell in that singular location, it is clear that the other houses did not disperse, and that eventually more were established.[97]

The Hospitaller sisters provide an interesting situation for gender studies because the order grew out of male Military Orders who specifically sought out a female presence for their endeavors. While the sisters apparently did not assist in the actual military maneuvers, they were present in most other aspects of order business. Significantly, unlike most other religious orders, the Hospitallers continued to welcome female association in male, female, and mixed-sex congregations throughout the thirteenth century, a time when other orders began to segregate monastic populations.[98] Further, sisters were welcome members of the Hospitallers while other orders not only isolated female members, but also discouraged them from joining.[99] Myra Struckmeyer observes that while the relative closeness between brothers and sisters was somewhat troubling, it was not enough to change the order's acceptance of women, and, furthermore, "the fear of women was mostly directed against secular women," especially since "the presence of female Hospitallers had practical implications for the organization of the Order."[100] Finally, in England more specifically, the opportunities for membership were more limited than on the Continent, as there are no examples of female lay associates with commanderies.[101] In fact, there are few records showing any interest at all in lay associations in England. The concept was embraced much more readily on the Continent. Instead, England had a larger population of anchoresses than most other countries. It appears as though the reclusive life was the English alternative to formal profession. If this is the case, it speaks to a desire for more autonomy than a public association with an order would bring.

NOTES

Introduction

1 The Norman Conquest of England was the invasion led by William, duke of Normandy, later William the Conqueror, who defeated Harold Godwinson, the last Anglo-Saxon king of England, on October 14, 1066. The cultural shift between the Anglo-Saxon period (449–1066 CE) and the "medieval" period of England is enormous primarily due to this event, which changed everything from the language to the governmental system. Medieval thus encompasses the Anglo-Norman period (1066–1154 CE), Plantagenet England (1154–1399 CE), and the fifteenth century (1400–85 CE). The Battle of Bosworth Field saw the defeat of Richard III, the last English king killed in battle, by Henry Tudor, later Henry VII on August 22, 1485. It traditionally marks the end of the medieval era in England, as well as the end of the Wars of the Roses, although technically that was the Battle of Stoke in 1487. Henry strove to present his victory as the beginning of a new era for the country, one unmarked by the internal turmoil of the Wars of the Roses, and went so far as to call his reign the "modern age."

2 Jeffrey Jerome Cohen, "Early Modern," *In the Medieval Middle*, November 30, 2012, http://www.inthemedievalmiddle.com/2012/11/early-modern.html.

3 Fredric Jameson, *The Political Unconscious: Narrative as a Socially Symbolic Act* (Ithaca: Cornell University Press, 1981), p. 28.

4 David Perkins, *Is Literary History Possible?* (Baltimore: Johns Hopkins University Press, 1992), p. 65.

5 Jeffrey Weeks, *Sexuality* (London: Routledge, 1986), p. 4.

6 Londa Schiebinger, *The Mind Has No Sex?: Women in the Origins of Modern Science* (Cambridge, MA: Harvard University Press, 1989), p. 189.

7 Among other sources, see especially Judith Butler, *Gender Trouble* (New York: Routledge, 2006; anniversary edition) and Judith Lorber, *Paradoxes of Gender* (New Haven: Yale University Press, 1994).

8 Lorber, *Paradoxes of Gender*, p. 117.

9 See especially Candace West and Don H. Zimmerman, "Doing Gender," *Gender and Society* 1.2 (1987): 125–51.

10 Chris Weedon, *Feminist Practice and Poststructuralist Theory* (Cambridge: Blackwell, 1987), p. 35.
11 Butler, *Gender Trouble*, p. 336.
12 See Chrys Ingraham, *Romancing Heterosexuality in Popular Culture* (New York: Routledge, 2008; 2nd ed.).
13 Heteronormative views align biology with sex, gender, and sexuality. The term is widely used now, but was first popularized by Michael Warner in *Fear of a Queer Planet: Queer Politics and Social Theory* (Minneapolis: University of Minnesota Press, 1993).
14 Karma Lochrie, *Heterosyncrasies: Female Sexuality when Normal Wasn't* (Minneapolis: University of Minnesota Press, 2005), pp. xiv, xxviii.
15 See, for example, the groundbreaking essay by Adrienne Rich, "Compulsory Heterosexuality and Lesbian Existence," *Signs: Journal of Women in Culture and Society* 5 (1980): 631–60. In this piece, Rich argues that heterosexuality is a political institution, constructed like any other, that employs a number of different methodologies to maintain its normative status. In order to stand up against it, Rich suggests that women engage in homosocial experiences.
16 See Eve Kosofsky Sedgwick, *Between Men: English Literature and Male Homosocial Desire* (New York: Columbia University Press, 1985). She argues that patriarchal structures make heterosexuality obligatory, but they also insist upon homosocial situations since power relations are dependent upon the relationships between men—homosocial desire—as much as they are dependent upon the suppression of women.
17 Richard Godbeer, "'The Cry of Sodom': Discourse, Intercourse, and Desire in Colonial New England." In *Long Before Stonewall: Histories of Same-Sex Sexuality in Early America*, ed. Thomas A. Foster (New York: NYU Press, 2007), pp. 81–113; p. 84.
18 Bruce R. Smith, *Homosexual Desire in Shakespeare's England: A Cultural Poetics* (Chicago: University of Chicago Press, 1991), pp. 10–11.
19 Karma Lochrie, Peggy McCracken, and James A. Schultz, "Introduction." In *Constructing Medieval Sexuality*, ed. Karma Lochrie, Peggy McCracken, and James A. Schultz (Minneapolis: University of Minnesota Press, 1997), pp. ix–xviii; p. xi.
20 Valerie Traub, *The Renaissance of Lesbianism* (Cambridge: Cambridge University Press, 2002), p. 268. Of course this purported ideal of friendship in marriage was not fully realized within society, and stood in direct opposition to the early modern ideal of friendship, which, based on the Classical model, held that only two men of similar station and degree could truly be friends.
21 See Michelle M. Sauer, "'Where Are the Lesbians in Chaucer?': Lack, Opportunity, & Female Homoeroticism in Medieval Studies Today," *The Journal of Lesbian Studies* 11.3–4 (2007): 331–45.
22 Lochrie, *Heterosyncrasies*, p. 2.
23 Natalie Zemon Davis, "Introduction." In *Worth and Repute: Valuing Gender in Late Medieval and Early Modern Europe Essays in Honour of Barbara*

Todd, ed. Kim Kippen and Lori Woods (Toronto: Centre for Reformation and Renaissance Studies, 2011), pp. 20–38; p. 27.

24 Diana Fuss, *Essentially Speaking* (New York: Routledge, 1989), p. 6.

Chapter 1

1 Rather horrifyingly, from a modern perspective, coverture remained the general practice in England, its colonies, and its former colonies—including the United States—well into the nineteenth century, and was not fully phased out until the 1970s.

2 Henry de Bracton, *Bracton on the Law and Customs of England*, ed. George E. Woodbine and trans. Samuel E. Thorne (Cambridge, MA: Harvard University Press, 1968).

3 Sara M. Butler, *Divorce in Medieval England: From One to Two Persons in Law* (New York: Routledge, 2013), p. 10.

4 Cordelia Beattie, "Married Women, Contracts and Coverture in Late Medieval England." In *Married Women and the Law in Premodern Northwest Europe*, ed. Cordelia Beattie and Matthew Frank Stevens (Woodbridge, Suffolk: Boydell, 2013), pp. 133–54; p. 153.

5 Butler, *Divorce in Medieval England*, p. 10.

6 Philippa Maddern, "Interpreting Silence: Domestic Violence in the King's Courts in East Anglia, 1422–1442." In *Domestic Violence in Medieval Texts*, ed. Eve Salisbury, Georgiana Donavin, and Merrall Llewelyn Price (Gainesville: University Press of Florida, 2002), pp. 31–56; p. 38.

7 See Gwen Seabourne, *Imprisoning Medieval Women: The Non-Judicial Confinement and Abduction of Women in England, c. 1170–1509* (Farnham, Surrey: Ashgate, 2011).

8 Frederick Pollock and F. W. Maitland, *The History of English Law before the Time of Edward I*, 2 vols (Cambridge: Cambridge University Press, 1968); vol. 2, p. 436.

9 See Sara Margaret Butler, *The Language of Abuse: Marital Violence in Later Medieval England* (Leiden: Brill, 2007).

10 Although coverture was specifically a matter of English common law, the principle behind it remained in effect throughout the areas formerly under Roman rule. Under ancient Roman law, women were generally under the direct protection of their husbands, although upper class women enjoyed some inheritance and property rights that were irrelevant to the lower classes. English common law codified this most strictly, giving husbands guardianship over their wives and their wives' property. Elsewhere in Northwest Europe, wives' property became community property, although women throughout Germany and Scandinavia still required permission for most transactions outside of those involving movable goods.

11 Obviously, there was some regional variation in just how extensively women were considered chattel, although in general few allowed women to enjoy the same privileges as men. See, for instance, Ellen E. Kittell, "Guardianship over Women in Medieval Flanders: A Reappraisal," *Journal of Social History* 31.4 (1998): 897–930.

12 Corrine J. Saunders, *Rape and Ravishment in the Literature of Medieval England* (Cambridge: D. S. Brewer, 2001), p. 29.

13 Bizarrely, this issue came up during the 2012 US election season a number of times. Perhaps most famously, Representative Todd Akin, a Republican from Missouri, said that in a "legitimate rape," women could not get pregnant because their bodies would shut down. See http://www.nytimes.com/2012/08/21/us/politics/rep-todd-akin-legitimate-rape-statement-and-reaction.html?_r=0 for a transcript of the interview. Unfortunately, Akin is not alone in holding this position, which has been thoroughly debunked by modern medicine.

14 *Fleta* (subtitle *seu Commentarius juris Anglicani*) is a common law tract from England dating to ca. 1290. It is debatable whether or not it is a derivative of *Bracton* or an expansion of it; nevertheless, the two are similar in nature. See *Fleta*, ed. H. G. Richardson and G. O. Sayles (London: Seldon Society, no. 72, 1955).

15 Saunders, *Rape and Ravishment*, pp. 29–30; translation hers. See also *The Prose Salernitan Questions*, ed. Brian Lawn (London: Oxford University Press, 1979).

16 Disturbingly, this is another trend that persists into the current age. The classic work on this phenomenon, and the one which put a name to it, is William Ryan's *Blaming the Victim* (New York: Vintage, 1971).

17 Saunders, *Rape and Ravishment*, p. 30.

18 See Kathryn Gravdal, "The Poetics of Rape Law." In *Rape and Representation*, ed. Lynn A. Higgins and Brenda R. Silver (New York: Columbia University Press, 1991), pp. 207–26; esp. p. 209.

19 See Thomas Laqueur, *Making Sex: Body and Gender from the Greeks to Freud* (Cambridge, MA: Harvard University Press, 1990).

20 See James A. Brundage, "Rape and Seduction in Medieval Canon Law." In *Sexual Practices and the Medieval Church*, ed. Vern L. Bullough and James Brundage (Amherst, NY: Prometheus Books, 1982), pp. 141–8.

21 See Kathryn Gravdal, *Ravishing Maidens: Writing Rape in Medieval French Literature and Law* (Philadelphia: University of Pennsylvania Press, 1991), p. 7.

22 Saunders, *Rape and Ravishment*, p. 35.

23 Dorothy Whitelock, ed., *English Historical Documents, I: c. 500–1042* (London: Eyre & Spottiswoode, 1955), p. 359.

24 "Selections from the Law of Adamnan (ca. 697)." In *Medieval Handbooks of Penance*, ed. McNeill and Gamer, p. 138.

25 See Brundage, "Rape and Seduction," p. 142. Gratian is considered the father of canon law. He was a teacher of theology at the monastery of Saints Nabor and Felix who wrote the *Decretum Gratiani* sometime around 1140–50.

26 2.2, q. 154, a. 7. Thomas Aquinas. *Summa Theologica*. Trans. Fathers of the English Dominican Province (Benziger Bros. edition, 1947). Part of the Christian Classics Ethereal Library, http://www.ccel.org/ccel/aquinas/summa.html.

27 Ranulf Glanvill, *The Treatise on the Laws and Customs of the Realm of England Commonly Called Glanvill*, ed. and trans. G. D. G. Hall (Oxford: Clarendon Press, 1993), p. 3.
28 See J. B. Post, "Ravishment of Women and the Statutes of Westminster." In *Legal Records and the Historian*, ed. John Hamilton Baker (London: Royal Historical Society, 1978), p. 151.
29 See John Marshall Carter, *Rape in Medieval England: An Historical and Sociological Study* (Lanham, MD: University Press of America, 1985), p. 95.
30 Saunders, *Rape and Ravishment,* pp. 50–6.
31 13 Edw. I Stat. Westm. Sec. 34 (Anglo Norman text), in Caroline Dunn, *Stolen Women in Medieval England: Rape, Abduction, and Adultery, 1100–1500* (Cambridge: Cambridge University Press, 2012), p. 30.
32 Post, "Ravishment of Women," p. 152.
33 See Ruth Kittel, "Rape in Thirteenth-Century England: A Study of the Common Law Courts." In *Women and the Law: A Social Historical Perspective*, ed. D. Kelly Weisberg (Cambridge: Schenkman, 1982), pp. 101–16; pp. 108–10.
34 See Barbara A. Hanawalt, *Of Good and Ill Repute: Gender and Social Control in Medieval England* (Oxford: Oxford University Press, 1998), especially pp. 124–41.
35 Dunn, *Stolen Women*, p. 76.
36 Hanawalt most directly says that this attitude is a refusal to acknowledge the brutality of rape. See *Of Good and Ill Repute*, pp. 132–3.
37 Daniel Klerman, "Settlement and the Decline of Private Prosecution in Thirteenth-Century England," *Law and History Review* 19.1 (2001): 1–65, p. 15.
38 John M. Carter, "Rape and Medieval English Society: The Evidence of Yorkshire, Wiltshire, and London, 1218–76," *Comitatus* 13 (1982): 33–63; p. 45 and Hanawalt, *Of Good and Ill Repute*, p. 132.
39 Kittel, "Rape in Thirteenth-Century England," p. 108. The length of time is significant because Westminster II called for a minimum sentence of two years imprisonment.
40 There are a number of studies regarding sexual violence and Chaucer's works. For more specific treatments of "The Wife of Bath's Tale," see, among others, Suzanne Edwards, "The Rhetoric of Rape and the Politics of Gender in the Wife of Bath's Tale and the 1382 Statute of Rapes," *Exemplaria* 23.1 (2011): 3–26; Robert J. Blanch, "'Al Was This Land Fulfild of Fayerye': The Thematic Employment of Force, Willfulness, and Legal Conventions in Chaucer's Wife of Bath's Tale," *Studia Neophililogica* 57 (1985): 41–51; Corrine Saunders, "Woman Displaced: Rape and Romance in Chaucer's Wife of Bath's Tale," *Arthurian Literature* 13 (1995): 115–31.
41 The fields of psychology, sociology, and criminology are primarily responsible for investigating the phenomenon of "secondary victimization." Although progress has been made toward understanding the intricacies, more work remains to be done. For a start, see Uli Orth, "Secondary Victimization of

Crime Victims by Criminal Proceedings," *Social Justice Research* 15.4 (2002): 313–25; Jenny Petrak and Barbara Hedge, eds, *The Trauma of Sexual Assault: Treatment, Prevention, and Practice* (West Sussex: John, Wiley & Sons, 2002); Rebecca Campbell and Sheela Raja, "Secondary Victimization of Rape Victims: Insights from Mental Health Professionals who Treat Survivors of Violence," *Violence and Victims* 14.3 (1999): 261–75.

42 R. Howard Bloch, "Medieval Misogyny," *Representations* 20 (1987): 1–24, pp. 3–5.

43 Diane Wolfthal, "'A Hue and a Cry': Medieval Rape Imagery and Its Transformation," *The Art Bulletin* 75.1 (1993): 39–64; p. 39.

44 Kathryn Gravdal, *Ravishing Maidens: Writing Rape in Medieval French Literature and Law* (Philadelphia: University of Pennsylvania Press, 1991), p. 123.

45 See Gravdal, *Ravishing Maidens*.

46 See Christian Gellinek, "Marriage by Consent in Literary Sources of Medieval Germany," *Studia Gratiana* 12 (1967): 555–79; Guido Ruggiero, *The Boundaries of Eros: Sex Crime and Sexuality in Renaissance Venice* (Oxford: Oxford University Press, 1985). Italy was not a unified country at this time, but the majority of the city-states reflected similar practices in regards to rape.

47 For an accessible collection of various medieval medical texts, see Faith Wallis, *Medieval Medicine: A Reader* (Toronto: University of Toronto Press, 2010).

48 Empiricists emphasized practical learning, while Dogmatists preferred logic. See Oswei Temkin, *Galenism: Rise and Decline of a Medical Philosophy* (Ithaca: Cornell University Press, 1973), pp. 15–19.

49 Siraisi, *Medieval and Early Renaissance Medicine*, p. 12. Muhammad ibn Zakariyā Rāzī, Latinized as Razi, was a Persian physician, alchemist, chemist, and philosopher, responsible for discovering a number of chemical compounds (e.g. alcohol and kerosene) and medical diagnoses (including differentiating smallpox and measles). Abū ʿAlī al-Ḥusayn ibn ʿAbd Allāh ibn Sīnā, Latinized as Avicenna, was a Persian physician, mathematician, and philosopher who most famously wrote *The Canon of Medicine*, which was used as a standard text at universities until 1650 CE, and supplies the complete system of medicine according to Galen and Hippocrates. Abū l-Walīd Muḥammad bin ʿAḥmad bin Rušd, Latinized as Averroes, was an Andalusian (present-day Spain) philosopher, theologian, and scientist. He is best known for his extensive defense of and commentaries on Aristotelian philosophy. Although his work was controversial in his Islamic homeland, it had a great impact on Western Christianity, and was the starting point of Scholasticism in medieval Europe.

50 A good overview of this system is set out in Robert M. Stelmack and Anastasios Stalikas, "Galen and the Humour Theory of Temperament," *Personality and Individual Differences* 12.3 (1991): 255–64.

51 Rebecca Flemming, *Medicine and the Making of Roman Women: Gender, Nature, and Authority from Celsus to Galen* (Oxford: Oxford University Press, 2000), p. 228.

52 John Trevisa, *On the Properties of Things: John Trevisa's Translation of Bartholomaeus Anglicus De proprietatibus rerum*, ed. M. C. Seymour, 3 vol. (Oxford: Clarendon, 1975–88), 1:306.

53 Vital heat was created in the heart (and, to some extent, the liver), maintained by the pneuma, and transmitted by blood vessels. See Richard J. Durling, "The Innate Heat in Galen," *Medizinhistorisches Journal* Bd. 23, H. 3/4 (1988): 210–12.

54 In Helen King, "The Mathematics of Sex: One to Two, or Two to One?" *Studies in Medieval & Renaissance History*, 3rd ser., 2 (2005): 47–58; p. 51.

55 Galen, *De usu partium*, XIV, vi, K, IV, pp. 158–60. In *Galen on the Usefulness of the Parts of the Body*, trans. Tallmadge May, 2 vol. (Ithaca, NY: Cornell University Press, 1986), 2:628–9. More specifically, Galen suggests the scrotum is analogous with the uterus; the penis becomes the vagina, with the head extending outward to create the labia, and the shaft making up the cervix; the testes are the equivalent of the ovaries; the "spermatic vessels" [*vas deferens*] change into the Fallopian tubes.

56 Thomas Laqueur, *Making Sex: Body and Gender from the Greeks to Freud* (Cambridge, MA: Harvard University Press, 1990), esp. ch. 2.

57 Ruth Mazo Karras, *Sexuality in Medieval Europe: Doing Unto Others* (New York: Routledge, 2005), p. 5.

58 See Michael Boylan, "The Galenic and Hippocratic Challenges to Aristotle's Conception Theory," *Journal of the History of Biology* 17.1 (1984): 83–112; Boylan, "Galen's Conception Theory," *Journal of the History of Biology* 19.1 (1986): 47–77; Joan Cadden, *Meanings of Sex Difference in the Middle Ages: Medicine, Science, and Culture* (Cambridge: Cambridge University Press, 1995), pp. 17–37.

59 *On the Nature of the Child*, pp. 12–18, trans. I. M. Lonie, *The Hippocratic Treatises* (Berlin: De Gruyter, 1981), pp. 6–9.

60 In Sabina Flanagan, *Hildegard of Bingen: A Visionary Life* (New York: Routledge, 1998, 2nd ed.), p. 97.

61 Cadden, *Meanings of Sex Difference in the Middle Ages*, esp. pp. 119–30.

62 In Hertz, "Pre-eminence," *Hau: Journal of Ethnographic Theory* 3.2 (2013): 335–57; p. 340; Reprint of Robert Hertz, "The Pre-eminence of the Right Hand." In *Right and Left: Essays on Dual Symbolic Classification*, ed. Rodney Needham, trans. Rodney and Claudia Needham (Chicago: University of Chicago Press, 1973), pp. 3–31; first published as "La prééminence de la main droite: étude sur la polarité religieuse," *Revue Philosophique* 68 (1909): 553–80.

63 See *Summa theologiae*, II–II, 156, 1.

64 See *Summa theologiae*, II–II, 138, 1, ad 1.

65 See *Summa theologiae*, II–II, 149, 4: In I ad Tim. II, 2, 75.

66 Cyrene was an ancient Greek and Roman city near present-day Shahhat, Libya. See John M. Riddle and J. Worth Estes, "Oral Contraceptives in Ancient and Medieval Times," *American Scientist* 80.3 (1992): 226–33; p. 226. Modern

experiments with silphion's surviving relatives demonstrate that it was likely quite successful.

67 The lovers in the *Song of Songs* mention a number of spices (such as honey, myrrh, and spikenard) that are commonly found in ancient contraceptive potions. See Athalya Brenner, *The Intercourse of Knowledge: On Gendering Desire and "Sexuality" in the Hebrew Bible* (Leiden: Brill, 1996), pp. 72–89.

68 See Numbers 5:18: "And when the woman shall stand before the Lord, he shall uncover her head, and shall put on her hands the sacrifice of remembrance, and the oblation of jealousy: and he himself shall hold the most bitter waters, whereon he hath heaped curses with execration," and 19–28. Here, giving an abortifacient to the accused, who would presumably lose an illicit fetus but retain a lawful one, tests the woman's alleged infidelity.

69 Margaret Higgins Sanger (1879–1966), who is considered the founder of the modern birth control movement, opened the first birth control clinic in the United States (1916), established the American Birth Control League (1921), which became Planned Parenthood Federation of America, and formed the National Committee on Federal Legislation for Birth Control (1929) as a lobbying group for the legalization of contraception. For more information, see Jean H. Baker, *Margaret Sanger: A Life of Passion* (New York: Hill and Wang, 2011); Patricia Walsh Coates, *Margaret Sanger and the Origin of the Birth Control Movement, 1910–1930: The Concept of Women's Sexual Autonomy* (Lewiston, NY: Edwin Mellen Press, 2008); Carole Ruth McCann, *Birth Control Politics in the United States, 1916–1945* (Ithaca, NY: Cornell University Press, 1994).

70 Letter 22, "To Eustochium," 13: "Some go so far as to take potions, that they may insure barrenness, and thus murder human beings almost before their conception. Some, when they find themselves with child through their sin, use drugs to procure abortion, and when (as often happens) they die with their offspring, they enter the lower world laden with the guilt not only of adultery against Christ but also of suicide and child murder." http://www.ccel.org/ccel/schaff/npnf206.v.XXII.html. Christian Classics Ethereal Library.

71 *Homily 24 on the Epistle to the Romans*: "For I have no name to give it, since it does not take off the thing born, but prevent its being born. Why then dost thou abuse the gift of God, and fight with His laws, and follow after what is a curse as if a blessing, and make the chamber of procreation a chamber for murder, and arm the woman that was given for childbearing unto slaughter? . . . Hence too come idolatries, since many, with a view to become acceptable, devise incantations, and libations, and love-potions, and countless other plans . . . For sorceries (poisonings) are applied not to the womb that is prostituted, but to the injured wife . . ." http://www.ccel.org/ccel/schaff/npnf111.vii.xxvi.html. Christian Classics Ethereal Library.

72 John M. Riddle, "Contraception and Early Abortion in the Middle Ages." In *Handbook of Medieval Sexuality*, ed. Vern L. Bullough and James A. Brundage (New York: Garland, 1996), pp. 261–78; p. 265.

73 For a thorough overview of the intricacies involved in this centuries-long debate, see David Albert Jones, *Soul of the Embryo: Christianity and the Human Embryo* (London: Continuum, 2004), esp. ch. 8.

74 Four Causes refers to an influential principle in Aristotelian thought whereby causes of change or movement are categorized into four fundamental types of answer to the question "why?": material cause ("that out of which"), formal cause ("the form"), the efficient cause ("the primary source of the change"), and final cause ("the end, for the sake of which something is done"). All four types of causes may enter into the explanation of a thing. See Alan Code, "Soul as Efficient Cause in Aristotle's Embryology," *Philosophical Topics* 15 (1987): 51–9; Mohan Matthen, "The Four Causes in Aristotle's Embryology," *Apeiron* 22.4 (1989): 159–80; Robert B. Todd, "The Four Causes: Aristotle's Exposition and the Ancients," *Journal of the History of Ideas* 37 (1976): 319–22.

75 *Summa Theologiae*, Ia, q. 118, a. 1, ad 4.

76 *Commentary on the Book of Sentences*, Bk. III, dist. 3, q. 5, a. 2, *Responsio*. This reflects basic Aristotelian philosophy as well.

77 Dante, *Purgatario* 25.130–40 identified by John T. Noonan, Jr, *Contraception: A History of Its Treatment by Catholic Theologians and Canonists* (Cambridge, MA: Harvard University Press, 1986), pp. 213–14; Chaucer's *Parson's Tale* references "drynkynge venenouse herbes thurgh which she may nat conceive," (see ll. 575–80), and the adulterous tryst in the pear tree during the *Merchant's Tale* may be reflecting Avicenna's belief in the contraceptive powers of styptic pears. See Carol Falvo Hefferman, "Contraception and the Pear Tree Episode of Chaucer's 'Merchant's Tale,'" *Journal of English and Germanic Philology* 94.1 (1995): 31–42; for contemporaneous French literary references, see Guy Mermier, "The Troubadours and Contraception," *Journal of the Minnesota Academy of Science* 2.2 (1970): 37–47.

78 Roberta Gilchrist, *Medieval Life: Archaeology and the Life Course* (Woodbridge, Suffolk: Boydell Press, 2012), p. 39.

79 For instance, Soranus of Ephesus wrote, "and during the sexual act, at the critical moment of coitus when the man is about to discharge the seed, the woman must hold her breath and draw away a little, so that the seed may not be hurled too deep into the cavity of the uterus. And getting up immediately and squatting down she should induce sneezing and carefully wipe the vagina all around; she might even drink something cold." See Angus McLaren, *A History of Contraception from Antiquity to the Present Day* (Cambridge, MA: Basil Blackwell, 1990), p. 58.

80 Marie-Jose Delage, *Césaire d'Arles: sermons au peuple*, Sources Chrétiennes 175 (Paris: Éditions du Cerf, 1971); 1.12, p. 248.

81 Pennyroyal (*Mentha pulegium*) oil is extremely toxic. Similarly, exposure to rue (*Ruta graveolens*) can cause severe phytophotodermatitis (hypersensitivity to ultraviolet light), resulting in burns and blisters. Sage (*Salvia officinalis*) is not nearly so destructive, but can indeed cause miscarriages if ingested in large quantities.

82 Most of these plants have been shown to have at least some effect on menses, and some can induce a miscarriage. See Riddle, "Contraception and Early Abortion," pp. 262–3 and 269–71. Many of these herbs continue to show up in "herbal abortion" products today. See Carmen Ciganda and

Amalia Laborde, "Herbal Infusions Used for Induced Abortion," *Journal of Toxicology—Clinical Toxicology* 41.3 (2003): 235–9.

83 Carole Rawcliffe, *Medicine & Society in Later Medieval England* (London: Stroud, 1999), p. 204. Barbara A. Hanawalt reports a case where the woman's death was directly attributed to "divers poisonous and dangerous draughts [meant to] destroy the child in her womb." See Barbara A. Hanawalt, *The Ties That Bound, Peasant Farmers in Medieval England* (Oxford: Oxford University Press, 1988), p. 101.

84 They were also clearly fairly common knowledge, as evidenced by Ophelia handing out flowers, including rosemary, fennel, and rue, in Act 4, Scene 5 of *Hamlet*. A number of scholars have written about this. For a brief overview, see Robert Painter and Brian Parker, "Ophelia's Flowers Again," *Notes & Queries* 41.1 (1994): 42–5.

85 John M. Riddle, *Eve's Herbs: A History of Contraception and Abortion in the West* (Cambridge, MA: Harvard University Press, 1997), p. 103.

86 See *Medieval Woman's Guide to Health: The First English Gynecological Handbook*, ed. and trans. Beryl Rowland (Kent, OH: Kent State University Press, 1981), p. xv.

87 From his treatise *Gynaecology*. See Renate Blumenfeld-Kosinski, *Not of Woman Born: Representations of Caesarian Birth in Medieval and Renaissance Culture* (Ithaca: Cornell University Press, 1990), p. 17.

88 This term was coined in Sara M. Butler, "Abortion by Assault: Violence against Pregnant Women in Thirteenth- and Fourteenth-Century England," *Journal of Women's History* 17.4 (2005): 9–31.

89 Hanawalt, *The Ties That Bound*, p. 101.

90 John M. Riddle, *Eve's Herbs*, pp. 94–5.

91 See also Sara M. Butler, "Abortion Medieval Style? Assaults on Pregnant Women in Later Medieval England," *Women's Studies* 40.6 (2011): 778–99.

92 See Johann Joseph Ignaz von Döllinger, "Charge 6, Allowing Ladies to Marry with the Lower Orders and Slaves." In *Hippolytus and Callistus,* trans. Alfred Plummer (Edinburgh: T&T Clark, 1876), pp. 147–74. The situation was surely exacerbated by the personal backgrounds of the two opponents—Callixtus had been born a slave, and the educated and eloquent Hippolytus was clearly not, yet Callixtus was pope.

93 Noonan, *Contraception*, p. 159.

94 See Germanus Morin, *Sancti Caesarii Arelatensis sermones*, CCSL 103–4 (Turnhout: Brepols, 1953). Morin discusses the classification of Caesarius' sermons in his introduction.

95 Noonan, *Contraception*, pp. 159–61.

96 Riddle, *Eve's Herbs*, p. 89.

97 See Venantius Fortunatus. *Vita Germani episcopi Parisiaci*. Ed. B. Krusch. MGH Auct. ant. 4,2. Venanti Honori Clementiani Fortunati presbyteri Italici Opera pedestria (Berlin, 1885), pp. 11–12.

98 John Kitchen, *Saints' Lives and the Rhetoric of Gender: Male and Female in Merovingian Hagiography* (Oxford: Oxford University Press, 1998), p. 29.

99 Maeve B. Callan, "Of Vanishing Fetuses and Maidens Made-Again: Abortion, Restored Virginity, and Similar Scenarios in Medieval Irish Hagiography and Penitentials," *Journal of the History of Sexuality* 21.2 (2012): 282–96; p. 289.

100 Callan, "Of Vanishing Fetuses," pp. 291–2, based on *Vita Prima Sanctae Brigidae*, trans. Sean Connolly, *Journal of the Royal Society of the Antiquaries of Ireland* 229 (1989): 45; *Cogitosus' Life of St. Brigit*, trans. Sean Connolly and J. M. Vicaid, *Journal of the Royal Society of the Antiquaries of Ireland* 117 (1987): 16.

101 Callan, "Of Vanishing Fetuses," pp. 289–90, based on *Vita sancti Ciarani episcopi Saigirensis,* in *Vitae sanctorum Hiberniae*, ed. W. W. Heist (Brussels: Société des Bollandistes, 1965), p. 348.

102 Callan, "Of Vanishing Fetuses," pp. 290–1.

103 Restoration of virginity is seemingly a theme in early Irish Christianity. The *Penitential of Finnian* says that if an unmarried woman "bears a child and her sin is manifest," but then lives on bread and water for six years, "in the seventh year she shall be joined to the altar; and then we say her honor (*coronam*) can be restored and she may don a white robe and be pronounced a virgin." In *Medieval Handbooks of Penance*, ed. McNeill and Gamer, p. 90. It is significant that the word *coronam* (crown) is used to indicate the woman's honor, as that is generally a reference to the crown of virginity worn by a Bride of Christ—a nun. Moreover, the penance for the impregnated woman is juxtaposed with that for a fallen cleric. While it is not specified that the woman in question is a nun, the contextual evidence strongly indicates it is so, making the need for "re-virgination" more vital.

104 Aelred of Rievaulx, "The Nun of Watton," trans. John Boswell. In *The Kindness of Strangers* by John Boswell (Chicago: University of Chicago Press, 1988), pp. 452–8; pp. 456–7. The infant's father did not fare so well, as he was castrated by his former lover and had his genitals stuffed in his mouth before being led back to the monastery.

105 For further analysis of the Early Irish abortion miracles, see Lisa Bitel, *Land of Women: Tales of Sex and Gender from Early Ireland* (Ithaca, NY: Cornell University Press, 1996); Zubin Mistry, "The Sexual Shame of the Chaste: 'Abortion Miracles' in Early Medieval Saints' Lives," *Gender & History* 25.3 (2013): 607–20.

106 This attitude is revealing in connection to the modern-day canonization cause of Dorothy Day who admitted to having an abortion early in her life before her conversion to Roman Catholicism. This has not hurt her cause for canonization, however, and Day is quite popular among American Catholics as well as being formally instated as a "servant of God," meaning that she is being officially investigated for possible sainthood.

107 M. K. K. Yearl, "Medieval Monastic Customaries on *Minuti* and *Infirmi*." In *The Medieval Hospital and Medical Practice*, ed. Barbara S. Bowers (Farnham, Surrey: Ashgate, 2007). "Minuti" is the term for those who had undergone the prophylactic bloodletting, while "infirmi" is an ill person. See

also Angela Montford, *Health, Sickness, and the Friars in the Thirteenth and Fourteenth Centuries* (Farnham, Surrey: Ashgate, 2004).

108 The word "venereal," was associated with overt sexual activity, desire, or sexual intercourse. See Byron Lee Grigsby, *Pestilence in Medieval and Early Modern English Literature* (New York and London: Routledge, 2004), pp. 53–4.

109 Amudsen, *Medicine, Society, and Faith*, p. 312.

110 M. A. Waugh, "Venereal Diseases in Sixteenth-Century England," *Medical History* 17 (1973): 192–9.

111 Cadden, *Meaning of Sex Difference*, esp. pp. 26–7.

112 Andrew Cunningham and Ole Peter Grell, *The Four Horsemen of the Apocalypse: Religion, War, Famine, and Death in Reformation Europe* (Cambridge: Cambridge University Press, 2000), p. 263.

113 See Kenneth Borris and George Rousseau, *The Sciences of Homosexuality in Early Modern Europe* (New York: Routledge, 2008); Kevin Siena, *Sins of the Flesh* (Toronto: Centre for Reformation and Renaissance Studies, 2005).

114 See, among other sources, Hanne Blank, *Virgin: The Untouched History* (New York: Bloomsbury, 2007), pp. 62–5. Disturbingly, this myth still persists today, particularly in connection with HIV.

115 Darrel W. Amundsen, *Medicine, Society, and Faith in the Ancient and Medieval Worlds* (Baltimore: Johns Hopkins University Press, 1996), p. 210.

116 Katherine Park, "Medicine and Society in Medieval Europe: 500–1500." In *Medicine in Society: Historical Essays*, ed. Andrew Wear (Cambridge: Cambridge University Press, 1998), pp. 59–91; p. 87.

117 See Rotha Mary Clay, *The Medieval Hospitals of England* (London: Methuen, 1909), pp. 273–6; Peter Richards, *The Medieval Leper and His Northern Heirs* (New York: Barnes & Noble, 1977), pp. 123–4.

118 There is evidence of special houses for lepers being built as early as the fifth century; however, full-scale leprosaria did not exist until after 1050 CE. In the twelfth century, however, over half of newly built hospitals were specifically for lepers. See Katherine Park, "Medicine and Society in Medieval Europe," pp. 70–2.

119 Carole Rawcliffe, *Leprosy in Medieval England* (Woodbridge, Suffolk: Boydell Press, 2006), esp. ch. 1.

120 Rawcliffe, *Leprosy in Medieval England*, esp. ch. 7. Rawcliffe also cites the Statute of Mortmain (1279), which was aimed at preventing land passing to the hands of immortal institutions, and thus out of the control and taxation system operated by the state, as an economic death blow to leprosaria in England (p. 347).

121 Susan Zimmerman, "Leprosy in the Medieval Imaginary," *Journal of Medieval and Early Modern Studies* 38.3 (2008): 559–87.

122 See Leviticus chapters 13 and 14. For an interpretation of these chapters in connection to the "unclean" nature of sexual sins, see Saul Brody, *The Disease of the Soul: Leprosy in Medieval Literature* (Ithaca: Cornell University Press, 1974), esp. pp. 108–11.

123 See Peter Lewis Allen, *The Wages of Sin* (Chicago: University of Chicago Press, 2000).

124 De Chauliac was particularly known for his study of the Black Plague, wherein he defined the two strands (bubonic and pneumonic). His major work, the *Chirurgia magna*, was completed in 1363, and comprises seven volumes covering anatomy, bloodletting, cauterization, drugs, anesthetics, wounds, fractures, ulcers, and antidotes, as well as surgical techniques such as intubation, suturing, and tracheotomy. See Guy de Chauliac, *The Middle English Translation of Guy de Chauliac's Anatomy*, ed. Bjorn Wallner (Lund: Lund University, 1964) and *The Cyrurgie of Guy de Chauliac*, ed. Margaret S. Ogden (London: Early English Text Society, 1971).

125 Zimmerman, "Leprosy in the Medieval Imaginary," pp. 561–2.

126 Danielle Jacquart and Claude Thomasset, *Sexuality & Medicine in the Middle Ages*, trans. Matthew Adamson (Princeton, NJ: Princeton University Press, 1988; Fr. org. 1985), p. 185.

127 See Grigsby, *Pestilence in Medieval and Early Modern English Literature*, esp. ch. 2.

128 Grigsby, *Pestilence in Medieval and Early Modern English Literature*, p. 55.

129 See Faye M. Getz, *Healing and Society in Medieval England: A Middle English Translation of the Pharmaceutical Writings of Gilbertus Anglicus* (Madison: University of Wisconsin Press, 2010).

130 John Gower, *Mirour de l'omme*, trans. William Burton Wilson (East Lansing, MI: Colleagues Press, 1992), ll. 9649–53.

131 *Book of Margery Kempe*, Part 2, ll. 22–3 and 27–8, from *The Book of Margery Kempe*, ed. Lynn Staley (Kalamazoo, MI: Medieval Institute Publications, 1996). Also see Rosalynn Voaden, "Beholding Men's Members: The Sexualizing of Transgression in *The Book of Margery Kempe*." In *Medieval Theology and the Natural Body*, ed. Peter Biller and Alastair Minnis (York: York Medieval Press, 1997), pp. 175–90.

132 The description of Cresseid's illness occurs on ll. 312–43. See *The Testament of Cresseid* in *The Poems of Robert Henryson*, ed. Robert L. Kindrick (Kalamazoo, MI: Medieval Institute Publications, 1997). For more about her leprosy, see Sanford V. Larkey, "Leprosy in Medieval Romance: A Note on Robert Henryson's *Testament of Cresseid*," *Bulletin of the History of Medicine* 25 (1958): 77–80; Julie Orlemanski, "Desire and Defacement in *The Testament of Cresseid*." In *Reading Skin in Medieval Literature and Culture*, ed. Katie L. Walter (New York: Palgrave Macmillan, 2013), pp. 161–81; Marion Wynne-Davies, "Spottis Blak: Disease and the Female Body in *The Testament of Cresseid*," *Poetica: An International Journal of Linguistic-Literary Studies* 38 (1993): 32–52.

133 See Irven M. Resnick, *Marks of Distinctions: Christian Perceptions of Jews in the High Middle Ages* (Washington, DC: Catholic University of America Press, 2012), esp. pp. 78 and 180.

134 In a fascinating example, Hugh of Orival (d. 1085), bishop of London, underwent this drastic treatment, and subsequently suffered censure because he was a eunuch, not because he was a leper. As a bishop, Hugh

was especially trapped, since his leprous state meant he could not serve as a Church official, and was clearly a mark of his sinful nature, yet even in the event that castration had cured him, as a eunuch, he would also have been barred from office. This incident is reported in William of Malmesbury's *Gesta pontificum Anglorum* (*Deeds of the English Bishops*; ca. 1125 CE). See William of Malmesbury, *Gesta pontificum Anglorum*, Vol. 1, ed. and trans. M. Winterbottom and R. M. Thomson, Vol. 2, ed. R. M. Thomson (Oxford: Oxford University Press, 2007).

135 More "normal" cures related to the prevailing humoral medical theory. Leprosy was a disease that was related to the element of fire, characterized by causing the body to become "hot and dry," so the advice was to eat and drink things that were "cold and wet," or, the opposite advice might be offered, to increase the dryness, the patient should consume scorpions or dirt from ant hills. Lepers were unclean, so to purify the blood, they might ingest a liquid containing powdered gold, and undergo regular bloodletting. See Rawcliffe, *Leprosy in Medieval England*, pp. 65–71; Charlotte Roberts and Margaret Cox, *Health and Disease in Britain: From Prehistory to Present Day* (Thrupp: Sutton Publishing, 2003), p. 270.

136 *Women's Secrets: A Translation of Pseudo-Albertus Magnus's "De secretis mulierum" with Commentaries*, ed. Helen Lemay (Albany: State University of New York Press, 1992), pp. 60 and 88.

137 Zimmerman, "Leprosy in the Medieval Imaginary," p. 565. Zimmerman more specifically connects women, Jews, and leprosy through ritual practices concerning pigs. For the background about Jewish male menstruation, see Willis Johnson, "The Myth of Jewish Male Menses," *Journal of Medieval History* 24.3 (1998): 273–95; David S. Katz, "Shylock's Gender: Jewish Male Menstruation in Early Modern England," *The Review of English Studies* 50.200 (1999): 440–62; Irven M. Resnick, "Medieval Roots of the Myth of Jewish Male Menses," *Harvard Theological Review* 93.3 (2000): 241–63.

138 Zimmerman, "Leprosy in the Medieval Imaginary," pp. 568–9.

139 See David Nirenberg, *Communities of Violence: Persecution of Minorities in the Middle Ages* (Princeton, NJ: Princeton University Press, 1996), pp. 43–68.

140 Nirenberg, *Communities of Violence*, pp. 101–3.

141 For more about the lesbian implications of this situation, see Sauer, "Representing the Negative." For medieval greensickness and its remedies, see *The Trotula: An English Translation of the Medieval Compendium of Women's Medicine*, ed. and trans. Monica H. Green (Philadelphia: University of Pennsylvania Press, 2001).

142 See Laqueur, *Solitary Sex*, esp. pp. 93–5.

143 For the early modern version of this illness, see Helen King, *The Disease of Virgins: Green Sickness, Chlorosis and the Problems of Puberty* (London: Routledge, 2003) and Valerie Traub, *Renaissance of Lesbianism in Early Modern England* (Cambridge: Cambridge University Press, 2002). For a modern analysis of the condition, see Irvine Loudon, "The Diseases Called

Chlorosis," *Psychological Medicine* 14.1 (1984): 27–36. He suggests that greensickness was actually a name applied to both a form of hypochromic anemia (chloro-anemia) and a disorder resembling anorexia nervosa (chloro-anorexia).

144 Sujata Iyengar, *Shades of Difference Mythologies of Skin Color in Early Modern England* (Philadelphia: University of Pennsylvania Press, 2004), p. 155.

145 The movie *Hysteria* (Dir. Tanya Wexler. Perf. Hugh Dancy and Maggie Gyllenhaal. Informant Media, Beachfront Films, Forthcoming Productions, Chimera Films LLC, 2011), set at the end of the nineteenth century, depicts the (slightly revised) invention of the vibrator by Dr Mortimer Granville, as a cure for hysteria. In fact, Granville intended his device as a relief for aching (male) muscles. Also see Rachel P. Maines, *The Technology of Orgasm: "Hysteria," Vibrators and Women's Sexual Satisfaction* (Baltimore: Johns Hopkins University Press, 1999).

146 The seminal text on this disorder is Ilza Veith, *Hysteria: The History of a Disease* (Chicago: University of Chicago Press, 1965).

147 Aretaeus of Cappadocia wrote sometime in the first century CE: "In the middle of the flanks of women lies the womb, a female viscus, closely resembling an animal; for it is moved of itself hither and thither in the flanks, also upwards in a direct line to the thorax, and also obliquely to the right or to the left, either to the liver or spleen; and it likewise is subject to prolapsus downwards, and, in a word, it is altogether erratic. It delights, also, in fragrant smells and advances towards them; and it has an aversion to fetid smells, and flees from them; and on the whole, the womb is like an animal within an animal." In *Women's Life in Greece and Rome: A Source Book in Translation*, ed. Mary R. Lefkowitz and Maureen B. Fant (Baltimore: Johns Hopkins University Press, 2005; 3rd ed.), p. 248.

148 Laurinda S. Dixon, "The Curse of Chastity: The Marginalization of Women in Medieval Art and Medicine." In *Matrons and Marginal Women in Medieval Society*, ed. Robert R. Edwards and Vickie Ziegler (Woodbridge, Suffolk: Boydell Press, 1995), pp. 49–74.

149 Bennett, *Ale, Beer, and Brewsters*, p. 154.

150 See Hanawalt, *The Wealth of Wives*, esp. pp. 160–2.

151 Anna Dronzek, "Women and Property Conflicts in Late Medieval England." In *Women, Wealth, and Power in Medieval Europe*, ed. Earenfight, pp. 187–208; p. 194.

152 Hanawalt, *The Wealth of Wives*, pp. 169–76.

153 Butler, *Divorce in Medieval England*, p. 10.

154 Karma Lochrie, *Covert Operations: The Medieval Uses of Secrecy* (Philadelphia: University of Pennsylvania Press, 1999), p. 164.

155 See Kari Elizabeth Børresen, *Subordinance and Equivalence: The Nature and Role of Woman in Augustine and Thomas Aquinas* (Washington, DC: University Press of America, 1981).

Chapter 2

1 Aldhelm, "De Virginitate." In *Aldhelm: The Prose Works*, trans. Michael Lapidge and Michael Herren (Totowa, NJ: Rowman and Littlefield, 1979), pp. 59–132; p. 75.

2 In *Anchoritic Spirituality: Ancrene Wisse and Associated Works*, ed. Anne Savage and Nicholas Watson (Mahwah, NJ: Paulist, 1991), p. 233.

3 Jane Tibbetts Schulenburg, *Forgetful of Their Sex: Female Sanctity and Society ca. 500–1100* (Chicago: University of Chicago Press, 2001), p. 128.

4 Ruth Mazo Karras, *Sexuality in Medieval Europe: Doing Unto Others* (New York: Routledge, 2005), p. 29.

5 In Gillian Cloke, *"This Female Man of God": Women and Spiritual Power in the Patristic Age, AD 350–450* (London: Routledge, 1995), p. 60.

6 This discussion will focus on female virginity, rather than male. Male virginity was a murky subject not only because there is no physical proof of such a status, but also because men did not necessarily tarnish their soul to the same extent as women did through giving into temptation. Since women were biologically constricted to give in to temptation, their resistance to such was seen as a greater achievement, even if the overall effect was a passive—virginity being the absence of sexual congress. Similarly, men were designed to resist temptation, and even if they yielded to temptation, it was an effeminate moment, not necessarily a regendering. Moreover, hagiographies often describe male resistance to sexual temptation in active, heroic terms that warrant praise.

7 See Joyce E. Salisbury, "The Latin Doctors of the Church and Sexuality," *Journal of Medieval History* 12 (1986): 279–89.

8 Kate Cooper and Conrad Leyser, "The Gender of Grace: Impotence, Servitude, and Manliness in the Fifth-Century West," *Gender & History* 12.3 (2000): 536–51; pp. 541–3.

9 See Jean Delumeau, *History of Paradise: The Garden of Eden in Myth and Tradition*, trans. Matthew O'Connell (Urbana/Chicago: University of Illinois Press, 2000; Fr. orig. 1992), esp. pp. 203–5.

10 See Cloke, *"This Female Man of God,"* esp. p. 28.

11 The *Romance of the Rose* is an allegorical French dream vision, begun circa 1230 CE by Guillaume de Lorris, and completed circa 1275 by Jean de Meun.

12 Rob Aben and Saskia deWit, *The Enclosed Garden: History and Development of the Hortus Conclusus and Its Reintroduction into the Present-Day Urban Landscape* (Rotterdam: 010 Publishers, 1999), p. 14.

13 In Cloke, *"This Female Man of God,"* p. 58. From Jerome's Letter 22.

14 Clarissa Atkinson, "'Precious Balsam in a Fragile Glass': The Ideology of Virginity in the Later Middle Ages," *Journal of Family History* 8 (1983): 131–43; p. 133.

15 Angela of Foligno (1248[?]–1309 CE) was a married mystic who had a number of children. She experienced a vision of St Francis when she was around 40; however, she did not undertake a wholly religious life until three years later

after her husband and children perished. She dictated a number of her visions to various scribes throughout her life, and was an active member of the Third Order of St Francis (a lay order). She was declared a saint on October 9, 2013 by Pope Francis I (r. 2013–pres.) Birgitta of Sweden (1303–73 CE) was another married mystic. She and her husband, Ulf, had eight children, of whom six survived. After Ulf's death in 1344, Birgitta joined the Third Order of St Francis. She continued to work among the poor and sick, go on pilgrimages, experience visions, and advise Church leaders. In 1370, Pope Urban V (r. 1362–70 CE) confirmed the establishment of the Bridgettines, which relied upon double monasteries. She was canonized in 1391 by Pope Boniface IX (r. 1389–1404 CE). Dorothea von Montau (1347–94 CE) was another married mystic. After her husband and eight of their nine children died, Dorothea devoted herself entirely to religion. In 1391, she received permission to become an anchoress attached to Marienwerder cathedral where she remained until her death in 1393. She was canonized by popular acclamation in 1976 by Pope Paul VI (1963–78 CE).

16 This was not a view shared by all theologians. Some believed that remarriage helped eliminate fornication.

17 Marie-Françoise Alamichel, *Widows in Anglo-Saxon and Medieval Britain* (New York: Peter Lang, 2008), p. 53.

18 Katherine Clark, "Putting on the Garment of Widowhood: Medieval Widows, Monastic Memory, and Historical Writing," *Quidditas* 31.1 (2010): 22–76, p. 25.

19 See Mary C. Erler, "Three Fifteenth-Century Vowesses." In *Medieval London Widows*, ed. Caroline M. Barron and Anne F. Sutton (London: Hambledon Press, 1994), pp. 165–83.

20 Although not quite as formal a process as the vowesses of Northern Europe, many widows in medieval Italy adopted a "fashion of piety" that allowed them to stay both unmarried and at home. See Patricia Skinner, "The Widow's Options in Medieval Southern Italy." In *Widowhood in Medieval and Early Modern Europe*, ed. Sandra Cavallo and Lyndan Warner (New York: Addison Wesley Longman, 1999), pp. 57–65.

21 See R. H. Helmholz, *The Spirit of Classical Canon Law* (Athens: University of Georgia Press, 2010), pp. 247–9.

22 I am speaking here about individual chaste marriages contracted between one man and one woman. There were some other forms of this choice. For example, the Humiliati of Italy was a penitential association of the laity formed ca. 1150 CE. A group of laymen who had rebelled in Lombardy were exiled to Germany. While there, they assumed penitential garb and devoted themselves to charity and chastity. Upon securing their pledge of obedience, Emperor Henry V (1081–1125 CE) allowed them to return to Italy. They were accompanied by their wives who established a similar penitential community nearby where they cared for lepers. These individuals, however, are different from a vowed chaste marriage arrangement, since at one point they actively engaged in sexual relations, and their vocational choice was made (at least initially) in response to political decimation.

23 Augustine, *De bono coniugali and De sancta virginitate*, ed. and trans. P. G. Walsh (Oxford: Oxford University Press, 2001), p. 7.

24 See Irven M. Resnick, "Marriage in Medieval Culture: Consent Theory and the Case of Joseph and Mary," *Church History* 69.2 (2000): 350–71.

25 Today, the Roman Catholic, Orthodox, and Anglo-Catholic communion uphold this doctrine, while the majority of Protestant denominations do not. Islam, which accepts the virgin birth, has no official position on Mary's eternal virginity.

26 For a good overview of Edward's life and reign, see Frank Barlow, *Edward the Confessor* (Berkeley: University of California Press, 1984).

27 See Jennifer N. Brown, "Body, Gender, and Nation in the Lives of Edward the Confessor." In *Barking Abbey and Medieval Literary Culture: Authorship and Authority in a Female Community*, ed. Jennifer N. Brown and Donna Alfano Bussell (Woodbridge, Suffolk: Boydell & Brewer, 2012), pp. 145–63.

28 Hedwig and her widowed daughter-in-law, Anne of Bohemia, founded a Benedictine abbey and retired to it. Dorothy ended her life as an anchoress.

29 Scholarship often refers to "Margery" when discussing the character of the *Book* and "Kempe" in reference to the authorial voice. I have used Margery because the two are collapsed, at least to some degree, here.

30 Helen L. Parish, *Clerical Celibacy in the West, c. 1100–1700* (Basingstoke, VT: Ashgate 2010), p. 88.

31 Dyan Elliott, *Spiritual Marriage: Sexual Abstinence in Medieval Wedlock* (Princeton: Princeton University Press, 1993), p. 5.

32 Eric Josef Carlson, *Marriage and the English Reformation* (Oxford: Blackwell, 1994), p. 18.

33 See Christine Fell, *Women in Anglo-Saxon England and the Impact of 1066* (Oxford: Blackwell, 1984) and Anne L. Klinck, "Anglo-Saxon Women and the Law," *Journal of Medieval History* 8 (1982): 107–21.

34 See Christopher N. L. Brooke, *The Medieval Idea of Marriage* (Oxford and New York: Oxford University Press, 1991).

35 Ralph A. Houlbrooke, *The English Family 1450–1700* (London and New York: Longman Press, 1984), p. 73.

36 David Herlihy, *Medieval Households* (Cambridge, MA: Harvard University Press, 1985), p. 98.

37 Beatrice Gottlieb, *The Family in the Western World from the Black Death to the Industrial Age* (New York and Oxford: Oxford University Press, 1993), pp. 52–4.

38 See Dyan Elliott, "Sex in Holy Places: An Exploration of a Medieval Anxiety," *Journal of Women's History* 6.3 (1994): 6–34.

39 *Book of Vices and Virtues*, ed. W. Nelson Francis (London: EETS, 1942).

Chapter 3

1 Noted in Alastair Minnis, *Fallible Authors: Chaucer's Pardoner and Wife of Bath* (Philadelphia, PA: University of Pennsylvania Press, 2007), p. 3.

2 Minnis, *Fallible Authors*, p. 2.

3   This is from an anonymous Middle English translation of Thomas à Kempis's *Imitatio Christi* originally composed in Latin ca. 1418–27 CE.
4   Any basic sociology text covers these ideas. See, for example, Margaret L. Andersen and Howard Francis Taylor, *Sociology: The Essentials* (Belmont, CA: Thomson Wadsworth, 2009).
5   Carolyn Dinshaw, *Getting Medieval: Sexualities and Communities, Pre- and Postmodern* (Durham, NC: Duke University Press, 1999), p. 7.
6   Elizabeth Grosz, *Volatile Bodies: Toward a Corporeal Feminism* (Bloomington, IN: Indiana University Press, 1994), p. 207.
7   Caroline Walker Bynum, *Fragmentation and Redemption: Essays on Gender and the Human Body in Medieval Religion* (New York: Zone Books, 1992), p. 114.
8   Joan Cadden, *Meanings of Sex Difference in the Middle Ages: Medicine, Science, and Culture* (Cambridge: Cambridge University Press, 1993), p. 174.
9   William Naphy, *Sex Crimes from Renaissance to Enlightenment* (Stroud, Gloucestershire: Tempus, 2004), pp. 103–4.
10 For a discussion of how the term transformed throughout the centuries, see Heike Bauer, "Sex, Popular Beliefs and Culture." In *A Cultural History of Sexuality in the Enlightenment*, ed. Julie Peakman (London: Berg, 2012), pp. 159–83.
11 See Ruth Mazo Karras, "Holy Harlots: Prostitute Saints in Medieval Legend," *Journal of the History of Sexuality* 1.1 (1990): 3–32.
12 This is called the "composite Magdalene" in Western Christianity, and includes the woman explicitly called Mary Magdalene in the Gospels, but also Mary of Bethany, sister of Martha and Lazarus, and the unnamed female sinner who washed Christ's feet with her tears. The Eastern Orthodox Churches did not accept this composite. See Susan Haskins, *Mary Magdalen: Myth and Metaphor* (New York: Riverhead, 1995) and Katherine Ludwig Jansen, *The Making of the Magdalen: Preaching and Popular Devotion in the Later Middle Ages* (Princeton, NJ: Princeton University Press, 2000).
13 Leah Lydia Otis, *Prostitution in Medieval Society: The History of an Urban Institution in Languedoc* (Chicago: University of Chicago Press, 1985), p. 13.
14 Aquinas's famous analogy is the comparison of a brothel to the sewer in a palace—stinking, but necessary. See *De regilnine principum* 4:14; *Summa* 2:2, 10. II.
15 The exception is medieval Spain, where male prostitutes were prized and often charged more money than women. See Abdelwahab Bouhdiba, *Sexuality in Islam* (London: Routledge, 1985); Gregory S. Hutcheson, "Desperately Seeking Sodom: The Nature of Queerness in the Chronicles of Álvaro de Luna." In *Queer Iberia*, ed. Gregory Hutcheson and Josiah Blackmore (Durham, NC: Duke University Press, 1999), pp. 222–49; Mary Elizabeth Perry, *Gender and Disorder in Early Modern Seville* (Princeton, NJ: Princeton University Press, 1990); Norman Roth, "'Deal Gently With The Young Man': Love of Boys in Medieval Hebrew Poetry of Spain," *Speculum* 57.1 (1982): 20–51.
16 See Ruth Mazo Karras, "Prostitution in Medieval Europe." In *Handbook of Medieval Sexuality*, ed. Bullough and Brundage, pp. 243–60, esp. p. 246.

17 Mark Jordan, *The Invention of Sodomy in Christian Theology* (Chicago: University of Chicago Press, 1997), p. 82.

18 Allen J. Frantzen, "Between the Lines: Queer Theory, the History of Homosexuality, and Anglo-Saxon Penitentials," *Journal of Medieval and Early Modern Studies* 26.2 (1996): 255–96, p. 266.

19 Jeffrey Richards, *Sex, Dissidence, and Damnation* (London: Routledge, 1990), pp. 198–9.

20 William E. Burgwinkle, *Sodomy, Masculinity, and Law in Medieval Literature* (Cambridge: Cambridge University Press, 2009), pp. 48–50.

21 CLRO, L-BL, fol. 189v (Sharpe, *Cal L-B L*, 216). In Ruth Mazo Karras, *Common Women: Prostitution and Sexuality in Medieval England* (Oxford: Oxford University Press, 1996), p. 16.

22 Otis, *Prostitution in Medieval Society*, p. 41.

23 Joyce E. Salisbury, "When Sex Stopped Being a Social Disease: Sex and the Desert Fathers and Mothers." In *Medieval Sexuality: A Casebook*, ed. April Harper and Caroline Proctor (New York: Routledge, 2008), pp. 47–58; p. 52.

24 Simon Lienyueh Wei, "The Absence of Sin in Sexual Dreams in the Writings of Augustine and Cassian," *Vigiliae Christianae* 66 (2012): 362–78.

25 See Peggy McCracken, *The Curse of Eve, The Wound of the Hero: Blood, Gender, and Medieval Literature* (Philadelphia, PA: University of Pennsylvania Press, 2003), p. 3.

26 Regarding repression and externalization, see Dyan Elliott, *Fallen Bodies: Pollution, Sexuality, and Demonology in the Middle Ages* (Philadelphia, PA: University of Pennsylvania Press, 1999), p. 29.

27 Louis Crompton, *Homosexuality and Civilisation* (Cambridge, MA: Harvard University Press, 2006), p. 188.

28 See Genesis 38: 1–10.

29 Kim M. Phillips, "'They Do Not Know the Use of Men': The Absence of Sodomy in Medieval Accounts of the Far East." In *Medieval Sexuality: A Casebook*, ed. Harper and Proctor, pp. 189–208; p. 195.

30 *Medieval Handbooks of Penance*, ed. McNeill and Gamer, p. 103.

31 Leah DeVun, "The Jesus Hermaphrodite: Science and Sex Difference in Premodern Europe," *Journal of the History of Ideas* 69.2 (2008): 193–218; pp. 197–8.

32 In Thomas W. Laqueur, *Solitary Sex: A Cultural History of Masturbation* (New York: Zone Books, 2003), p. 142.

33 *Medieval Handbooks of Penance*, ed. McNeill and Gamer, p. 191.

34 In Allen J. Frantzen, *Before the Closet: Same-Sex Love from Beowulf to Angels in America* (Chicago, IL: University of Chicago Press, 1998), p. 150.

35 *Medieval Handbooks of Penance*, ed. McNeill and Gamer, p. 185.

36 *Ancrene Wisse* 2, lines 813–15, ed. and trans. Robert Hasenfrantz (Kalamazoo, MI: Medieval Institute Publications, 2000); also archived at http://d.lib.rochester.edu/teams/text/hasenfratz-ancrene-wisse-introduction. Hasenfrantz

includes a number of parenthetical remarks that I have removed for the sake of clarity.

37 See Michelle M. Sauer, "Uncovering Difference Encoded Homoerotic Anxiety within the Christian Eremitic Tradition in Medieval England," *Journal of the History of Sexuality* 19.1 (2010): 133–52, esp. pp. 149–50.
38 Frantzen, *Before the Closet*, p. 150.
39 *Medieval Handbooks of Penance*, ed. McNeill and Gamer, p. 254.
40 "General Prologue," l. 691.
41 In Hebrew, the term is *saris*, and in Greek, *eunouchos*. However, these terms can also be translated as "court official," rather than referring only to a man without working genitals.
42 See Lynn E. Roller, *In Search of God the Mother: The Cult of Anatolian Cybele* (Berkeley, CA: University of California Press, 1999).
43 *Story of His Misfortunes*, written ca. 1132, is an epistolary autobiographical work.
44 Larissa Tracy (ed.), "Introduction: A History of Calamities: The Culture of Castration." In *Castration and Culture in the Middle Ages* (Cambridge: D. S. Brewer, 2013), pp. 1–28; p. 5.
45 See Aelred of Rievaulx, "The Nun of Watton," trans. John Boswell. In *The Kindness of Strangers* by John Boswell (Chicago: University of Chicago Press, 1988), pp. 452–8. This is also discussed briefly in Chapter Four.
46 Edward II (1284–1327 CE) reigned as King of England from 1307 until 1327, when he was deposed by his wife, Isabella, and her lover, Roger Mortimer. During his life, Edward was openly accused of having male lovers, including Piers Gaveston and Hugh le Despenser, although he also fathered five children.
47 See *Self and Society in Medieval France: The Memoirs of Abbot Guibert of Nogent*, ed. John F. Benton (New York: Harper & Row, 1970).
48 *Codex Calixtinus* is a twelfth-century illuminated manuscript formerly attributed to Pope Callixtus II that provides background information and advice to pilgrims on their way to the shrine of St James in Compostela.
49 For there are eunuchs, who were born so from their mother's womb: and there are eunuchs, who were made so by men: and there are eunuchs, who have made themselves eunuchs for the kingdom of heaven. He that can take, let him take it.
50 See Jacqueline Murray (ed.), "Mystical Castration: Some Reflections on Peter Abelard, Hugh of Lincoln and Sexual Control." In *Conflicted Identities and Multiple Masculinities* (New York: Taylor & Francis, 1999), pp. 73–110.
51 See *The Sanctity and Miracles of St. Thomas Aquinas from the First Canonisation Enquiry* (Naples, at the Archbishop's Palace; July 21 to September 18, 1319). http://sedevacantist.com/stthomas/stcanonise.html.
52 Mathew S. Kuefler, "Castration and Eunuchism in the Middle Ages." In *Handbook of Medieval Sexuality*, ed. Vern L. Bullough and James A. Brundage (New York/London: Routledge, 1996), pp. 279–306; p. 283. Also see Mathew

S. Kuefler, *The Manly Eunuch: Masculinity, Gender Ambiguity, and Christian Ideology in Late Antiquity* (Chicago: University of Chicago Press, 2001).

53 Tracy, "Introduction," p. 1.
54 Translation Irvine's in Martin Irvine, "The Pen(is), Castration, and Identity: Abelard's Negotiations of Gender." Archived at http://www8.georgetown.edu/departments/medieval/labyrinth/conf/cs95/papers/irvine.html. See also Martin Irvine, "Abelard and (Re)Writing the Male Body: Castration, Identity, and Remasculinization." In *Becoming Male in the Middle Ages*, ed. Jeffrey Jerome Cohen and Bonnie Wheeler (New York: Garland, 1997), pp. 87–106.
55 London, British Library MS Egerton 881, f. 132r.
56 Valeria Finucci, *The Manly Masquerade: Masculinity, Paternity, and Castration in the Italian Renaissance* (Durham, NC: Duke University Press, 2003), p. 6.
57 See Sander L. Gilman, *Making the Body Beautiful: A Cultural History of Aesthetic Surgery* (Princeton, NJ: Princeton University Press, 2001), esp. pp. 61–4.
58 Culley C. Carson III (ed.), "History of Urologic Prostheses." In *History of Urologic Prostheses* (Totowa, NJ: Humana Press, 2001), pp. 1–7; p. 1.
59 Ambroise Paré, *On Monsters and Marvels*, trans. Janis L. Pallister (Chicago, IL: University of Chicago Press, 1995).
60 Jacqueline Murray (ed.), "Mystical Castration." In *Conflicted Identities and Multiple Masculinities: Men in the Medieval West* (New York: Garland Press, 1999), pp. 73–91; p. 76.
61 *Deut* 22:5: "A woman shall not be clothed with man's apparel, neither shall a man use woman's apparel: for he that doeth these things is abominable before God."
62 The word "transvestite" was coined in 1910 by Magnus Hirschfield, although he more specifically connected it to sexual desire, rather than a lifestyle choice. Today, the term "cross-dresser" is preferred over transvestite, and will be used here. Both terms are significantly different from transgender, however, and should not be extended to that gender identification.
63 John Anson, "The Female Transvestite in Early Monasticism: The Origin and Development of a Motif," *Viator* 5 (1974): 1–32.
64 Suzanne J. Kessler and Wendy McKenna, "Toward a Theory of Gender." In *The Transgender Studies Reader*, ed. Susan Stryker and Stephen Whittle (New York: Routledge, 2006), pp. 165–82; p. 175.
65 See *Primary Sources and Context Concerning Joan of Arc's Male Clothing*, ed. Robert Wirth (Historical Association for Joan of Arc Studies, 2006). http://www.joan-of-arc-studies.org/.
66 Valerie R. Hotchkiss, *Clothes Make the Man: Female Cross Dressing in Medieval Europe* (New York/London: Garland, 1991), p. 22.
67 There were exceptions to this practice. Some nuns put on Easter pageants within their convents, and in France, women were occasionally allowed on stage.
68 See Katie Normington, *Gender and Medieval Drama* (Cambridge: D. S. Brewer, 2004), p. 41.

69 Michelle Szkilnik, "The Grammar of the Sexes in Medieval French Romance." In *Gender Transformations: Crossing the Normative Barrier in Old French Literature*, ed. Karen J. Taylor (New York: Garland, 1998), pp. 61–88; p. 65.
70 For more on male cross-dressing, see Keith Busby, "*Plus ascesmez qu'une popire*: Male Cross-Dressing in Medieval French Narrative." In *Gender Transformations*, ed. Taylor, pp. 45–60.
71 See David Lorenzo Boyd and Ruth Mazo Karras, "The Interrogation of a Male Transvestite Prostitute in Fourteenth Century London," *GLQ* 1 (1995): 459–65 and David Lorenzo Boyd and Ruth Mazo Karras, "'Ut cum muliere': A Male Transvestite Prostitute in Fourteenth Century London." In *Premodern Sexualities*, ed. Louise Fradenburg and Carla Freccero (London: Routledge, 1996), pp. 99–116.
72 For a discussion of this incident, see Nancy F. Partner, "No Gender, No Sex," *Speculum* 68.2 (1993): 419–43.
73 See *Medieval Handbooks of Penance*, ed. McNeill and Gamer.
74 As discussed in Introduction, there was no "homosexual identity" in the premodern world, or, really, until the twentieth century. However, modern scholarship often uses the term for convenience's sake. I have attempted to use homosexuality, same-sex activity, and other terms somewhat interchangeably in the spirit of scholarship, but do want to point out that I am in no way presuming a premodern homosexual identification.
75 See James Boswell, *Same-Sex Unions in Pre-Modern Europe* (New York: Villard, 1994).
76 Pierre J. Payer, *Book of Gomorrah: An Eleventh-Century Treatise against Clerical Homosexual Practices* (Waterloo, ON: Wilfrid Laurier University Press, 1982), p. 68.
77 Payer, *Book of Gomorrah*, p. 70.
78 In Michael Goodich, ed., *Other Middle Ages: Witnesses at the Margins of Medieval Society* (Philadelphia, PA: University of Pennsylvania Press, 1998), p. 135.
79 Burgwinkle, *Sodomy, Masculinity, and Law*, p. 49.
80 The infamous details about Edward's murder, supposedly by means of a red-hot poker inserted into his anus, is believed to be a later fabrication for political purposes. See, among other sources, Roy Martin Haines, *King Edward II: His Life, His Reign, and its Aftermath, 1284–1330* (Waterloo, ON: Mcgill Queens University Press, 2003).
81 Although the pope ordered that their lands be given to the Hospitallers, Philip ignored this directive and held the lands himself, as did a number of other monarchs.
82 In September 2001, while examining the Vatican Secret Archives, Barbara Frale discovered a copy of a document, now called the Chinon Parchment, dated August 17–20, 1308. In it, Clement V absolves all the Templar leaders and restores them to communion with the Church. See Barbara Frale, "The Chinon Chart: Papal Absolution to the Last Templar, Master Jacques de Molay," *Journal of Medieval History* 30.2 (2004): 109–34.

83 See Sylvia Federico, "Queer Times: Richard II in the Poems and Chronicles of Late Fourteenth-Century England," *Medium Aevum* 79.1 (2010): 25–46.

84 Warren Johansson and William A. Percy, "Homosexuality." In *Handbook of Medieval Sexuality*, ed. Bullough and Brundage, pp. 155–89; p. 175.

85 See *The Lesbian Premodern*, ed. Noreen Giffney, Michelle M. Sauer, and Diane Watt (New York: Palgrave, 2011).

86 See Bernadette J. Brooten, *Love Between Women: Early Christian Responses to Female Homoeroticism* (Chicago, IL: University of Chicago Press, 1996), p. 59.

87 Seneca the Younger, *Moral Epistles* 95.21. In *Homosexuality in Greece and Rome: A Sourcebook of Basic Documents*, ed. Thomas K. Hubbard (Berkeley, CA: University of California Press, 2003), p. 394.

88 *Epistles* 211; *PL* 33:964.

89 From *In Epistolam ad Romanos*, homily 4 (*PG*, 60: 415–22).

90 In John Boswell, *Christianity, Social Tolerance, and Homosexuality* (Chicago, IL: University of Chicago Press, 1980), p. 185.

91 One exception was fourteenth-century legislation from Orléans, which operated under the three-strike system. For the first two offenses, the punishment for lesbian activity was "dismemberment." The third infraction resulted in death by burning. This coincides with the rise of witchcraft trials in the area.

92 See McNeill and Gamer, *Handbooks of Penance*.

93 In Edith Benkov, "The Erased Lesbian: Sodomy and the Legal Tradition in Medieval Europe." In *Same Sex Love and Desire among Women in the Middle Ages*, ed. Francesca Canadé Sautman and Pamela Sheingorn (New York: Palgrave, 2001), pp. 101–22; p. 104.

94 See Michelle M. Sauer, "Representing the Negative: Positing the Lesbian Void & Medieval English Anchoritism," *thirdspace* 3.2 (2004): 70–88.

95 Bernd-Ulrich Hergemoller, *Sodom and Gomorrah: On the Everyday Reality and Persecution of Homosexuals in the Middle Ages*, trans. John Phillips (London: Free Association, 2001), pp. 14–5.

96 See Helmut Puff, *Sodomy in Reformation Germany and Switzerland* (Chicago, IL: University of Chicago Press, 2003), pp. 60–1.

97 Barbara K. Newman, *From Virile Woman to WomanChrist* (Philadelphia, PA: University of Pennsylvania Press, 1995), p. 34.

98 Although the term "hermaphrodite" is the historically accepted one, it is no longer in use today. Modern medicine recognizes individuals born exhibiting genetic characteristics of both biological sexes, which may or may not include nonstandard external genitalia, or may have a condition in which an individual's phenotypic sex (genitals) and chromosomal sex do not match. Such individuals are called intersex.

99 See *Plato's Symposium*, trans. Seth Benardete, with commentaries by Allan Bloom and Seth Bernadete (Chicago, IL: University of Chicago Press, 2001), p. 19.

100 DeVun, "The Jesus Hermaphrodite," p. 196.

101 DeVun, "The Jesus Hermaphrodite," p. 197.

102 Laqueur, *Making Sex*, esp. p. 135.

103 In Miri Rubin, "The Person in the Form: Medieval Challenges to Bodily 'Order.'" In *Framing Medieval Bodies*, ed. Sarah Kay and Miri Rubin (Manchester: Manchester University Press, 1994), pp. 100–22; p. 102.

104 See also Cary J. Nederman and Jacqui True, "The Third Sex: The Idea of the Hermaphrodite in Twelfth-Century Europe," *Journal of the History of Sexuality* 6 (1996): 497–517.

105 Alice Dreger, *Hermaphrodites and the Medical Invention of Sex* (Cambridge, MA: Harvard University Press, 1998), p. 6.

106 John Trevisa, *On the Properties of Things: John Trevisa's Translation of Bartholomaeus Anglicus De proprietatibus rerum*, ed. M. C. Seymour, 3 vols (Oxford: Clarendon, 1975–88), 1:196. Bartholomeus Anglicus (before 1203–1272 CE) was a Scholastic scholar and member of the Franciscan order who authored the compendium *De proprietatibus rerum* (*On the Properties of Things*, ca. 1240), a heavily annotated 19-volume work covering the entirety of heaven and earth. John of Trevisa (ca. 1342–1402) was a Cornishman educated at Exeter College, generally considered the greatest translator of his time.

107 Jacobus de Voragine, *The Golden Legend: Readings on the Saints*, trans. William Granger Ryan, 2 vols (Princeton, NJ: Princeton University Press, 1993), 1:349.

108 Anne Rosalind Jones and Peter Stallybrass, "Fetishizing Gender: Constructing the Hermaphrodite in Renaissance Europe," in *Body Guards: The Cultural Politics of Gender Ambiguity*, ed. Julia Epstein and Kristina Staub (London: Routledge, 1991), 81.

109 Rubin, "The Person in the Form," p. 101.

110 Henry de Bracton, *Bracton on the Law and Customs of England*, ed. George E. Woodbine, trans. Samuel E. Thorne (Cambridge: Harvard University Press, 1968), sec. 2:31. See also http://bracton.law.harvard.edu/Unframed/English/v2/32.htm.

111 Rubin, "The Person in the Form," p. 104.

112 Dreger, *Hermaphrodites*, p. 33.

113 DeVun, "The Jesus Hermaphrodite," p. 197. Also see Pseudo-Albertus Magnus, *Women's Secrets: A Translation of Pseudo-Albertus Magnus's De Secretis Mulierum With Commentaries*, ed. Helen Rodnite Lemay (Albany, NY: State University of New York Press, 1992), esp. pp. 116–7.

114 Bettina Bildhauer and Robert Mills, "Introduction: Conceptualizing the Monstrous." In *The Monstrous Middle Ages*, ed. Bildhauer and Mills (Toronto: University of Toronto Press, 2003), pp. 1–27; pp. 20 and 22.

115 David Williams, *Deformed Discourse: The Function of the Monster in Medieval Thought and Literature* (Montreal: Mcgill Queens University Press, 2002), p. 108.

116 John Block Friedman, *The Monstrous Races in Medieval Art and Thought* (Syracuse, NY: Syracuse University Press, 2000), p. 30.

117 Dana Oswald, *Monsters, Gender, and Sexuality in Medieval English Literature* (Woodbridge, Suffolk: D. S. Brewer, 2010), p. 12.
118 Homi K. Bhabha, *The Location of Culture* (London: Routledge, 2004), p. 121.
119 Jacques Gélis, *History of Childbirth: Fertility, Pregnancy, and Birth in Early Modern Europe*, trans. Rosemary Morris (Boston, MA: Northeastern University Press, 1991), p. 259.
120 Sarah Alison Miller, *Medieval Monstrosity and the Female Body* (New York: Routledge, 2010), p. 87. Citing Commentator B, speaking about Aristotle's *Generation of Animals*.
121 Miller, *Medieval Monstrosity*, p. 87.
122 See sections 57, 60, and 62.
123 See Jeffrey Jerome Cohen (ed.), "Monster Culture." In *Monster Theory: Reading Culture* (Minneapolis, MN: University of Minnesota Press, 1996), pp. 3–25 as well as Oswald and Miller.
124 Rubin, "The Person in the Form," p. 110.
125 Misty Urban suggests that female monsters create a new "thirdspace," in which the constructiveness of patriarchal society is exposed primarily through the establishment of woman as absolute Other. See Misty Urban, *Monstrous Women in Middle English Romance: Representations of Mysterious Female Power* (Lewiston, NY: The Edwin Mellen Press, 2010).

Chapter 4

1 Joan Cadden, "Western Medicine and Natural Philosophy." In *Handbook of Medieval Sexuality*, ed. Vern L. Bullough and James A. Brundage (New York: Garland, 1996), pp. 51–80; p. 62.
2 Joyce E. Salisbury, "Gendered Sexuality." In *Handbook of Medieval Sexuality*, ed. Bullough and Brundage, pp. 81–102; p. 84.
3 Karma Lochrie, *Covert Operations: The Medieval Uses of Secrecy* (Philadelphia, PA: University of Pennsylvania Press, 1999), p. 182.
4 Salisbury, "Gendered Sexuality," p. 85.
5 Jeffrey Jerome Cohen and Bonnie Wheeler (eds), "Becoming and Unbecoming." In *Becoming Male in the Middle Ages* (New York/London: Routledge, 1997), pp. vii–xx; p. xiii.
6 Michael Uebel, "On Becoming Male." In *Becoming Male in the Middle Ages*, ed. Cohen and Wheeler, pp. 367–84; p. 378.
7 Vern Bullough, "On Being Male." In *Medieval Masculinities*, ed. Clare A. Lees; Ruth Mazo Karras, *From Boys to Men: Formations of Masculinity in Late Medieval Europe* (Philadelphia, PA: University of Pennsylvania Press, 2003), pp. 31–46; pp. 40–1.

8 Maureen C. Miller, "Masculinity, Reform, and Clerical Culture: Narratives of Episcopal Holiness in the Gregorian Era," *Church History* 72 (2003): 25–52, p. 50.

9 Jo Ann McNamara, "The *Herrenfrage*: The Restructuring of the Gender System, 1050–1150." In *Medieval Masculinities: Regarding Men in the Middle Ages*, ed. Clare A. Lees, Thelma Fenster, and Jo Ann McNamara (Minneapolis, MN: University of Minnesota Press, 1994), pp. 3–29; p. 20.

10 See Maureen C. Miller, "Masculinity, Reform, and Clerical Culture: Narratives of Episcopal Holiness in the Gregorian Era," *Church History* 72 (2003): 25–52.

11 Lynda L. Coon, *Dark Age Bodies: Gender and Monastic Practice in the Early Medieval West* (Philadelphia, PA: University of Pennsylvania Press, 2011), esp. pp. 2–11 and 8–96.

12 See Conrad Leyser, "Masculinity in Flux: Nocturnal Emissions and the Limits of Celibacy in the Middle Ages." In *Masculinity in Medieval Europe*, ed. Dawn M. Hadley (New York: Addison Wesley, 1998), pp. 103–19.

13 Jacqueline Murray, "Masculinizing Religious Life: Sexual Prowess, and Battle for Chastity and Monastic Identity." In *Holiness and Masculinity in the Middle Ages*, ed. P. H. Cullum and Katherine J. Lewis (Cardiff: University of Wales Press, 2004), pp. 24–42; p. 27.

14 See Megan McLaughlin, "Secular and Spiritual Fatherhood in the Eleventh Century." In *Conflicted Identities and Multiple Masculinities: Men in the Medieval West*, ed. Jacqueline Murray (New York: Garland, 1999), pp. 25–43.

15 See Dyan Elliott, "Pollution, Illusion, and Masculine Disarray: Nocturnal Emissions and the Sexuality of the Clergy." In *Constructing Medieval Sexuality*, ed. Karma Lochrie, Peggy McCracken, and James A. Schultz (Minneapolis, MN: University of Minnesota Press, 1997), pp. 1–23.

16 See François Piponnier and Perrine Mane, *Dress in the Middle Ages*, trans. Caroline Beamish (New Haven, CT: Yale University Press, 1997).

17 Jennifer D. Thibodeaux, "Man of the Church, or Man of the Village? Gender and the Parish Clergy in Medieval Normandy," *Gender & History* 18.2 (2006): 380–99; p. 395.

18 See Natalie Zemon Davis, "Women on Top: Symbolic Sexual Inversion and Political Disorder in Early Modern Europe." In *The Reversible World: Symbolic Inversion in Art and Society*, ed. Barbara A. Babock (Ithaca, NY: Cornell University Press, 1978), pp. 147–90.

19 See Fiona Harris Stoertz, "Young Women in France and England, 1050–1300," *Journal of Women's History* 12.4 (2001): 22–46.

20 See Ann W. Astell, *The Song of Songs in the Middle Ages* (Ithaca, NY: Cornell University Press, 1990) and Denys Turner, *Eros and Allegory: Medieval Exegesis of the Song of Songs* (Kalamazoo, MI: Cistercian Publications, 1995).

21 See *Listen, Daughter: The Speculum Virginum and the Formation of Religious Women in the Middle Ages*, ed. Constant J. Mews (New York: Palgrave, 2001), which contains a translation of much of the *Speculum* by Barbara Newman in the Appendix as well as essays about the text and related lyrics.

22 See *Speculum Inclusorum/A Mirror for Recluses: A Late-Medieval Guide for Anchorites and its Middle English Translation*, ed. and trans. E. A. Jones (Liverpool: University of Liverpool Press, 2013).

23 Caroline Walker Bynum, *Holy Feast, Holy Fast: The Religious Significance of Food to Medieval Women* (Berkeley, CA: University of California Press, 1987), pp. 209–10.

24 See Geoffrey Galt Harpham, *The Ascetic Imperative in Culture and Criticism* (Chicago, IL: University of Chicago Press, 1986). He discusses sacrifice as the surrender of a desire, or "a denial of desire," and concludes that critics in the past focused too strongly on the denial aspect of asceticism and consequently ignored the importance of desire.

25 This was one of the major objections to the Beguine movement, since the women did not enjoy the "safety" of the convent.

26 In Elizabeth Makowski, *Canon Law and Cloistered Women: Periculoso and Its Commentators, 1298–1545* (Washington, DC: Catholic University Press, 1997), p. 135.

27 See Laura Wertheimer, "Children of Disorder: Clerical Parentage, Illegitimacy, and Reform in the Middle Ages," *Journal of the History of Sexuality* 15 (2006): 382–407; p. 393.

28 Ambrose, *On Virginity*, trans. Daniel Callam (Toronto: Pergrina, 1989), p. 22.

29 Jerome, Commentary on Ephesians, III ch. 5.

30 To be fair, they felt the same way about men who were married, too, although being superior and rational beings, men could overcome this failing more easily than women.

31 Thomas Aquinas, I Cor. ch.11, lectio 2.

32 For some unpacking of this complicated term, see Judith Bennett, "Queens, Whores and Maidens: Women in Chaucer's England." Hayes Robinson Lecture Series (Egham, Sussex: Royal Holloway, University of London, 2002), p. 22.

33 Ambrose, *Letter to Syagrius, Epistola 5, PL* 16. Cited in Kathleen Coyne Kelly, *Performing Virginity and Testing Chastity in the Middle Ages* (London: Routledge, 2000), p. 34.

34 Bennett, "Queens, Whores and Maidens," p. 24.

35 Margaret R. Miles, *Carnal Knowing: Female Nakedness and Religious Meaning in the Christian West* (Boston, MA: Beacon Press, 1989), p. 62.

36 Thomas J. Heffernan, in *Sacred Biography: Saints and Their Biographers in the Middle Ages* (Oxford: Oxford University Press, 1988), outlines the archetypal narrative structure of virgin martyr hagiographies; see pp. 265–75. See also Karen A. Winstead, *Virgin Martyrs: Legends of Sainthood in Late Medieval England* (Ithaca, NY: Cornell University Press, 1997), pp. 5–10.

37 Allen J. Frantzen, "When Women Aren't Enough," *Speculum* 68.2 (1993): 445–71; p. 462.

38 Julie E. Fromer, "Spectators of Martyrdom: Corporeality and Sexuality in the Liflade Ant Te Passiun of Seinte Margarete," *Intersections of Sexuality and the*

Divine in Medieval Culture, ed. Susannah Mary Chewning (Aldershot, VT: Ashgate, 2005), pp. 89–106; p. 90.

39 Ruth Mazo Karras, *From Boys to Men: Formations of Masculinity in Late Medieval Europe* (Philadelphia, PA: University of Pennsylvania Press, 2003), p. 10.

40 Judith Halberstam, *Female Masculinity* (Durham, NC: Duke University Press, 1998).

41 Carol Clover, "Regardless of Sex: Men, Women, and Power in Early Northern Europe," *Speculum* 68.2 (1993): 363–87.

42 See, among numerous other sources, James Marrow, *Passion Iconography in Northern European Art of the Late Middle Ages and Early Renaissance* (Kortrijk, Belgium: Van Ghemmert, 1979) and Martin O'Kane, "Picturing 'The Man of Sorrows': The Passion-Filled Afterlives of a Biblical Icon," *Religion and the Arts* 9.1–2 (2005): 62–100.

43 See Amy Hollywood, "'That glorious slit': Irigaray and the Medieval Devotion to Christ's Side Wound." In *Luce Irigaray and Premodern Culture: Thresholds of History*, ed. Theresa Krier and Elizabeth D. Harvey (New York: Routledge, 2004), pp. 105–25.

44 Clarissa W. Atkinson, *The Oldest Vocation: Christian Motherhood in the Middle Ages* (Ithaca, NY: Cornell University Press, 1991), pp. 238–9.

45 Caroline Walker Bynum, *Jesus as Mother: Studies in the Spirituality of the High Middle Ages* (Berkley: University of California Press, 1982), pp. 132–3, original emphasis.

46 Bynum, *Jesus as Mother*, p. 115.

47 In 1373, Julian almost died from a serious illness, during which she experienced mystical visions of Jesus on the cross and in glory. Immediately upon recovery, Julian dictated her visions in the version known traditionally as *The Short Text*. Later Julian revised this text, expanding the theological discussions, and this version is often called *The Long Text*. However, recent scholarship has suggested that the two texts are more deeply intertwined than "short" and "long" imply, preferring instead *A Vision Showed to a Devout Woman* (the short text) and *A Revelation of Love* (the long text). See *The Writings of Julian of Norwich: A Vision Showed to a Devout Woman and a Revelation of Love*, ed. Nicholas Watson and Jacqueline Jenkins (University Park, PA: Pennsylvania State University Press, 2006).

48 Valerie M. Lagorio, "Variations on the Theme of God's Motherhood in Medieval English Mystical and Devotional Writings," *Studia Mystica* 8 (1985): 15–37.

49 Barbara Newman, *Sister of Wisdom: St Hildegard's Theology of the Feminine* (Berkeley, CA: University of California Press, 1998), esp. p. 35. "Chosenness" traditionally refers to the idea of the Jews as God's chosen people.

50 See Michelle M. Sauer, "Divine Orgasm and Self-Blazoning: The Fragmented Body of the Female Medieval Visionary." In *Sexuality, Sociality and Cosmology in Medieval Literary Texts*, ed. Jennifer N. Brown and Marla Segol (New York: Palgrave, 2013), pp. 123–43.

51 See John Bugge, *Virginitas: An Essay in the History of a Medieval Ideal* (The Hague: Martinus Nijhoff, 1975). Bugge discusses the concept of the *sponsa* Christi as one that transcends gender, tracing it back to the Gnostic Gospels where it indicated a nonsexual union between human and divine, and where either gender could temporarily assume the posture of the other for purposes of this union.

52 Sermon 7.2. See Bernard of Clairvaux, *Sermons on the Song of Songs*. In four volumes: Cistercian Fathers Series nos 4, 7, 31, 40. Trans. Killian Walsh (Kalamazoo, MI: Cistercian Publications, 1971).

53 Judith M. Bennett and Ruth Mazo Karras (eds), "Women, Gender, and Medieval Historians." In *The Oxford Handbook of Women and Gender in Medieval Europe* (Oxford: Oxford University Press, 2013), pp. 1–17; p. 9.

54 See Michel Foucault, *A History of Sexuality: An Introduction* (New York: Pantheon, 1978).

55 See Dyan Elliott, "The Three Ages of Joan Scott," *American Historical Review* 113 (2008): 1390–403.

56 Jo Ann McNamara, *Sisters in Arms: Catholic Nuns through Two Millennia* (Cambridge, MA: Harvard University Press, 1996), p. 144.

57 Jacqueline Murray, "One Flesh, Two Sexes, Three Genders?" In *Gender and Christianity in Medieval Europe: New Perspectives*, ed. Lisa M. Bitel and Felice Lifshitz (Philadelphia, PA: University of Pennsylvania Press, 2008), pp. 34–51; p. 49.

58 Sarah Salih, *Versions of Virginity in Late Medieval England* (Cambridge: D. S. Brewer, 2001), p. 24.

59 Stacey Schlau, "Following Saint Teresa: Early Modern Women and Religious Authority," *Modern Language Notes* 117 (2002): 286–309; p. 288.

60 Tertullian, *De virginibus velandis*, sections 3.5 and 7.1. In *Sarah Alison Miller, Medieval Monstrosity and the Female Body* (New York/London: Routledge, 2010), pp. 64–5.

61 P. H. Cullum, "Clergy, Masculinity and Transgression in Late Medieval England." In *Masculinity in Medieval Europe*, ed. D. M. Hadley (Boston, MA: Addison Wesley Longman, 1999), pp. 178–96.

62 R. N. Swanson, "Angels Incarnate: Clergy and Masculinity from Gregorian Reform to Reformation," in *Masculinity in Medieval Europe*, p. 160.

63 Ruth Mazo Karras, "Thomas Aquinas's Chastity Belt: Masculinity in Medieval Europe," *Gender and Christianity in Medieval Europe*, ed. Bitel and Lifshitz, pp. 52–67; p. 53.

64 Bennett and Karras, "Women, Gender, and Medieval Historians," p. 2.

Chapter 5

1 Judith M. Bennett, Elizabeth A. Clark, Jean F. O'Barr, B. Anne Vilen, and Sarah Westphal-Wihl (eds), "Introduction." In *Sisters and Workers in the Middle Ages* (Chicago: University of Chicago Press, 1989), pp. 1–10; p. 2.

2 See Barbara A. Hanawalt, *The Wealth of Wives: Women, Law, and Economy in Late Medieval London* (Oxford: Oxford University Press, 2007), p. 161ff.
3 See Theresa Earenfight (ed.), "Introduction." In *Women, Wealth, and Power in Medieval Europe* (New York: Palgrave, 2010), pp. 1–12; p. 2.
4 Christopher Cannon, "The Rights of Medieval English Women: Crime and the Issue of Representation." In *Medieval Crime and Social Control*, ed. Barbara A. Hanawalt and David Wallace (Minneapolis, MN: University of Minnesota Press, 1999), pp. 156–85; p. 179, emphasis his. He goes on to propose that women often transformed "disadvantage into an opportunity."
5 See, among others, Frances Gies and Joseph Gies, *Women in the Middle Ages* (New York: Barnes & Noble, 1978).
6 Diane Bornstein, *The Lady in the Tower: Medieval Courtesy Literature for Women* (Hamden, CT: Archon Books, 1983), esp. p. 96.
7 Carol Adams, Paula Bartley, Hilary Bourdillon, and Cathy Loxton, *From Workshop to Warfare: The Lives of Medieval Women* (Cambridge: Cambridge University Press, 1983), p. 5.
8 In Bornstein, *The Lady in the Tower*, pp. 105–7.
9 See Derek G. Neal, *The Masculine Self in Late Medieval England* (Chicago: University of Chicago Press, 2008), esp. pp. 7–8.
10 See *The Paston Letters: A Selection in Modern Spelling*, ed. Norman Davis (Oxford: Oxford University Press, 2009).
11 See Barbara A. Hanawalt, *Women and Work in Preindustrial Europe* (Bloomington, IN: Indiana University Press, 1986), esp. pp. 148–55.
12 Stephen A. Epstein, *Wage, Labor, and Guilds in Medieval Europe* (Chapel Hill, NC and London: University of North Carolina Press, 1991), p. 118. He goes on to note that discrepancies existed across the board. For instance, a master mason could earn the yearly income of a woman in 25 days or less, and male dyers could make more than double what a female dyer did.
13 In Judith M. Bennett, *Ale, Beer, and Brewsters in England: Women's Work in a Changing World, 1300–1600* (New York: Oxford University Press, 1996), p. 145; from Thirsk's presentation "Women's Initiatives in Early Modern England: Where are They?" June 4, 1999.
14 Although the office of abbess was supposed to be an elected one, in reality abbesses were often nominated by founders or wealthy donors, invited from other monasteries, or even ensconced as children. Such practices dominated through the twelfth century, and continued throughout the Middle Ages depending on external politics.
15 See Gary Macy, *The Hidden History of Women's Ordination: Female Clergy in the Medieval West* (Oxford: Oxford University Press, 2007), esp. pp. 80–6.
16 See Martha C. Howell, "Citizenship and Gender: The Problem of Women's Political Status in Late Medieval Cities of Northern Europe." In *Women and Power in the Middle Ages*, ed. Mary Erler and Maryanne Kowaleski (Athens, GA: University of Georgia Press, 1987), pp. 37–60. The cities under review are Bruges, Leiden, Lille, Cologne, and Frankfurt.

17 This practice continued past the Reformation, with Martin Luther explaining that it was just to exclude women from participation in government as retribution for their complicity in Original Sin.
18 Howell, "Citizenship and Gender," p. 38.
19 Ruth Mazo Karras, *From Boys to Men: Formations of Masculinity in the Later Middle Ages* (Philadelphia, PA: University of Pennsylvania Press, 2003), p. 109.
20 Neal, *The Masculine Self*, p. 7.
21 Lois Huneycutt, "Medieval Queenship," *History Today* 39.6 (1989): 16–22; p. 22.
22 At this time, Sweden included what is now Finland, and Norway also encompassed its exterior dependencies—Iceland, Greenland, and the Faroe Islands.
23 The Giudicati (judgeships) were the indigenous kingdoms of Sardinia ca. 900–1420 CE, after which time they were all absorbed into the Crown of Aragon. The rulers of each region were titled *giudici* or *giudicessa* ["judge"].
24 See *Queens and Queenship in Medieval Europe*, ed. Anne J. Duggan (Woodbridge, Suffolk: Boydell Press, 1997); William Layher, *Queenship and Voice in Medieval Northern Europe* (New York: Palgrave, 2010); *Queens and Power in Medieval and Early Modern England*, ed. Carole Levin and Robert Bucholz (Lincoln, NE: University of Nebraska Press, 2009); Lois L. Huneycutt, *Matilda of Scotland: A Study in Medieval Queenship* (London: Boydell Press, 2003); Maria Paula Marçal Lourenço, "The Household of Portuguese Queens in Modern Times: Patronage and Powers," *Mediterranean Studies* 14 (2005): 17–26.
25 Theresa Earenfight, "Without the Persona of the Prince: Kings, Queens and the Idea of Monarchy in Late Medieval Europe," *Gender and History* 19.1 (2007): 1–21; p. 1.
26 Earenfight, "Without the Persona of the Prince," p. 8.
27 A. Lynn Martin, "The Role of Drinking in the Male Construction of Unruly Women." In *Medieval Sexuality: A Casebook*, ed. April Harper and Caroline Proctor (New York/London: Routledge, 2008), pp. 98–112; p. 98.
28 A *brewster* is a female brewer, with *-ster* being the feminine ending for professions (e.g. *spinster*). The gender distinction held until 1500 CE or so, when *brewer* became the term for a beer maker of either biological sex. See the entry for *brewster* in the *Oxford English Dictionary* for reference.
29 Elizabeth Ewan, "'For Whatever Ales Ye': Women as Producers in Late Medieval Scottish Towns," in *Women in Scotland, c. 1100–c. 1750*, ed. Elizabeth Ewan and Maureen M. Meikle (East Linton, Scotland: Tuckwell Press, 1999), pp. 125–35; p. 130. Ewan specifically discusses Scotland, but the principle still applies to English brewsters. Scottish brewing regulations were slightly different than English, especially with their (mostly failed) attempts to restrict the craft to the burgess rank, but also in the establishment of guilds and ordinances. Besides Ewan, see also Nicholas Mayhew, "The Status of Women and the Brewing of Ale in Medieval Aberdeen," *Review of Scottish Culture* 10 (1997): 16–21.

30 See Richard W. Unger, *Beer in the Middle Ages and the Renaissance* (Philadelphia, PA: University of Pennsylvania Press, 2004), esp. pp. 11–3.
31 Bennett, *Ale, Beer, and Brewsters*, p. 9.
32 The first recorded instance of European hops (*Humulus lupulus*) cultivation dates to 736 CE in Bavaria, although they were apparently not used in beer brewing until 1079. Hops are a perennial plant of the *Cannabaceae* family, and in the premodern world also had several medical uses, primarily as a sleep-aid or calming agent, similar to valerian. For a good introduction to the subject in relation to England, see George Clinch, *English Hops: A History of Cultivation and Preparation for the Market from the Earliest Times* (London: McCorquodale, 1919).
33 Bennett, *Ale, Beer, and Brewsters*, pp. 88–9.
34 See Bennett, *Ale, Beer, and Brewsters*, pp. 92–5.
35 Hanawalt, *The Wealth of Wives*, p. 181.
36 See *The Book of Vices and Virtues* (fourteenth century), *Dives and Pauper* (ca. 1405–10 CE), *Ayenbite of Inwit* or *The Pricke of Conscience* (mid-fourteenth century), *Jacob's Well* (early fifteenth century), and *Handlyng Synne* (early fourteenth century), all of which have ties to *La Somme le roi* a moral compendium assembled in 1279 CE by the Dominican Friar Laurent for King Philip III of France (r. 1270–85 CE).
37 Martin, "The Role of Drinking," p. 106. See also A. Lynn Martin, *Alcohol, Sex, and Gender in Late Medieval and Early Modern Europe* (Basingstoke: Palgrave, 2001).
38 Hanawalt, *The Wealth of Wives*, p. 194. See also Barbara A. Hanawalt, "The Host, the Law, and the Ambiguous Space of Medieval London Taverns." In *Medieval Crime and Social Control*, ed. Barbara A. Hanawalt and David Wallace (Minneapolis, MN: University of Minnesota Press, 1998), pp. 204–23.
39 Bennett, *Ale, Beer, and Brewsters*, p. 128.
40 James Davis notes that the existence of Alianora recorded in Leatherhead in 1525 "lends a veneer of authenticity to Skelton's misogynistic satire." See *Medieval Market Morality: Life, Law and Ethics in the English Marketplace, 1200–1500* (Cambridge: Cambridge University Press, 2012), n. 337, pp. 109–10.
41 Steven Earnshaw, *The Pub in Literature: England's Altered State* (Manchester: Manchester University Press, 2000), p. 25.
42 Miriam Gill, "Reading Images: Church Murals and Collaboration between Media in Medieval England." In *Collaboration in the Arts from the Middle Ages to the Present*, ed. Silvia Bigliazzi and Sharon Wood (Burlington, VT: Ashgate, 2006), pp. 17–32; pp. 27–8.
43 Holy Trinity Church, Coventry, is located in Coventry City Centre, West Midlands, England. It dates to the twelfth century, and the Doom wall painting was restored in 2002. The official site is found at http://www.holytrinitycoventry.org.uk/Groups/170794/Holy_Trinity_Church/Our_History/Our_History.aspx.
44 Gill, "Reading Images," p. 28.

45 This standard image was found as early as the Holkham Bible Picture Book (London: British Library, MS ADD 47682), an early fourteenth-century (ca. 1320–30 CE) bible supplement. See W. O. Hassall, *The Holkham Bible Picture Book* (London: Dropmore Press, 1954), fol. 42v.

46 Juanita Ballew Wood, *Wooden Images: Misericords and Medieval England* (Cranbury, NJ: Associated University Presses, 1999), p. 44. Wood also notes that the demon in this carving is playing the bagpipes, which were specifically thought to arouse animal passions in people.

47 Bennett, *Ale, Beer, and Brewsters*, p. 128.

48 See Peter Clark, *The English Alehouse: A Social History, 1200–1830* (London/New York: Longman, 1983); Beat Kümin and Ann B. Tlusty, *The World of the Tavern: The Public House in Early Modern Europe* (Aldershot, VT: Ashgate, 2002); Lynn A. Martin, *Alcohol, Sex, and Gender in Late Medieval and Early Modern Europe* (Basingstoke: Palgrave, 2001).

49 The word "guild" derives from the Old English words *gegyld* "guild" and *gild*, *gyld* "payment, tribute, compensation." The guilds both required an entrance fee and recurring membership payments, and also regulated production and payments received; thus, the blending of words is quite appropriate.

50 There were other types of guilds as well, more social in nature, such as drinking groups and parish collectives. However, the Merchant Guilds and Craft Guilds were the only ones who had such an enormous impact on economics and politics and large memberships.

51 One notable exception to this was two female members of the powerful merchants of the Staple in the fifteenth century, as discussed by Kay. E. Lacey, "Women and Work in Fourteenth and Fifteenth Century London." In *Women and Work in Preindustrial England*, ed. Lindsey Charles and Lorna Duffin (London: Croom Helm, 1985), pp. 24–83. For a more typical perspective, see P. J. P. Goldberg, "Female Labour, Service, and Marriage in the Late Medieval Urban North," *Northern History* 22 (1986): 18–38, esp. pp. 31–3, and Shulamith Shahar, *The Fourth Estate: A History of Women in the Middle Ages*, trans. Chaya Galai (London: Metheun, 1983), esp. pp. 192–8.

52 Eleanora Carus-Wilson called this period the "Industrial Revolution of the Middle Ages" (see especially "An Industrial Revolution of the Thirteenth Century," *Economic History Review* 11 [1941]: 39–60), while Richard H. Britnell merely refers to this as "commercialization." See *The Commercialization of English Society, 1000–1500* (Cambridge: Cambridge University Press, 1993). In either case, in England, the period extends from the close of the Anglo-Norman period through the beginnings of early modern society.

53 Sylvia Thrupp, *The Merchant Class of Medieval London 1300–1500* (Chicago: University of Chicago Press, 1989), esp. p. 19. Rpt. University of Michigan Press, 1948.

54 For a solid overview of religious activities of guilds, see Gary Richardson, "Craft Guilds and Christianity in Late-Medieval England: A Rational-Choice Analysis," *Rationality and Society* 17.2 (2005): 139–89.

55 See Maryanne Kowaleski and Judith M. Bennett, "Crafts, Gilds, and Women in the Middle Ages: Fifty Years After Marian K. Dale." In *Sisters and Workers in the Middle Ages*, ed. Bennett et al., pp. 11–25.
56 See Simone Roux, *Paris in the Middle Ages*, trans. Jo Ann McNamara (Philadelphia, PA: University of Pennsylvania Press, 2009).
57 See for example, Martin Raiser, "Informal Institutions, Social Capital and Economic Transition." In *Transition and Institutions: The Experience of Gradual and Late Reformers*, ed. Giovanni Andrea Cornia and Vladimir Popov (Oxford: Oxford University Press, 2001), pp. 218–39.
58 See especially Sheilagh Ogilvie, *A Bitter Living: Women, Markets, and Social Capital in Early Modern Germany* (Oxford: Oxford University Press, 2003). Although this book addresses Germany, the concept of limiting participation of women due to patriarchal fears of relinquishing power is fairly universal.
59 Epstein, *Wage, Labor, and Guilds in Medieval Europe*, p. 122.
60 Epstein, *Wage, Labor, and Guilds in Medieval Europe*, p. 122.
61 Karras, *From Boys to Men*, esp. pp. 148–51.
62 Elasticity is an economic term meaning changes in the quantity supplied have little effect on the price of the product. In elastic markets, sellers maximize profits by expanding output until the costs of manufacture rise to the market price, whereupon the cycle begins again with a price change.
63 See Hanawalt, *The Wealth of Wives*, p. 176. The rebellious apprentices were not confined to any particular type of guild.
64 Kowaleski and Bennett, "Crafts, Gilds, and Women," p. 16.
65 For more information on women and the guild system in early modern society, see Clare Crowston, "Women, Gender and Guilds in Early Modern Europe: An Overview of Recent Research," *International Review of Social History* 53 (2008): 34–9; S. D. Smith, "Women's Admission to Guilds in Early-Modern England: The Case of the York Merchant Tailor's Company, 1693–1776," *Gender & History* 17 (2005): 99–126.
66 See Teresa Earenfight, "Introduction," *Women, Wealth, and Power*, pp. 1–12; Victoria de Grazia and Ellen Furlough, *The Sex of Things: Gender and Consumption in Historical Perspective* (Berkeley, CA: University of California Press, 1996).
67 Monica H. Green, "Women's Medical Practice and Health Care in Medieval Europe." In *Sisters and Workers in the Middle Ages*, ed. Bennett et al., pp. 39–78; p. 41. Originally in *Signs* 14.2 (1989): 434–73.
68 See Carole Rawcliffe, *Medicine and Society in Later Medieval England* (Stroud: Sutton, 1995), ch. 9.
69 Muriel Joy Hughes, *Women Healers in Medieval Life and Literature* (New York: King's Crown Press, 1943), p. 110.
70 See Frances Gies and Joseph Gies, *Daily Life in Medieval Times* (New York: Black Dog Laventhal Publishers, 1990), esp. p. 258, and Hughes, *Women Healers*, p. 122. Hildegard of Bingen also accepted the widely held beliefs about the healing properties of certain stones.

71 This was likely due to the widespread belief that witches roasted and ate the flesh of newborn infants and made candles from the fat of unbaptized children. The *Malleus Maleficarum* (*Hammer of Witches*) is the most famous and influential text about identifying and prosecuting witches. It was written in 1486 CE by two German Dominican friars, Heinrich Kramer and James Sprenger. It became the standard witch-hunt manual, used by Protestants and Catholics alike, for 300 years.

72 See Robin Briggs, *Witches and Neighbors* (New York: Penguin, 1998), esp. pp. 77–9; Thomas R. Forbes, "Midwifery and Witchcraft," *Journal of History of Medicine* 16 (1962): 264–82; David Harley, "Historians as Demonologists: The Myth of the Midwife Witch," *Journal of the Society for the Social History of Medicine* 3 (1990): 1–26.

73 Cupping therapy relies upon creating a local suction to mobilize blood flow in order to promote healing. Small "cups," usually made of glass or bone, are placed on the skin for a period of time to create a suction lock. Sometimes this is followed with a small incision to the cupped skin and the removal of a minor amount of blood. Cupping was written about by Hippocrates and known to Galen. Although it fell out of wide use in Western medicine, it was not completely forgotten, and made a resurgence in the early twentieth century.

74 In England, barbers and surgeons originally had separate guilds, but these were merged in 1540 by Henry VIII into The Company of the Barber-Surgeons of London. See J. O. Robinson, "The Barber-Surgeons of London," *Archives of Surgery* 119.10 (1984): 1171–5.

75 Because they also sold spices, herbs, and roots, the apothecaries, along with spicers and pepperers, originally fell under the jurisdiction of the Grocers' guilds across Europe. For instance, in Barcelona, apothecaries identified themselves as sellers of rare goods and only later as medical professionals. See Michael R. McVaugh, *Medicine before the Plague: Practitioners and Their Patients in the Crown of Aragon, 1285–1345* (Cambridge: Cambridge University Press, 1993), esp. 116–23. In England, a separate Society of Apothecaries was finally established in 1617. There are few sources dedicated to the history of the English apothecary practice. For some background, see Juanita G. L. Burnby, *A Study of the English Apothecary from 1660–1760* (London: Wellcome Trust Centre, 1983).

76 Rawcliffe, *Medicine and Society*, pp. 187–90.

77 Nancy G. Siraisi, *Medieval and Early Renaissance Medicine* (Chicago: University of Chicago Press, 1990), p. 27.

78 Siraisi, *Medieval and Early Renaissance Medicine*, p. 19.

79 The *Scuola Medica Salernitana*, which many scholars believe holds the distinction of being the first medical school of the Western world, was the most prestigious medieval school of the time. Women were both permitted to study there and to teach there. It featured a very progressive curriculum that fused European (based on Greek and Roman traditions), Islamic, and Jewish approaches. See Victor A. Ferraris and Zoë Alaina Ferraris, "The Women of Salerno: Contribution to the Origins of Surgery from Medieval Italy," *The Annals of Thoracic Surgery* 64.6 (1997): 1855–7.

80 Hughes notes that an attempt by the university in 1220 to prohibit all but the bachelors among the faculty to practice medicine was considered so unreasonable that men and women alike ignored it, and women were regularly registered during Paris censuses. See Hughes, *Women Healers in Medieval Life and Literature*, pp. 83–4.

81 Siraisi, *Medieval and Early Renaissance Medicine*, p. 27.

82 In the United States, the first medical school opened at the University of Pennsylvania in 1765, but did not admit its first female student, Elizabeth Blackwell, until 1847. The American Medical Association was founded the same year and accepted its first female member in 1876, but did not elect a female board member until 1989. By the end of the nineteenth century, 5 percent of American physicians were women; in 1949, 5.5 percent; in 1974, 22 percent, and by the close of the twentieth century, 46 percent. In England, the first openly female doctor was Elizabeth Garrett Anderson who, after being refused admittance to all British universities, graduated with a medical degree from the University of Sorbonne, Paris in 1870. In 1873, she became a member of the British Medical Association. Finally, in 1876, an act was passed that allowed women to study medicine. Interestingly enough, however, the first woman in Britain to graduate as a medical doctor was Margaret Ann Bulkley. She graduated in 1812 from Edinburgh University; however, she did so by cross-dressing as a man, and living as her alter ego, James Barry, for more than 50 years.

83 See the following by Monica H. Green: "In Search of an 'Authentic' Women's Medicine: The Strange Fates of Trota of Salerno and Hildegard of Bingen," *Dynamis: Acta Hispanica ad Medicinae Scientiarumque Historiam Illustrandam* 19 (1999): 25–54; "Reconstructing the Oeuvre of Trota of Salerno," in *La Scuola medica Salernitana: Gli autori e i testi*, ed. Danielle Jacquart and Agostino Paravicini Bagliani (Florence: SISMEL/Edizioni del Galluzzo, 2007), pp. 183–233; *Making Women's Medicine Masculine: The Rise of Male Authority in Premodern Gynaecology* (Oxford: Oxford University Press, 2008), esp. ch. 1, 5, and 6.

84 "The Wife of Bath's Prologue," ll. 669–85; l. 677. For a discussion thereof, see Lorrayne Y. Baird-Lange, "Trotula's Fourteenth-Century Reputation, Jankyn's Book, and Chaucer's Trot," *Studies in the Age of Chaucer* (1985): 245–56.

85 Jutta was born Countess Jutta von Sponheim, the youngest daughter of Count Stephen of Sponheim. She became an anchoress at an early age, and tutored a number of female pupils from wealthy families who lived with her in her anchorhold. Jutta practiced strict asceticism and enforced it on her pupils as much as possible, although Hildegard herself later urged moderation in such matters.

86 There are numerous books and articles about Hildegard of Bingen. To name a few that concern her ideas about medicine and the female body: Joan Cadden, "It Takes All Kinds: Sexuality and Gender Differences in Hildegard of Bingen's 'Book of Compound Medicine,'" *Traditio* 40 (1984): 149–74; Timothy P. Daaleman, "The Medical World of Hildegard of Bingen," *American Benedictine Review* 44.3 (1993): 280–9; Florence Eliza Glaze, "Medical Writer: 'Behold the Human Creature.'" In *Voice of the Living*

Light: Hildegard of Bingen and Her World, ed. Barbara Newman (Berkeley, CA: University of California Press, 1998), pp. 125–48; Barbara Newman, *Sister of Wisdom: St. Hildegard's Theology of the Feminine* (Berkeley, CA: University of California Press, 1987); Victoria Sweet, "Hildegard of Bingen and the Greening of Medieval Medicine," *Bulletin of the History of Medicine* 73.3 (1999): 381–403, and Victoria Sweet, *Rooted in the Earth, Rooted in the Sky: Hildegard of Bingen and Premodern Medicine* (New York: Routledge, 2006). For an accessible translation, see *Hildegard von Bingen's Physica: The Complete English Translation of Her Classic Work on Health and Healing*, trans. Priscilla Throop (Rochester, VT: Healing Arts Press, 1998). The actual texts of the works are difficult for nonscholars to read, but the most usable editions include: Hildegard von Bingen, *Physica: Liber subtilitatum diversarum naturarum creaturarum*, ed. Reiner Hildebrandt and Thomas Gloning (Berlin: Walter de Gruyter, 2010), and *Beate Hildegardis Cause Et Cure*, ed. Laurence Moulinier and Rainer Berndt (Berlin: Akademie Verlag, 2003).

87 The *Physica* consists of nine sections, the first of which records more than 200 plants, followed by books devoted to the elements, trees, precious stones, fish, birds, mammals, reptiles, and metals, as well as the medicinal uses of all of these, including recipes. The *Causae et Curae* consists of five sections covering cosmology, cosmography, and humanity, along with theory about the four humors, followed by a list of some two hundred diseases and conditions, two sections with cures for various ailments, and, finally, a section on "diagnostic" tools, such as uroscopy and astrology.

88 For an overview of Hildegard in contemporary cultural context, including the reception of her ideas, see *A Companion to Hildegard of Bingen*, ed. Beverly Mayne Kienzle, Debra L. Stoudt, and George Ferzoco (Leiden: Brill, 2013).

89 For further reading on Jewish medieval medicine, see Susan L. Einbinder, "Theory and Practice: A Jewish Physician in Paris and Avignon," *Association for Jewish Studies Review* 33.1 (2009): 135–53; Harry Friedenwald, *The Jews and Medicine: Essays*. 2 vols (Baltimore, MD: Johns Hopkins University Press, 1944), 1:146–80 and 217–20; 2:551–74 and 613–700; Peter Kay Jankrift, "Jews in Medieval European Medicine," trans. Frankie Sue Kann. In *The Jews of Europe in the Middle Ages (Tenth to Fifteenth Centuries)*, ed. Christoph Cluse (Turnhout, Belgium: Brepols, 2004), pp. 331–9; Cedi Roth, "The Qualification of Jewish Physicians in the Middle Ages," *Speculum* 28 (1953): 834–43.

90 Siraisi, *Medieval and Early Renaissance Medicine*, p. 31.

91 The Avignon Papacy was the period from 1309 to 1378 CE, during which seven successive popes resided in Avignon, France, rather than in Rome.

92 Anne Witz, *Professions and Patriarchy* (London: Routledge, 1992), p. 74.

93 Siraisi, *Medieval and Early Renaissance Medicine*, pp. 21–2.

94 M. Conner Verluysen, "Old Wives' Tales? Women Healers in English History." In *Rewriting Nursing History*, ed. Celia Davies (London: Croom, 1980), p. 194.

95 It is important to remember that medieval hospitals were also institutions of charity, where the needy could go for succor, rather than just establishments for healing the sick. In fact, they were an important part of the spiritual life of the Middle Ages, providing an outlet for charitable works and donations, much like the leprosaria. Hospitals themselves preserved both the symbolic and material link to the Church and religion, based on the idea that the body and the soul were closely connected and mutually influenced. Patients were often encouraged, or even required, to follow monastic patterns while recuperating. Even hospital architecture inspired religious devotion, with many built-in cross-shaped patterns, like churches, and decorated with religious artworks, wall paintings, windows, and statues.

96 See Jonathan Riley-Smith, *The Knights of St John in Jerusalem and Cyprus, c. 1050–1310* (London: St Martin's Press, 1967); Riley-Smith, "The Origins of the Commandery in the Temple and the Hospital." In *La commanderie: Institution des ordres militaires dans l'Occident médiéval*, ed. Anthony Luttrell and Léon Pressouyre (Paris: CTHS, 2002), pp. 9–18; *The Hospitallers' Riwle (Miracula et Regula Hospitalis Sancti Johannis Jerosolimitani)*, ed. Keith Val Sinclair (London: Anglo-Norman Text Society, 1984).

97 See Elizabeth M. Hallam, "Henry II as a Founder of Monasteries," *Journal of Ecclesiastical History* 28.2 (1977): 113–32.

98 In the canonical orders, the men lived as canons and the women dwelled separately as nuns, and they were dependent on male guidance and religious leadership.

99 Sharon K. Elkins, *Holy Women of Twelfth-Century England* (Chapel Hill, NC: University of North Carolina Press, 1988).

100 Myra Struckmeyer, "The Sisters of the Order of St John at Minchin Buckland." In *Hospitaller Women in the Middle Ages*, ed. Anthony Luttrell and Helen J. Nicholson (Aldershot, VT: Ashgate, 2006), pp. 89–112; p. 95.

101 Lay sisters were women who had a formal association with the Order of Saint John, but were not fully professed. Therefore, they had a lesser status in the Hospital and usually did not live in a commandery.

FURTHER READING

This is a short, not comprehensive, list of some of the major books a student of gender(ed) history might wish to consult. The notes within each chapter provide a more detailed list. For the most part, articles are excluded. Edited collections are cited as a single work.

Arnold, John and Sean Brady (eds) *What is Masculinity? Historical Dynamics from Antiquity to the Contemporary World* (Palgrave, 2011).
Atkinson, Clarissa. *Becoming Male in the Middle Ages.* Ed. Jeffrey Cohen and Bonnie Wheeler (Garland, 1997).
—. *The Oldest Vocation: Christian Motherhood in the Middle Ages* (Cornell University Press, 1991).
Bennett, Judith M. *Ale, Beer, and Brewsters in England: Women's Work in a Changing World, 1300–1600* (Oxford University Press, 1996).
—. "'Lesbian-Like' and the Social History of Lesbianisms." *Journal of the History of Sexuality* 9.1 (2000): 1–24.
Bennett, Judith and Amy M. Froide (eds) *Singlewomen in the European Past, 1250–1800* (University of Pennsylvania Press, 1998).
Bennett, Judith M., Elizabeth A. Clark, Jean F. O'Barr, B. Anne Vilen, and Sarah Westphal-Wihl (eds) *Sisters and Workers in the Middle Ages* (University of Chicago Press, 1989).
Bitel, Lisa. *Land of Women: Tales of Sex and Gender from Early Ireland* (Cornell University Press, 1996).
Børresen, Kari Elizabeth. *Subordinance and Equivalence: The Nature and Role of Woman in Augustine and Thomas Aquinas* (University Press of America, 1981).
Brooten, Bernadette J. *Love between Women: Early Christian Responses to Female Homoeroticism* (University of Chicago Press, 1996).
Brown, Peter. *The Body and Society: Men, Women, and Sexual Renunciation in Early Christianity* (Columbia University Press, 1988).
Brundage, James. *Law, Sex, and Christian Society in Medieval Europe* (University of Chicago Press, 1987).
Bullough, Vern L. and James A. Brundage (eds) *Handbook of Medieval Sexuality* (Garland, 1996).
—. (ed.) *Sexual Practices and the Medieval Church* (Prometheus Books, 1982).
Burger, Glenn and Steven F. Kruger (eds) *Queering the Middle Ages* (University of Minnesota Press, 2001).
Butler, Sara M. *Divorce in Medieval England: From One to Two Persons in Law* (Routledge, 2013).
Bynum, Caroline Walker. *Fragmentation and Redemption: Essays on Gender and the Human Body in Medieval Religion* (Zone, 1992).

—. *Holy Feast and Holy Fast: The Religious Significance of Food to Medieval Women* (University of California Press, 1987).
—. *Jesus as Mother: Studies in the Spirituality of the High Middle Ages* (University of California Press, 1984).
Cadden, Joan. *Meanings of Sex Difference in the Middle Ages: Medicine, Science, and Culture* (Cambridge University Press, 1995).
Cantarella, Eva. *Bisexuality in the Ancient World*. Trans. Cormac Ó Cuilleanáin (Yale University Press, 1992; Ital. org. 1988).
Dinshaw, Carolyn. *Chaucer's Sexual Poetics* (University of Wisconsin Press, 1989).
—. "A Kiss Is Just a Kiss: Heterosexuality and Its Consolations in *Sir Gawain and the Green Knight*." *Diacritics* 24.2–3 (1994): 205–26.
Elliott, Dyan. *The Bride of Christ Goes to Hell* (University of Pennsylvania Press, 2011).
—. *Fallen Bodies: Pollution, Sexuality, and Demonology in the Middle Ages* (University of Pennsylvania Press, 1998).
—. *Spiritual Marriage: Sexual Abstinence in Medieval Wedlock* (Princeton University Press, 1995).
Foucault, Michel. *The History of Sexuality. Vol. 1: An Introduction*. Trans. Robert Hurley (Vintage, 1978; Fr. org. 1976).
Fradenburg, Louise and Carla Freccero (eds) *Premodern Sexualities* (Routledge, 1996).
Frantzen, Allen J. "Between the Lines: Queer Theory, the History of Homosexuality, and the Anglo-Saxon Penitentials." *Journal of Medieval and Early Renaissance Studies* 26 (1996): 245–96.
Garber, Marjorie. *Vested Interests: Cross-Dressing and Cultural Anxiety* (HarperCollins, 1993).
Giffney, Noreen, Michelle M. Sauer, and Diane Watt (eds) *The Lesbian Premodern* (Palgrave, 2011).
Gilchrist, Roberta. *Gender and Material Culture: The Archaeology of Religious Women* (Routledge, 1994).
Gravdal, Kathryn. *Ravishing Maidens: Writing Rape in Medieval French Literature and Law* (University of Pennsylvania Press, 1991).
Green, Monica H. *Making Women's Medicine Masculine: The Rise of Male Authority in Premodern Gynaecology* (Oxford University Press, 2008).
Greenberg, David F. *The Construction of Homosexuality* (University of Chicago Press, 1988).
Hamburger, Jeffrey. *Nuns as Artists: The Visual Culture of a Medieval Convent* (University of California Press, 1997).
Hanawalt, Barbara A. *Of Good and Ill Repute: Gender and Social Control in Medieval England* (Oxford University Press, 1998).
—. *The Wealth of Wives: Women, Law, and Economy in Late Medieval London* (Oxford University Press, 2007).
—. *Women and Work in Preindustrial Europe* (Indiana University Press, 1986).
Hollywood, Amy. *The Soul as Virgin Wife: Mechtild of Magdeburg, Marguerite Porete, and Meister Eckhardt* (University of Notre Dame Press, 1995).
Jacquart, Danielle and Claude Thomasset. *Sexuality & Medicine in the Middle Ages*. Trans. Matthew Adamson (Princeton University Press, 1988; Fr. org. 1985).

Johnson, Penelope. *Equal in Monastic Profession: Religious Women in Medieval France* (University of Chicago Press, 1991).
Karras, Ruth Mazo. *Common Women: Prostitution and Sexuality in Medieval England* (Oxford University Press, 1998).
—. *Sexuality in Medieval Europe: Doing Unto Others* (Routledge, 2005).
—. *Unmarriages* (University of Pennsylvania Press, 2012).
Kruger, Steven F. "Claiming the Pardoner: Toward a Gay Reading of Chaucer's *Pardoner's Tale*." *Exemplaria* 6.1 (1994): 115–39.
Laqueur, Thomas. *Making Sex: Body and Gender from the Greeks to Freud* (Harvard University Press, 1990).
Lees, Clare A. (ed.) *Medieval Masculinities: Regarding Men in the Middle Ages* (University of Minnesota Press, 1994).
Lochrie, Karma. *Covert Operations: The Medieval Uses of Secrecy* (University of Pennsylvania Press, 1999).
Lochrie, Karma, Peggy McCracken, and James Schultz (eds) *Constructing Medieval Sexuality* (University of Minnesota Press, 1997).
McAvoy, Liz Herbert. *Medieval Anchoritisms: Gender, Space and the Solitary Life* (D.S. Brewer, 2011).
Murray, Jacqueline (ed.) *Conflicted Identities and Multiple Masculinities: Men in the Medieval West* (Garland, 1999).
Newman, Barbara. *From Virile Woman to WomanChrist: Studies in Medieval Religion and Literature* (University of Pennsylvania Press, 1995).
—. *Sister of Wisdom: St. Hildegard's Theology of the Feminine* (Berkeley: University of California Press, 1987).
Normington, Katie. *Gender and Medieval Drama* (D. S. Brewer, 2006).
Payer, Pierre J. *The Bridling of Desire: Views of Sex in the Later Middle Ages* (University of Toronto Press, 1993).
Rawcliffe, Carole. *Medicine and Society in Later Medieval England* (Sutton, 1995).
Riddle, John M. *Eve's Herbs: A History of Contraception and Abortion in the West* (Harvard University Press, 1997).
Ringrose, Kathryn. *The Perfect Servant: Eunuchs and the Social Construction of Gender in Byzantium* (University of Chicago Press, 2004).
Salih, Sarah. *Versions of Virginity in Late Medieval England* (Boydell & Brewer, 2001).
Sauer, Michelle M. "Architecture of Desire: Mediating the Female Gaze in the Medieval English Anchorhold." *Gender & History* 25.3 (2013): 541–60.
—. "Uncovering Difference: Encoded Homoerotic Anxiety within the Medieval English Eremitic Tradition." *Journal of the History of Sexuality* 19.1 (2010): 133–52.
Saunders, Corrine J. *Rape and Ravishment in the Literature of Medieval England* (D. S. Brewer, 2001).
Schulenburg, Jane Tibbetts. *Forgetful of Their Sex: Female Sanctity, ca. 500–1100* (University of Chicago Press, 1998).
Schultz, James A. *Courtly Love, the Love of Courtliness, and the History of Sexuality* (University of Chicago Press, 2006).
Sedgwick, Eve Kosofsky. *Between Men: English Literature and Male Homosocial Desire* (Columbia University Press, 1985).
Shahar, Shulamith. *The Fourth Estate: A History of Women in the Middle Ages*. Trans. Chaya Galai (Metheun, 1983).

van Houts, Elisabeth. *Memory and Gender in Medieval Europe, 900–1200* (Macmillan, 1999).
Watt, Diane. *Amoral Gower. Language, Sex, and Politics* (University of Minnesota Press, 2003).
Wemple, Suzanne. *Women in Frankish Society: Marriage and the Cloister, 500–900* (University of Pennsylvania Press, 1981).
Wiesner, Merry. *Women and Gender in Early Modern Europe* (Cambridge University Press, 1994).

GLOSSARY

Abbess: Female head of a convent for nuns.
Anchorite/Anchoress: An individual who lives a life of extreme isolated religious contemplation in a small cell, often attached to a church or erected in a churchyard.
Apothecary: A medieval general practitioner of sorts who sold medicines, ingredients for prescriptions, and dispensed medical advice.
Apprentice: A young person, age 7 through early teens, who wanted to learn a trade or craft. The apprentice lived with the Master and received no wages, but did get room and board in exchange for learning the trade.
Black Death: The illness that ravaged Europe predominantly during the years 1348–50 CE, killing an estimated 30–60 percent of the population. Modern studies have shown that the *Yersinia pestis* bacterium was likely responsible, presumably spread by fleas and rats. Medieval people did not know this, and believed that causes included sin, outsiders, earthquakes, livestock, deviance, misalignment of stars, and "bad air."
Bloodletting: Also called phlebotomy. It is the oldest tradition in medicine and is found in numerous world cultures. It involves the withdrawal of small quantities of blood from a patient to cure or prevent illness and disease, usually done according to elaborate charts and graphs.
Castration: The act of rendering male genitals useless through removal or impairment.
chanson de geste: Literally "song of great deeds." An Old French epic poem, most of which involved Charlemagne and/or his knights.
Chaste marriage: A marriage in which both parties agree to refrain from sexual relations with each other or anyone else. Formal declaration of such is usually required in order to avoid complications caused by lack of consummation.
Chastity: Remaining within your proscribed sexual boundaries, not necessarily remaining a virgin. For instance, a married woman was chaste if she only had sexual relations with her lawful spouse.
Cosmology: The study of the origin, evolution, and eventual fate of the universe.
Coverture: A legal doctrine under which a married woman had no rights, as all were assumed by her husband.
Cross-dressing: The act of wearing clothing and other accoutrements commonly associated with the opposite biological sex within a particular society. May or may not be attached to sexual excitement.
Embryology: Branch of biological science that deals with the formation, early growth, and development of living organisms, including humans.
Ensoulment: Philosophical or religious concept referring to the moment at which a human being gains a soul.

Essentialism: The position that men and women have innate characteristics that distinguish them from each other, and therefore sex roles are defined by nature and/or God.

feme sole: Under medieval English law, a married woman, who, by the custom of London, engages in business on her own account, independently of her husband.

Gender: Refers to the socially constructed and/or performed roles, behaviors, activities, and attributes that a given society considers appropriate for humans.

Guild: Exclusive organization created for the benefit of its members. Craft Guilds were comprised of members of the same profession, while Merchant Guilds formed for protection of goods while traveling. Both types controlled access to materials and price points.

Gynecology: Medical specialty dealing with the health of the female reproductive system, which may or may not include childbirth.

Hegemony: An indirect form of dominance and control.

Hermaphrodite: An antiquated term for humans possessing the sexual characteristics or chromosomes of both biological sexes. Today these individuals are referred to as "intersexed."

Heterosexual: Sexual preference directed toward members of the opposite biological sex.

Homosexual: Sexual preference directed toward members of the same biological sex.

Hysteria: Literally "wandering womb." A condition characterized by extreme emotional excess, once thought only to affect women and to be caused by movements of the uterus.

Journeyman: An individual who is partially trained in a craft and paid for his/her labor, but is still supervised by a Guild Master.

Master: A master crafter who could set up his/her own workshop, train apprentices, and supervise journeymen. In order to become a master, an individual produced a "masterpiece" demonstrating skill that was judged by other Masters.

Masturbation: Self-stimulation of the sexual organs to produce erotic pleasure.

Midwife: Women who assisted in the birthing process across all social classes. Informally trained through apprenticeship.

Military orders: Christian society of knights founded for purposes of crusading.

Misericord: Wooden ledges in church choir stalls that allowed the user a small degree of comfort during extended periods of prayer, often exquisitely carved with elaborate images, both secular and sacred.

Misogyny: Hatred of women.

Nocturnal emission: A spontaneous (male) orgasm involving the involuntary ejaculation of semen, usually occurring at night during sleep.

Obstetrics: Medical specialty that deals with the care of women during pregnancy, childbirth, and immediately afterward.

Original Sin: The Christian doctrine identified within the Patristic church, but refined most importantly by Augustine of Hippo, that aligns humans with a sinful, "fallen" state, originating from the disobedience of Adam and Eve in the Garden of Eden. Often thought to bring about sexual desire, reproduction, and menstruation.

Patriarchy: The social system in which men are the primary authority figures central to social organization. This has been the dominant form of society throughout human existence.

Premodern: Human society before the Renaissance, often more specifically referring to the time period between the end of the Classical era and the beginning of the Renaissance.

Pre-Reformation Church: The Christian church prior to the Protestant Reformation (1517 CE). It is distinct from the Roman Catholic Church, although that denomination retains a number of its beliefs and practices. Often reductively refers to the Roman church alone, excluding the Byzantine branch, which became the Orthodox churches.

Prostitution: The so-called oldest profession, in which an individual exchanges sex acts for money or gifts.

Romances: Tales of chivalry and adventure involving the nobility (knights, kings, and ladies), often including quests, the supernatural, and courtly love.

Sex: The biological characteristics of a human being that mark an individual as male or female.

Sexology: The study of human sexuality, including human sexual interests, behaviors, and functions. Often involves identification and classification.

Social construction: Theoretical position that says human identity is formed due to interactions with the world around them, including other people and society as a whole.

Sodomy: A complicated concept in the Middle Ages that could involve any "unnatural" form of sexual intercourse (e.g. any deviation from heterosexual intercourse in the missionary position) as well as treason and heresy.

Teratology: The study of human developmental abnormalities, sometimes referred to as "monster studies."

Transgender: The state of one's gender identity (self-identification as woman, man, neither, or both) or gender expression not matching one's assigned or biological sex.

INDEX

abbesses 54, 87, 128–9, 145, 146, 179n. 14
abduction (raptus) *see* rape
Abelard, Peter 79, 81–2
abstinence 7, 34, 42, 56, 58, 104
abortion 31–8, 156n.70, 157n. 82, 159nn. 105–6
  comparison with birth control 32
  condemning women for 35
  definition of 35
  as manslaughter 34–5
  methods 34
  miracles 37
  sanctity and 36
Abū ʿAlī al-Ḥusayn ibn ʿAbd Allāh ibn Sīnā *see* Avicenna
Abū l-Walīd Muḥammad bin ʿAḥmad bin Rušd *see* Averroes
adultery 8, 32, 61, 99, 137, 156n. 70, 157n. 77
  annulment and 65
  as deviant 69
  heterosexual 68
  innocent spouse in 55
  procreation and 67–70, 75
Áed mac Brice 37
Aelred of Rievaulx 37, 79
Æthelthryth 57
Agatha, Saint 114
"agayns kynde" 98, 102
Alan of Lille 73
Albert the Great 95, 97
Aldhelm 47, 73
alewives 134–7
Alexander of Hales 49
Alexis, Saint 57
Ambrose 49, 59, 84, 108, 111–14
Amis and Amiloun 42
Anastasia the Patrician (of Constantinople) 85

anchoress 77–8, 94, 118, 119, 145, 148, 165n. 15, 166n. 28, 185n. 85
anchorite 110
Ancrene Wisse (Guide for Anchoresses) 77
Andreae, Johannes 36
Angela of Foligno 52, 164–5n 15
Anglo-Saxon laws, on rape 19
anima (soul) 120
Anna/Euphemianos of Constantinople 85
Anne, Saint 58
Anne of Bohemia 91, 166n. 28
annulments, in marriage 64–5
Anselm of Canterbury 89
Apollinaria/Dorotheos 85
apothecaries 144, 184n. 75
Aquinas, Thomas 20, 27, 29–33, 50, 65, 72, 75–6, 80, 91, 112, 167n. 14
Aretaeus of Cappadocia 163n. 147
Aristotle 24, 27, 29, 30, 32, 33, 46, 94–5, 157n. 74
ascetics, asceticism, ascetic discipline 12, 48, 58, 71, 75, 88, 98, 108, 110, 176n. 24, 185n. 85
Athanasia of Antioch 85
Athanasius 75
Augustine of Hippo 32, 49, 56, 58, 71, 72, 75, 92, 98
autocastration 79, 81–3
Averroes 24, 154n. 49
Avicenna 24, 34, 154n. 49, 157n. 77
Avignon Papacy 186n. 91

Baldwin III, King of Jerusalem 130
"Ballade on an Ale-Seller" 136
barber-surgeons 144
Bartholomeus Anglicus 173n. 106
Basil of Caesarea 75

Battle of Bosworth Field 149n. 1
"becoming male," notion of 113
　see also chastity and regendering
Bede 92
behaviors/appearances, gender-defined 4
Bernard of Clairvaux 108, 118, 120
betrothal theory see consent theory
biology and reproduction 25–9
　Aristotelian principles and 25
　differences in male and female bodies and 26
Birgitta of Sweden 52, 58, 59, 165n. 15
birth control vs. abortion 32
Black Death 32, 41, 63, 140
bloodletting 38–9, 43, 144, 159n. 107, 161n. 124, 162n. 135
bodily humors 24–5
Bonaventure 50
Boniface IX, Pope 165n. 15
Boniface VIII, Pope 111
Book of Gomorrah see *Liber Gomorrhianus (Book of Gomorrah)*
Book of Margery Kempe 41, 59, 161n. 131
Book of Vices and Virtues 66
Bourges, Council of 111
breasts 28, 37, 96, 110, 113, 114, 117, 118
Brewer's Guild of London 135
brewsters 132, 180nn. 28–9
　alcoholic preferences 133–4
　from brewing to serving in taverns and inns 135
　consumption, pattern of 135
　guild control and 137
　literary and artistic depictions and 136–7
　marketing 134
　as women dominated 133
　trade transformation and 137
Bride of Christ metaphor 108–9, 111–12, 119, 159n. 103
Brigid of Kildare 37
Bruinnech 37

Caesarius of Arles 34, 35
Cainnech of Aghaboe 37
Callisthene 85
Callixtus, Pope 35, 158n. 92

Callixtus II, Pope 169n. 48
The Canon of Medicine 154n. 49
Canterbury Tales 57, 78, 145
Carthage, Council of 59
Cassian 59, 75, 81
castration 12, 20, 42, 69, 78–83, 159n. 104, 162n. 134
　as curative 80
　divine 80–1
　as punishment 78–80, 82
　as purification 82
　self- 79, 81, 82
　unlawful 79
Catherine of Siena 105
Causae et Curae (Causes and Cures) 146, 186n. 87
Cecilia, Saint 56–7
celibacy 50
　clerical 56, 59, 103–6, 111
　Church on 47, 48
　perpetual 120
chanson de geste 12, 85–6
chaste marriage 55–60, 165n. 22
　by ending sexual interactions 56, 58
　historical records of 57–8
　legends and 57
chastity 11, 12, 38, 43, 47, 48, 50, 51, 54, 57, 66, 71, 76, 86, 106, 108, 109, 110, 119, 132, 165n. 22
　as birth control 34
　chastity test 31
　as distinct sexual orientation 121–2
　regendering and 107, 111–12
　resistant 80
　sworn or vowed chastity 20, 55, 57
　virgin martyrs and 113
Chaucer, Geoffrey 22, 42, 57, 67, 68, 78, 100, 136, 145, 153n. 40, 157n. 77
Chirurgia magna 161n. 124
Christ 116, 119–20
　fluidity of 115–20
　as infant 120
　as man 117
　as nun's husband 108–9
　side wound 117
　see also Bride of Christ metaphor
Christina of Markyate 85
Christine de Pizan 126
Chrysostom, John 32, 92, 109

Church councils
  Council of Bourges 111
  Council of Carthage 59
  Council of Clermont 111
  Council of Elvira 59
  Council of Ephesus 116
  Council of Trent 61, 64
  Lateran Council 64
  Nicaea Council 81, 128
Ciarán of Saigir 37
City of God 98
Classical world 3, 4, 18, 24, 31–3, 39, 78, 91, 94, 104, 150n. 20
Clement V, Pope 90, 171n. 82
clerical wife 60, 111
Clermont, Council of 111
clothing 20, 40, 49, 55, 63, 85, 87, 106, 121, 140
Codex Calixtinus 79–80, 169n. 48
coinage, women in 128–9
coitum habet 77
coitus interruptus 33
commanderies 147, 148
Commentary on Aristotle's Metaphysics 29
Commentary on St. Paul's First Epistle to the Corinthians 29
The Complaint of Nature 73
composite Magdalene 167n. 12
conception, theories of 27–8
concupiscence 49
consanguinity 64, 65
consent theory 56
Constantine the Great, emperor of Rome 19
construction, gender and sexuality and 5, 10, 24, 30, 102
consummation theory 56
conventions, gender 11–12
convents 7, 54, 79, 81, 94, 108, 110, 120, 128, 170n. 67, 176n. 25
coverture 10, 15, 16, 45, 46, 151nn. 1
Craft Guilds 138, 182n. 50
cross-dressing 83–8, 170n.62, 171n. 70
  in fiction 85
  in hagiographies 84–5
  legends and 84–5
  records of male in 87

  as renunciation of sex 85
Crown of Aragon 180n. 23
cupping therapy 184n. 73
Cynethryth, Queen of Mercia 128

Damian, Peter 76, 88–9
d'Argenteuil, Héloïse 79, 82
Dark Ages 2
De animalibus 95
de Chauliac, Guy 41, 161n. 124
Decretum 62
De Generatione Animalium 33
De legibus et consuetudinibus Angliae (*On the Laws and Customs of England*) 15, 20, 96
demasculinization 73, 146
De miraculis Sancti Jacobi 79
De proprietatibus rerum (*On the Properties of Things*) 173n. 106
derivation technique 38
De secretis mulierum (*On the Secrets of Women*) 42, 97
Desert Harlots 71
De spermate 94
deviance and transgression 67–70
  castration and 78–83
  cross-dressing and 83–8
  hermaphrodites and 94–7
  homosexuality and 88–94
  masturbation and nocturnal emission and 74–8
  monsters and 97–100
  prostitution and 70–4
disease and illness 38–44
distaff 126
divine castration 80
divorce 16, 60–1, 64–5
Dogmatists 24
Dorothy of Montau 52, 58, 59, 165n. 15, 166n. 28

Ebner, Margaretha 120
ecclesiastical court and world
  fertility control and dominance of 24, 32, 36, 37
  marriage and 56
  queenship 130
  rape victims, treatment on 21
  sex, beliefs on 60

Ecgfrith of Northumbria 57
economy, women's importance and 45, 125
  abortion contemplation and 35–6
  ban on full citizenship and 129
  brewsters and 131–2
  guilds limiting 142
  as managers of resources 127
  marriage and reproduction and 7
  as members of guilds 127–8
  peasant women and 126
  queens and 131
  see also guilds
Edith 57, 58
Edward the Confessor, King of England 57–8
Edward I, King of England 21, 89–90, 138
Edward II, King of England 79, 89–91, 169n. 46
Edward III, King of England 90
Edward VI, King of England 138
effeminacy 31, 73, 89, 90, 91, 115, 164n. 6
  see also femininity
Egbert 92
elasticity 183n. 62
Eleanor of Arborea 131
Elias 81
Elisabeth of Bosnia 130
Elvira, Council of 59
Empiricists 24
English law, on rape 19–20
ensoulment 27, 30, 32, 35, 98
Ephesus, Council of 116
Equitius of Valeria 81
essentialism 4
Etymologiae 98
eucrasia 38
Eugenia/Eugenius 85
eunuchization 69
eunuchs 67, 69, 82, 105, 121, 161–2n 134, 169n. 49
  in Classical world, types of 78
Euphrosyne/Smaragdus 85
Euphrosyne Jr 85
Eusebia 36
Eusebius 80

Eustochium 108, 156n. 70
Eve, reference to 50, 107, 126

Fall (from Paradise)
  caused by Eve's unwise choice 50
  consequences of 49–50
female body, view on 17–18
feme covert (being under the coverture of spouse) 45
feme sole (single woman) 12, 45, 135
femininity 30–1, 35, 38, 46, 51, 82, 88–9, 102, 116, 117, 118, 122, 132, 146
  "becoming male" and 113
  definition of 107
  female activities and 127
  female masculinity and 115
  female medical practitioners and 143–8
  gender-defined rules and 114
  marriage and 107–8
  monasticism and 108
  orgasm and 28
  practicing virtue and 110
  religious 107–15
  rigorous self-mortification and 110
  sex change and 12–13
  virgin martyrs and 113–14
  virginity and religious 111
  see also effeminacy
feminization threat, within clerical masculinity 105–6
fertility control 24, 31–8
  abortion methods and 34
  abstinence as Church endorsed method for 34
  birth control *vs.* abortion and 32
  condemning 32
  medieval contraceptive practices for 33
  sanctions against birth control and 32–3
feudalism, impact on marriage 61–2
First Baptismal Instruction 109
Fleta 17, 34, 152n. 14
Fontevrault Abbey 128
fornication 36, 37, 39, 53, 63, 71, 74, 92, 106, 137, 165n. 16
Four Causes principle 157n. 74
France (medieval), on rape 23

Frances of Rome 58
Francis I, Pope 165n. 15
Fulbert 79

Galen 17, 18, 24–8, 38–9, 46, 94, 154n. 49, 155n. 55, 184n. 73
Galenic theory 43
Galla 95
Galli 79
Garden of Eden 49–51, 72
Gaveston, Piers 79, 90, 169n. 46
genitals, genitalia 26, 40, 44, 49, 65, 76, 78, 79, 80, 82, 83, 84, 93, 94, 96, 101, 105, 112, 117, 159n. 104, 169n. 41, 172n. 98
Germain of Paris 36–7
Germany (medieval), on rape 23
Gilbertine Order 37, 128
Gilbert the Englishman 41
Giudicati (judgeships) 180n. 23
God
  the Father 116
  Holy Spirit and 116, 118
  sexuality of 115–16
  see also Christ
  the Son *see* Christ
Godwin, the Earl of Wessex 57
Godwinson, Harold 57, 149n. 1
Golden Legend 56–7, 84, 85, 95
Gower, John 41
Granville, Mortimer 163n. 145
Gratian, Johannes 20, 62, 152n. 25
Great Rising (Peasants' Revolt) 91
greensickness 24, 43–4, 76, 162n. 141, 163n. 143
Gregorian masculinity 104
Gregorian Reform 59
Gregory I, the Great, Pope 75
Gregory VII, Pope 59
Gregory of Nyssa 32, 52
Gregory of Tours 87
Guibert of Nogent 79
guilds 54, 138–42, 182nn.49–50, 183n. 65, 184nn. 74–5
  in medical practice 144, 147
  membership 140–1
  role of 139
  widows and 140, 144

Guillaume de Lorris 164n. 11
Guy de Chauliac 41, 161n. 124

Haakon VI, King of Norway 131
hagiographies 1, 36, 37, 54, 56, 58, 80, 83–5, 114, 164n. 6, 176n. 36
Hebrew Bible 116
Hedwig of Silesia 58, 131, 166n. 28
Henry II, King of England 147
Henry V, King of England 165n. 22
Henry VII, King of England 149n. 1
Henry VIII, King of England 149n 1, 184n. 74
Henry of Bracton 15, 17, 20, 34, 96, 99
Henryson, Robert 41–2
hermaphrodites 67, 70, 77, 83, 94–7, 172n. 98
Hermaphroditus 94
heteronormativity 8, 90, 150n. 13
heterosexuality 5, 7–9, 47, 150nn. 15–16
  and adultery 68
  domestic 10
  and motivation for masturbation 77
  presumptive 88, 91
  see also deviance and transgression
Hetzeldorfer, Katherine 93
Hilda of Whitby Abbey, Saint 128
Hildefonsus of Toledo 81
Hildegard of Bingen 28, 118, 145–6, 183n. 70, 185nn. 85–6
Hincmar of Reims 92–3
Hippocrates 27, 28, 31, 38, 94, 154n. 49, 184n. 73
Hippolytus 35, 81, 158n. 92
Historia Calamitatum 79
Holkham Bible Picture Book 182n. 45
Holy Maidenhood 47, 111
Holy Spirit *see under* God
Holy Trinity 115
homoeroticism 92–3
homosexuality 10, 79, 88–94, 171n. 74
  female 91 *see also* lesbianism
hops 181n. 32
hortus conclusus 50–1
hospitaller sisters 147–8
Hospitaller Sisters of St John of Jerusalem 147

Hospital of Saint John of Jerusalem 147
hospitals, significance of 187n. 95
Hugh of Lincoln 80
Hugh of Orival 80, 161–2n 134
Hugh of Pisa 96
Humiliati of Italy 165n. 22
humoral system 24, 25, 38–9, 186n. 87
hymen 49, 51, 114
hypostatic union, doctrine of 116
hysteria 24, 36, 44, 163n. 145

identity 6, 171n. 74
  gender, sex, and sexuality and 3–4, 9, 12, 121
  as "fixed" by biology 12
  women before marriage 15–16
  heterosexual 7–9
  masculine 104, 115, 141
  signs of gender and 121
  for women 45, 91
image of God 29
The Imitation of Christ 68
Incarnation 51, 116, 117, 120
"inside out" men 4–5, 12, 18, 26
Irish Penitential of Cummean (seventh century) 76
Isabella, Queen of England 79, 90, 169n. 46
Isidore of Seville 98
Islam 166n. 25
Italy (medieval), on rape 23–4

James, Saint 80, 169n. 48
Jelena of Bosnia 130
Jerome, Saint 31, 32, 48, 49, 52, 59, 84, 108, 111, 113, 114
Jews, Judaism 42, 72, 74, 109, 146, 162n. 137, 177n. 49, 184n. 79
Joachim, Saint 58
Joan of Arc (Jeanne d'Arc; "The Maid of Orléans") 85
John of Trevisa 173n. 106
Julian of Norwich 118, 177n. 47
Justinian 19
Jutta 145, 185n. 85

Kempe, John 59
Kempe, Margery 58–60, 120, 166n. 29
Kramer, Heinrich 184n. 71

Langland, William 136
Lateran Council 64
law 125, 151n. 10, 152n. 14
  existence after marriage and 45, 61, 126
  medical science and 46
  rape *see* rape
  sex discrimination and 15–16
  widowhood and 52
  women as legal property and 17
lay sisters 187n. 101
lechery 41, 68, 74, 113, 135, 137
le Despenser, Hugh 79, 90, 169n. 46
Le Livre des trois vertus à l'enseignement des dames (Treasure of the City of Ladies) 126
Leo the Great, Saint, Pope 59
leprosy 40–2, 80, 120, 137, 160nn. 118, 161–2n 134, 161n. 132, 162nn. 135, 165n. 22
lesbianism 10, 91–3, 162n. 141, 172n. 91
  penalties for 93
  see also homosexuality
Liber compositae medicinae (Book of Compound Medicine) see Causae et Curae (Causes and Cures)
Liber Gomorrhianus (Book of Gomorrah) 76, 88
Liber monstrorum (Book of Monsters) 92, 98
Liber simplicis medicinae (Book of Simple Medicine) see Physica (Natural History)
Louis I, King of Hungary 130
lust 23, 28, 71, 73–4, 110, 136
  calming of 80
  leading to fall 49–50
  leprosy and 41
  masturbation as 78
  nocturnal emission and 74–5
  as women's fault 50, 85
Lydgate, John 136

Magdalene, Mary 71, 167n. 12
maidenhood 47, 111, 112
male prostitution 73, 87, 167n. 15

Malleus Maleficarum (*Hammer of Witches*) 144, 184n. 71
Man of Sorrows (*vir doloris*), image of 116
Margaret, Saint 114
Margareta/Pelagius 85
Margaret I, Queen of Denmark, Norway, and Sweden 131
Maria, the niece of Abraham 71
Marian iconography 50–1
Marina/Marinos of Antioch 85
Marina/Marinus of Alexandria 85
Marina of Sicily 85
marriage 7, 15, 43, 47–8, 107–8, 164–5n 15, 165nn. 16,22, 176n. 30
　age of 62–3
　annulment of 64–5
　chastity in 55–60, 165n. 22
　conjugal debt in 63
　consent in 63–4
　consummation of 64
　dowry in 62
　feudalism and impact on 61–2
　friendship in 150n. 20
　natural law and 65–6
　parity of rank in 63
　as social contract 61
　spiritual 55–6, 59
　superiority of male in 63
Mary (Virgin) 48–9, 51, 58, 107, 112, 119, 166n. 25
Mary, Queen of Hungary and Croatia 130
Mary Magdalene 71, 167n. 12
Mary of Egypt 71
masculinity 30, 60, 63, 69, 81–2, 86–7, 95–6, 102, 105, 112, 116, 117, 122, 129–30
　Christianity and 104
　clerical clothing and 106
　definition of 103
　dominance over men 141
　female 93, 113–15, 123, 127, 129, 132
　Gregorian 104
　and identity 104, 115, 141
　manhood and 106
　religious 103–6
masturbation 33, 43, 69, 70, 106
　bodily purity and 75

female 77
male 76–8
sodomy and 76
thwarting procreation 76
see also nocturnal emission
Matrona 84, 85
Maximus 57
medical practitioners, female 143–8
medicine
　philosophy, and theology and 29–31
　in premodern world 24–6, 96, 181n. 32
　science, gender, and sexuality and 24–5
Melisende, Queen of Jerusalem 130
men and women, difference between 29–31
menstruation 27, 28, 30, 33, 38, 42, 46, 69, 94, 162n. 137
Merchant Guilds 138, 182n. 50
Merlin 75, 86
midwifery 34, 43, 143–4
Mirour de l'omme (*The Mirror of Humanity*) 41
miscegenation 79
misogyny 24, 29, 137, 142, 145, 181n. 40
monasteries 7, 81, 108, 110, 128, 130, 152n. 25, 159n. 104, 165n. 15, 179n. 14, 187n. 95
　widows in 53–5
monsters 97–100, 174n. 125
moral virtues 31
Mortimer, Roger 79, 90, 169n. 46
mothers, in Middle Ages 117

Natalia 85
Natural History 98
Natural Law 28, 32, 65–6, 99
New Testament 53, 80
Nicaea, Council of 81, 128
nocturnal emission 76, 105, 106
　demonology and 75
　as sin 74–5
Norman Conquest 20, 57, 58, 149n. 1
normativity 8, 10–11, 16, 47, 60, 100, 103, 107, 115, 150n. 15
Nun of Watton 37, 159n. 104

Old Testament 156n 68, 160n. 122, 170n. 61
onanism 76

one-seed theory 27
one-sex model 4–5, 18, 26–7, 95
On Monsters and Marvels 83, 96
On the Nature of the Child 27
On the Temperaments 25
On Virginity 108, 111
Ordinance of Jean le Bon 140
orgasm 27, 39, 43, 75, 119
  female 17, 28–9, 44, 65, 146
Origen of Alexandria 80, 82, 109
Original Sin 30, 48–50, 66, 69, 180n. 17

Pachon of Scetis 81
Paesia 71
Palladius 80
Papula of Gaul 85
Pardoner (Canterbury Pilgrim) 78, 82
Paré, Ambroise 82–3, 96
Parson's Tale 68
Paston, John 127
Paston, Margaret 127
patriarchy 4–5, 107–8, 150n.16, 174n. 125, 183n. 58
  clerical chastity and 122
  Eve and need for 107
  fertility control and 24
  guild system and 141
  human body and 25
  laws equalizing gender constraints and 45
  marriage and 108
  one-sex model and 18
  queenship and 132
  sexuality and 3–4
Paul, Saint 59
Paul VI, Pope 165n. 15
Peasants' Revolt *see* Great Rising (Peasants' Revolt)
Pelagia, the actress of Antioch 71
Pelagia of Antioch/Pelagius 85
penis 4, 12, 26, 39, 78, 79, 82, 83, 84, 87, 93, 95, 96, 100, 155n. 55
Penitential of Columban 78
Penitential of Finnian 159n. 103
Penitential of Theodore 77, 92
performance theory 6–7, 11
"performative essentialism" 12, 31, 94, 101, 112
Periculoso 110

periodization 2, 10
  significance of 3
perpetual virginity 56, 60
Peter, Saint 114
Peter the Chanter 77, 96
Peter of Poitiers 77
Philip IV, King of France 90, 171n. 81
Physica (*Natural History*) 146, 186n. 87
Piers Plowman 136
Plato 94
pleasure 9, 16, 17, 27, 32, 41, 49–50, 59, 63, 66, 77, 110, 146
Pliny 98
political sphere
  brewsters and 132–7
  female medical practitioners and 142–8
  guilds and 138–42
  medieval queenship and 130–2
post-Enlightenment essentialism 4
poststructuralism 6
premodern world 2, 10, 12, 33, 47, 69, 80, 84
  dualism in 28
  essentialism and 4
  medicine in 24–6, 96, 181n. 32
  sexuality in 8, 9, 91, 171n. 74
  women in 32, 91
pre-Reformation Christianity 47, 115
primogeniture 61–2
private prosecution 21
procreation 7, 10, 32, 34, 47, 49, 50, 50, 58, 63, 78, 86, 156n. 71
  and adultery 67–70, 75
  masturbation thwarting 76
The Prose Salernitan Questions 17
prostitution 42, 69, 70, 136
  casual 74
  Church on 72–3
  male 73, 87, 167n. 15
  redemption practice and 71
Protestant Reformation 43
Pseudo-Albertus 69
purity 50
  bodily 75, 83

queenship, medieval 128, 130–2
queer theory 5, 8, 88

Radegund, Saint 87
rape 17, 37, 153n. 36
  Anglo-Saxon laws on 19
  definition, medieval 19
  English law on 19–20
  France (medieval) on 23
  Germany (medieval), on 23
  Italy (medieval), on 23–4
  "legitimate" 152n. 13
  and *raptus* 18–24
  Roman law on 19
ravishment 17, 19, 21, 23, 54
Raymond of Capua 105
Rāzī, Muhammad ibn Zakariyā 154n. 49
"real" sex 91
redemption
  bleeding and suffering as 116–17
  of prostitutes 71
Reformation 7, 48, 85, 180n. 17
religion and sexuality *see* sexuality
Renaissance 43
Revelations of Divine Love 118
revulsion technique 38
Rhazes 24
Richard, Earl of Warwick 85
Richard II, King of England 90
Richard III, King of England 149n. 1
Romance of the Rose 50, 67, 68, 82, 164n. 11
Roman de Silence 85–6
Roman followers of Cybele (Magna Mater) 79
Roman law, on rape 19
Romyng, Alianora 136, 181n. 40
Roscelin of Compiegne 81–2
Rufus, William (William II), King of England 73, 89, 90
Rykener, John 73, 87

Salmacis 94
salvation 29, 40, 47, 48, 71, 97–8, 113, 114, 141
Sanger, Margaret 32, 156n. 69
Sappho of Lesbos 91
Scriftboc 77
Scuola Medica Salernitana 184n. 79
secondary victimization 23, 153n. 41
Second Diocesan Statues 77

semen 18, 27, 32–3, 39, 46, 69, 75
Seneca the Younger 92
Serenus 80
sexology 9
sexual intercourse 56, 77, 96
  Edenic 49
  leprosy and 40–2
  sin-tree 65
sexuality 3–4, 12, 34, 47, 101–3, 122, 157n. 79, 160nn. 108, 164n. 6, 165n. 22, 170n. 62
  earthly 49
  femininity, religious and 107–15
  fluidity of Christ and 115–20
  gender and sex ideologies and 4–5
  gender construction and 10
  marital sex and 66
  masculinity, religious and 103–6
  as part of marital debt 60
  power and 8–9
  premodern 8, 9, 91, 171n. 74
  restraint of female 23
  sex and 9
  social construction of 5–6
  third gender and 120–3
  "will-not-to-know" and 4
sexually transmitted diseases 39, 41
  orgasms and 43
Shepherd's Crusade (1320) 42
Sigismund of Luxembourg 131
Sir Gowther 75
Skelton, John 136
skilled professions, women in 127
social constructionism 5–6
social world 15–18
  biology and reproduction and 25–9
  disease and illness and 38–44
  fertility control and 31–8
  medicine, philosophy, and theology and 29–31
  medicine, science, gender, and sexuality and 24–5
  rape and *raptus* and 18–24
Society of Apothecaries 184n. 75
sodomy 8, 70, 75–7, 88–90, 93, 106
Song of Songs 51, 108–9, 120, 156n. 67
Soranus of Ephesus 34, 39, 157n. 79
Speculum Inclusorum (*Mirror for Recluses*) 110

Speculum Virginum (*Mirror of Virgins*) 109
spiritual death 55
spiritual marriage 48, 55–6, 59, 60
spiritual widows 55, 56
sponsa Christi 119–20, 178n. 51
Sprenger, James 184n. 71
Statute of Mortmain 160n. 120
Stoicism 48, 116
subjectivity 6, 76, 91, 103
Subtililates diversarum naturarum creaturarum (*The Subtleties of the Diverse Nature of Created Things*) 145–6
Summa Theologica 50, 75, 76
Susanna 85
Sweden 128, 180n. 22
Swedish Bridgettines 128
Symposium 94
syphilis 24, 39, 40, 41, 74, 82

taverns 74, 135, 137
Tertullian 122
testicles 26, 78, 79, 96
The Testament of Cresseid 42
The Testament of Love 67
Thaïs the harlot 71
Thecla 85
Theodora 71
Theodora/Theodorus 85
Theodulf 77
third gender 120–3
Thomas of Coucy 79
Tiburtius 57
Traditio Apostolica 81
"transvestite" saints *see* cross-dressing
Trent, Council of 61, 64
Tristan de Nanteuil 85–6
Troilus and Criseyde 42
Trotula 34
Trotula of Salerno 145
Tudor, Henry *see* Henry VII, King of England
Tudor Dynasty 2
"The Tunning of Elinor Rumming" 136
two-seed model 18, 27
two-sex model 18

unnatural vs. natural 5
unveiled virgins 122
upper class women 126
Urban I, Pope 57
Urban V, Pope 165n. 15
Usk, Thomas 67
uterine suffocation 36–7

vagina, vaginal 4, 26, 33, 63, 92, 96, 102, 117, 155n. 55, 157n 79
Valerian 57
venereal disease 39–40
violence, sexual and domestic 16, 23, 85, 153n. 40
violentus concubitus 20
virgin
  consecrated 37
  cure, myth of 40
  as distinct from women 122
  martyrs 113–14, 176n. 36
  unveiled 122
  see also virginity
virginity 8, 43, 47–52
  Bride of Christ metaphor and 108–9, 111–12, 119
  chaste marriage and 55–60
  Church on 48
  female 51, 164n. 6
  male 50, 75, 164n. 6
  marriage and 60–6
  perpetual 56, 60
  physical 51–2, 112
  restoration of 37, 159n. 103
  secular 48
  spiritual 52, 112
  widow(er)hood and 52–5
  see also virgin
Virgin Mary *see* Mary (Virgin)
virtus formativa 33
Vita Aedwardi Regis 58
vital heat, theory of 26
Vitalis, Orderic 89
"vowed widowhood" 48
vowess 54, 55, 165n. 20

Wallace, William 80
Wars of the Roses 149n. 1

Western Christendom 1–2
Westminster II, statutes of 21, 22, 153n. 39
widow(er)hood 52–6, 165n.20, 166n. 28
　guilds and 140, 144
　monasteries and 53–5
　vowed 48
　"The Wife of Bath's Prologue" 136, 145
"Wife of Bath's Tale" 22–3
Wilgefortis 95
William of Conches 17
William of Malmesbury 73, 89
William of Tocco 80
William the Conqueror 73, 149n. 1

wives 44, 45, 52, 60, 63, 111, 125, 151n. 10
　acting in their husband's stead 126–7
　coverture and 16
　expectation from 125–6
woman–woman eroticism, in Classical world 91–2
wombs 32, 34, 36–7, 44, 99, 114, 117, 118, 144, 158n. 83, 163n. 147, 169n. 49
Wonders of the East 98
The Wooing of Our Lord 119

Yde et Olive 12, 85–6

www.ingramcontent.com/pod-product-compliance
Lightning Source LLC
LaVergne TN
LVHW010341260326
834688LV00036B/815